The Book of Remembrance

And Other Visions, Dreams, & Revelations

The Church of Jesus Christ in Christian Fellowship
2019-2024

The Church of
Jesus Christ
in Christian Fellowship

ISBN: 978-0-359-56542-9

The Church of Jesus Christ in Christian Fellowship
Post Office Box 1503
Miamisburg, Ohio, 45342
www.CJCCF.org

Table Of Contents

Dedication

To everyone in the Latter Day Saint Movement, may we be one, even as the Father and the Son are one; Amen.

Acknowledgements

Thank you to everyone that contributed for their work and encouragement. And, special thanks to the families and friends of those involved for the time taken to accomplish this sacred work. Alexie Christopher Mattanovich, Victoria Ramirez, and other anonymous editors.

Introduction

David's path of faith has been defined by profound spiritual experiences from a young age, which have shaped his deep understanding of God's presence in his life and the world around him. His journey is rooted in the belief that God speaks directly to individuals and forms personal covenants with them. David sees God as actively involved in all aspects of life, guiding and inspiring him at every turn.

This journey began when David was just four years old, following the divine direction his mother received to join the Church of Jesus Christ of Latter-day Saints. From this point, he became aware of God's guiding presence. At the age of six, seeking to know God's reality for himself, David received a vision where God revealed the history of the Latter Day Saint movement to him. This sacred experience confirmed his faith and led to a year filled with angelic visitations that profoundly deepened his spiritual understanding. Around the same age, David entered into a personal covenant with God, pledging to serve Him. This moment filled him with immense joy and solidified his lifelong dedication to God's work.

As a teenager, David had a vision that reconciled his understanding of creation with the scientific view of evolution, teaching him that God transcends time and that revelation comes in many forms. This vision broadened his understanding of God's mysteries and solidified his belief in a world that holds both spiritual and scientific truths.

A pivotal moment in David's journey came through a powerful dream about the Garden of Eden, which served as his divine calling to ministry. This calling was affirmed by multiple dreams and revelations that directed him toward creating a new spiritual fellowship. David was ordained as a High Priest by the angel Raphael, who entrusted him with the keys of the priesthood and revealed his mission to translate God's word and preach peace. Through continuing revelation, he went on to establish the Church of Jesus

Christ in Christian Fellowship, an inclusive space where people of all denominations can gather, study scripture, and grow in faith without judgment.

David's frequent visions and revelations have strengthened his conviction that God communicates personally with each individual. One such dream involved a mall, where different stores represented various denominations, leading David to see that God's grace is available to all who accept Christ, regardless of their specific church affiliation. His persistent quest for understanding and the divine answers he received have shaped his view of God as a God of truth, knowledge, and personal revelation.

David's life has been marked by numerous instances of divine intervention, further affirming his belief that God is actively involved in the lives of individuals and the course of human history. His story underscores the transformative power of personal spiritual experiences and highlights the importance of direct revelation, personal covenants, and an inclusive approach to faith. Through these experiences, David has come to see God as a personal, loving, and active presence, guiding individuals and shaping the world according to His divine plan.

2024 Preface

"And the Lord God said, 'Behold, the man is become as one of us, to know good and evil: and now, lest he put forth his hand, and take also of the tree of life, and eat, and live forever:' therefore the Lord God sent him forth from the garden of Eden, to till the ground from whence he was taken." – Genesis 3:22-23 KJV

With the exception of the first three chapters, the Book of Remembrance is a series of revelations David Ferriman, First Elder of the Church of Jesus Christ in Christian Fellowship received in January of 2016. After receiving the revelations, he felt inspired only to share a portion of what he was given with the world. However, in the summer of 2018 he felt moved by the Holy Spirit to share the revelation in full.

When putting the Book of Remembrance together, some portions of the revelations were reorganized to make for a better narrative. This changed neither the meaning or nature of the original. He also discovered that a portion of the revelations already existed as a part of the Book of Raziel apparently first printed in 1701. However, it was not an exact copy, nor was it laid out in the same format.

After finding and reading the Book of Raziel (included in the appendix), he prayed to discover why it was included in the work and was informed that Raziel was Raphael and that he did in fact speak to Adam, and this record taught his message more clearly for the world to understand. Of this David said, *"the skeptic might say that as a student of pseudepigraphal works, I may have read this book and merely not remembered; that this may have affected my revelations. However, the Lord has told me these words are of Him, and this has satisfied my conscience."*

Like the Holy Bible and the Book of Mormon, the Book of Remembrance is not perfect and should not always be taken literally. Though Joseph Smith Jr. on at least one occasion declared the Book of Mormon to be the "most correct book," no one ever declared it perfect. The book itself admits that it has flaws as it was compiled by men. Likewise, the Book of Remembrance is not a perfect record. As the title page of the Book of Mormon states:

"And now, if there are faults they are the mistakes of men; wherefore, condemn not the things of God, that ye may be found spotless at the judgment-seat of Christ."

We echo Moroni's words and encourage all to read this book prayerfully that the Spirit may speak to mankind through it, just as we would the Holy Bible and any other work of scripture.

This work will help guide readers in preparing for and understanding the purpose of the Endowments. These are not secret works of the occult, but rather sacred works of the Lord. They are not a light to be hidden under a bushel, but rather to be place upon a hill. It is our prayer that Latter Day Saints of all denominations may use these revelations, with the scriptures of their branches of the kingdom, to better understand the works of the Lord.

In May of 2022, David was asked a question in regards to those that do not identify as male or female. After going to the Lord for answers, David received a lengthy revelation he was told to add to this Book of Remembrance. He was also told that he would receive additional revelations in November of that same year. These revelations came and have been added to this sacred work.

In addition, we have added more of the visions, dreams, and revelations David received. These revelations can be found in Doctrines of the Saints and the dreams and vision in Epistles of the Saints. We have added them to this volume that all Saints may read, study, and pray on them to receive their own witness. We have also included two revelations from the other members of the First Presidency of the Fellowship of Christ. Any further dreams, visions, or revelations may be found in the afore mentioned volumes. While Doctrines of the Saints and Epistles of the Saints are open books, David has been instructed to close the Book of Remembrance itself as a finished work. The Lord has stated that if any other separate books are required, they will be their own titles, and as such may be added to further versions of this, the collection of David's dreams, prophecies, visions, and revelations.

The Book of Remembrance

and other dreams, visions, & revelations

The Book of Remembrance

Revelations given on the origins of God's dealing with mankind.

Chapter 1

Revelation received by David, his call to the ministry received November 16, 2015, recorded here as an introduction to the Book of Remembrance.

1 This book is a collection of revelations from the Lord unto the prophet David,

2 Having been called of God and ordained an Elder by the Church of Jesus Christ of Latter-day Saints, a High Priest by the Lord–given by the administering hands of His holy angels, and an apostle by the witness and testimony of the living Jesus Christ,

3 ¶ The Lord has commanded me saying: Behold, I say into thee, my servant David: Write ye the words of the Lord.

4 Keep my words in a Book of Remembrance that shall stand as a testimony at the last day;

5 That ye are my covenanted servant, and that I have called and sanctified thee to speak for me in these, the last days;

6 Not to declare a new Gospel, for behold the trump of the angel has sounded, and the Everlasting Gospel has been sent unto them that dwell on the earth, and shall go forth to every nation, and kindred, and tongue, and people:

7 Yea, even the Book of Mormon, to bear witness of me and my Word, that I am the Lord thy God, and I am the same yesterday, today, and forever.

8 ¶ Behold, I say unto thee: Fear not, for I am with thee; if the world should reject thee, know that thou art whole in me;

9 And I say unto thee that even if thou should suffer at the hands of men, I am with thee; I shall be thy strength and my Spirit shall be thy constant companion.

10 And if my Church, even the Church of Jesus Christ of Latter-day Saints, shall persecute thee and those that follow thee in my name; if

they are to cast you out for speaking in my name, all will be well for thee;

11 For behold: man cannot destroy that which the Lord creates, nor can man take away that which the Lord gives;

12 Therefore, thy priesthoods and thy covenants, these shall thou still carry with thee even so long as you remain steadfast unto me, the Lord thy God.

13 ¶ And behold, I will provide a pathway forward for thee to create a place for my people that my Church has cast out; and their baptisms and their covenant shall still be whole in my sight;

14 And yea, there shall be no need for a second baptism for those already baptized in my name by one with authority;

15 But I say unto thee that as my people find pleasing, they may be baptized in my name by the desires of their hearts.

16 ¶ And thus I say unto my servant, David: Go and make a place that my people may find peace and rest in my holy name;

17 For I am He who was with the Father from the beginning, even Jesus Christ. Amen.

Chapter 2

Revelation on the pre-mortal world/existence received approximately 1989.

1 Worlds without number have I created; and these were created for a purpose, and by the Son, YHVH were they created; which is Jesus Christ, the Only Begotten.

2 Yet only an account of this earth and the inhabitants thereof are given unto mankind;

3 For behold, there are many worlds that have passed away by the Word of my power, and there are many that now stand; and innumerable are they unto mankind;

4 But all things are numbered unto Elohim, for they are YHVH's and I know them.

5 And as one earth shall pass away and the heavens thereof, even so shall another come; and thus there is no end to my works, neither to my Word.

6 Behold, this is the work and the glory of Elohim, of YHVH and of the gods: to bring to pass the immortality and eternal life of mankind; and the works of this creation shall I reveal unto you.

7 ¶In the beginning was the counsel, even a counsel of the gods, and YHVH, the Lord Jesus Christ premortal, was God, and chief or head of the gods; the same was in the beginning with Elohim and is the Only Begotten.

8 ¶ Well did my servant John say: All things were made by him, and without Him was not anything made that was made.

9 For behold, in Christ was and is life; and this life was and is the light of men and women, and the light shineth in darkness; yet the darkness comprehended it not.

10 ¶ And before this world was, in the flesh, I gathered the intelligences that were organized before the world was; and among all these there were many of the noble and great ones.

11 And I, Elohim; that is to say, God Aviad our Heavenly Father, and Godess Asyma, the Queen of Heaven our Heavenly Mother, and their Son YHVH, God our Christ; saw these souls that they were good, and We stood in the midst of them;

12 And, speaking as one, Elohim said: These I will make my rulers, for we now stood among those that were spirits, and saw that they were good.

13 And by the Only Begotten, YHVH who is Jesus Christ, were these things created; yea, in the beginning I created the heaven, and the earth upon which thou standest.

14 And the earth was without form, and void; and I caused darkness to come up upon the face of the deep; and the Spirit of God moved upon the face of the water; for these are God's.

15 ¶ And the earth, after it was formed, was empty and desolate, because nothing had been formed but the earth; and darkness reigned upon the face of the deep, and the spirit of the gods was brooding upon the face of the waters.

16 And there stood one among them that was like unto God, YHVH, and the Lord Jesus Christ premortal who was before these with me, and He said unto those who were with Him:

17 We will go down, for there is space there, and we will take of these materials, and we will make an earth whereon these may dwell,

18 And we will prove them herewith, to see if they will do all things whatsoever the Lord their God shall command them;

19 And they who keep their first estate shall be added upon,

20 And they who keep not their first estate shall not have glory in the same kingdom with those who keep their first estate;

21 And they who keep their second estate shall have glory added upon their heads forever and ever.

22 And this was the counsel of the gods.

23 ¶ And Elohim said: Whom shall be sent?

24 And one answered like unto the Son of Man, even YHVH, the great I AM; saying: Here am I, send me.

25 And another answered saying: Behold, here am I, send me; I will be thy son, and I will redeem all mankind, that one soul shall not be lost, and surely I will do it; wherefore give me thine honor.

26 But, behold, YHVH, which was my Beloved and Chosen from before the beginning, said: thy will be done, and the glory be thine forever.

27 And Elohim said: I will send the first.

28 ¶ And the second was angry, and was called Perdition, for the heavens wept over him; for he was Lucifer, a Son of the Morning.

29 Yet he kept not his first estate; and at that day many followed after him.

30 ¶ And there was war in heaven; Michael and his angels fought against the dragon; and the dragon fought and his angels,

31 And they prevailed not; neither was their place found anymore in heaven.

32 For the great dragon and his seed was cast out;

33 That old serpent, called the Devil, and Satan, which deceiveth the whole world:

34 He was cast out into the earth, and his angels were cast out with him.

35 And thus he became Satan, yea, even the devil: the father of all lies;

36 And he thrives now only to deceive and to blind men, and to lead them captive at his will, even as many as would not hearken unto the voice of God.

37 And the angels which kept not their first estate, these left their own habitation,

38 And I have reserved unto them, and those that would join them, the everlasting chains of Hell and their place in outer darkness, unto the judgment of the great day.

39 ¶ And behold, it is this that has led the prophets to say: How art thou fallen from heaven, O Lucifer, son of the morning! How art thou cut down to the ground, which did weaken the nations!

40 For thou hast said in thine heart, I will ascend into heaven; I will exalt my throne above the stars of God;

41 I will sit also upon the mount of the congregation, in the sides of the north;

42 Yea, I will ascend above the heights of the clouds; I will be like the Most High.

43 Yet thou shalt be brought down to hell, to the sides of the pit.

44 Therefore, because Lucifer, that Satan, rebelled against me, and sought to destroy the agency of man,

45 And also desired that he should be given my power,

46 By the power given of Elohim to YHVH, the Only Begotten, I caused that he should be cast down.

47 ¶ And here is a mystery: The holy number unto God is three, thus Lucifer and his servants declared themselves holy as represented by the number six,

48 But behold seven is the holy number of the Lord and thus the first shall be last and the last shall be first and the devil was not numbered above Elohim in power nor in righteousness.

49 And yea, the number of man is nine; for behold man hath the power to be as the gods and receive, through Christ, all that the Father hath;

50 Yet behold, so too doth mankind have the power to follow that Satan that deceived even a third of the hosts of heaven, lifting himself up in pride to fall even as these did into darkness.

51 And thus there are ten sefirot, for man is not above God, yea nothing is before nor is anything after.

52 And these are the blessings and the curse of agency which was given him of God.

Chapter 3

Revelation on the creation of this world, received approximately 1989.

1 Then said Elohim unto YHVH and Michael: Yonder is matter unorganized; go ye down and organize it into a world like unto the worlds that we have heretofore formed; call your labors the first day and bring word.

2 And then mine Only Begotten said unto Michael and the gods and angels: Let us go down.

3 ¶ And they went down at the beginning; and they, that is the gods, organized and formed the heavens and the earth, thus creating their second estate that they might prove themselves.

4 And Elohim said to the gods: Let there be light; and they, the gods, said: Let there be light; and there was light.

5 And behold, Elohim, saw the light; and that light was good.

6 And they, the gods, comprehended the light, for it was bright; and they, by the command of Elohim, divided the light, or caused it to be divided, from the darkness.

7 And Elohim called the light Day and the darkness he called Night; and this was done by the Word of their power; and it was done even as Elohim spake.

8 And thus the gods too called the light Day and the darkness they called Night.

9 And it came to pass that from the evening until morning we called night and from the morning until the evening called we day;

10 And this was the first, or the beginning, of that which was called day and night, not by the reckoning of time as to man, but by the order or direction of Elohim and by the counsel of the gods.

11 And the evening and the morning were the first day.

12 ¶ And again, Elohim spake and said: Let there be a firmament in the midst of the water, and it was so;

13 For behold, Elohim said: Let it divide the waters from the waters; and it was done, for the gods obeyed the Word of Elohim.

14 And they, the gods, said: Let there be an expanse in the midst of the waters, and it shall divide the waters from the waters.

15 And the gods ordered the expanse so that it divided the waters which were under the expanse from the waters which were above the expanse; and it was so, even as they ordered.

16 And Elohim called the firmament Heaven; and the gods followed, calling the expanse Heaven.

17 And it came to pass that it was from evening until morning that was called night by the reckoning of the gods; and it came to pass that it was from morning until evening that they called day;

18 And this was the second time that they called night and day, and thus the evening and the morning were the second day.

19 ¶ And Elohim, said unto the Only Begotten and Michael: Let the waters under the heaven be gathered together unto one place.

20 And they, the gods, under the direction of YHVH and Michael ordered, saying: Let the waters under the heaven be gathered together unto one place; and it was so.

21 And Elohim said: Let there be dry land, yea and let the earth come up dry; and it was so as they ordered in the name of the Only Begotten.

22 And Elohim called the dry land Earth and the gathering together of the waters called He the Sea.

23 And the gods too pronounced the dry land earth; and the gathering together of the waters, pronounced they, Great Waters; and the gods saw that they were obeyed.

24 And Elohim saw that all things which had been made were good.

25 And Elohim said: Let the earth bring forth grass, the herb yielding seed, the fruit tree yielding fruit, after his kind, and the tree yielding fruit, whose seed should be in itself upon the earth.

26 And the gods organized the earth to bring forth grass from its own seed, and the herb to bring forth herb from its own seed, yielding seed after his kind;

27 And they caused the earth to bring forth the tree from its own seed, yielding fruit, whose seed could only bring forth the same in itself, after his kind.

28 And it came to pass that they numbered the days; from the evening until the morning they called night; and it came to pass, from the morning until the evening they called day; and it was the third time.

29 And the evening and the morning were, by the reckoning of time by the gods, the third day.

30 ¶ And behold, Elohim said unto them: Let there be lights in the firmament of the heaven, to divide the day from the night, and let them be for signs, and for seasons, and for days, and for years; and let them be for lights in the firmament of the heaven to give light upon the earth.

31 And they, the gods, organized the lights in the expanse of the heaven in the manner required by Elohim, and caused them to divide the day from the night; and organized them to be for signs and for seasons, and for days and for years.

32 And they organized them to be for lights in the expanse of the heaven to give light upon the earth; and it was so.

33 And Elohim desired there be made two great lights; the greater light to rule the day, and the lesser light to rule the night, and the greater light was the sun, and the lesser light was the moon; and the stars also were made even according to their word.

34 And the gods obeyed his commands, and having thus organized the two great lights; the greater light to rule the day, and the lesser light to rule the night; with the lesser light they set the stars also;

35 Yea and behold, these were even created in their own time, the sun even before the earth; yet all things at this time did fall into their place that these things should work for the benefit of man.

36 For Elohim desired the gods to set them in the firmament of the heaven to give light upon the earth;

37 Thus the gods set them in the expanse of the heavens upon the direction of Elohim, to give light upon the earth, and to rule over the day and over the night, and to cause to divide the light from the darkness.

38 And the gods watched those things which they had ordered until they obeyed.

39 And Elohim saw that all things which they had made were good.

40 And it came to pass that from evening until morning that it was night; and it came to pass that it was from morning until evening that it was day,

41 And it was the fourth time; and thus the evening and the morning were the fourth day.

42 ¶ And behold, Elohim said unto the Only Begotten and the Only Begotten unto Michael, and Michael said unto the gods: Let the waters bring forth abundantly the moving creature that hath life, and fowl which may fly above the earth in the open firmament of heaven.

43 And the gods prepared the waters that they might bring forth the monsters and the great ones, and every living creature that moveth, which the waters were to bring forth abundantly after their kind; and every winged fowl after their kind.

44 And the gods saw that they would be obeyed and that the plan was good.

45 ¶ And Elohim required the gods that they should create the monsters and the great ones, and every living creature that moveth, which the waters brought forth abundantly, after their kind; and every winged fowl after his kind;

46 And the gods saw that all things were created, and that they were good.

47 And Elohim required they blessed them, saying: Be fruitful, and multiply, and fill the waters in the sea; and let fowl multiply in the earth.

48 And the gods said: We will bless them, and cause them to be fruitful and multiply, and fill the waters in the seas or great waters; and cause the fowl to multiply in the earth.

49 And it came to pass that it was from evening until morning that we called night; and it came to pass that it was from morning until evening that we called day; and it was the fifth time.

50 And the evening and the morning were the fifth day by the reckoning of the gods.

51 ¶ And Elohim said: Let the earth bring forth the living creature after his kind, cattle, and creeping things, and beasts of the earth after their kind, and it was so.

52 For they, the gods organized the earth to bring forth the beasts after their kind, and cattle after their kind, and everything that creepeth upon the earth after its kind; and the gods saw they would obey.

53 And thus Elohim, through the gods, by the power of the Only Begotten given him by Elohim, made the beasts of the earth after their kind, and cattle after their kind, and everything which creepeth upon the earth after his kind;

54 And Elohim saw that all these things were good.

55 And Elohim said unto the Only Begotten, which was with Elohim, and thus with the gods, from the beginning: Let us make man in our image, after our likeness.

56 And the gods took counsel among themselves and said: Let us go down and form man in our image, after our likeness.

57 And the gods went down to organize man in their own image, and in the image of the Only Begotten; and in the image of the gods to form they him, male and female to form they them.

58 And Elohim said: Let them have dominion over the fishes of the sea, and over the fowl of the air, and over the cattle, and over all the earth, and over every creeping thing that creepeth upon the earth.

59 And Elohim required the gods bless them, and to say unto them: Be fruitful, and multiply, and replenish the earth, and subdue it, and have dominion over the fish of the sea, and over the fowl of the air, and over every living thing that moveth upon the earth.

60 And the gods said: We will bless them.

61 And the gods said: We will cause them to be fruitful and multiply, and replenish the earth, and subdue it, and to have dominion over the

fish of the sea, and over the fowl of the air, and over every living thing that moveth upon the earth.

62 And Elohim caused YHVH to say unto man: Behold, I have given you every herb bearing seed, which is upon the face of all the earth, and every tree in the which shall be the fruit of a tree yielding seed; to you it shall be for meat.

63 And to every beast of the earth, and to every fowl of the air, and to everything that creepeth upon the earth, wherein I grant life, there shall be given every clean herb for meat; and it was so, even as they spake through the voice of their servants, the gods or the Holy Spirit.

64 And Elohim saw everything that had been made, and behold, all things which had been made were very good.

65 And it came to pass that it was from evening until morning they called night; and it came to pass that it was from morning until evening that they called day; and they numbered the sixth time.

66 And the evening and the morning were the sixth day by the reckoning of the Gods.

67 ¶ And thus Elohim; by the works of the only begotten, and Michael, and the gods, did finish the heavens and the earth, and all the hosts of them.

68 And the morning stars sang together, and all the sons of God, or the children of Elohim, shouted for joy.

69 And on the seventh day Elohim ended the work; and Elohim rested on the seventh day from all work, and all things which they had made were finished, and Elohim saw that they were good;

70 And the gods saw this and said among themselves: On the seventh time we will end our work, which we have counseled; and we will rest on the seventh time from all our work which we have counseled.

71 And thus the gods too concluded upon the seventh time, because that on the seventh time they would rest from all their works which they, the gods, counseled among themselves to form; and sanctified it.

72 And thus were their decisions at the time that they counseled among themselves to form the heavens and the earth created.

73 And thus Elohim blessed the seventh day, and sanctified it calling it Sabbath; because that in it Elohim had rested from all the work which was made.

Chapter 4

Revelation on Adam, Eve, and Lilith received in Ohio on January 12, 2016.

1 Verily, thus saith the Lord: It shall come to pass that every soul who calleth on my name, and obey my voice, and keep my commandments, thus forsaking sin and coming unto me shall see my face and know that I am;

2 Yea even they shall know that that I AM the Father of their Salvation, and that the Father, Elohim, and I are one:

3 I am the Father because They gave unto me of Their fullness, and I am the Son because I was in the world and made flesh my tabernacle and dwelt among the sons of men.

4 And behold, it is I AM that is YHVH and that spoke to your first parents in the garden.

5 ¶ Behold, I spake the words of Elohim when I said unto man:

6 We have created you this earth and have placed upon it vegetation of all kinds and animal life of all kinds.

7 Yea, we have commanded all these to multiply in their own sphere and element;

8 And behold, we give thee dominion over all these things and make you lord over the whole earth and all things on the face thereof.

9 We now command thee that thou shalt multiply and replenish the earth, that ye may have joy and rejoicing in thy posterity.

10 And I also spake unto mankind, giving them commandments, saying: We have also planted for thee in this garden all manner of fruits, flowers, and vegetation.

11 Yea, and of every tree of the garden thou may freely eat, but of the tree of knowledge of good and evil thou shalt not eat;

12 Nevertheless, thou may choose for thyself, for it is given unto thee;

13 But remember that I forbid it, for in the day thou eatest thereof thou shalt surely die.

14 And this I spake unto Adam and unto his wives, Lilith and Eve, that they mayest choose for themselves to follow these my first commandments unto mankind.

15 And thus said I, the Lord God, even YHVH of Elohim: Remember, O mankind, this commandment which we have given unto you.

16 And I commanded them saying: Go now to dress this garden, and care for the good of it; yea, be happy and have joy therein;

17 And I shall go my way but shall visit thee again from time to time and thus give unto thee further instructions.

18 ¶ And behold, whence I departed, the Devil came among the children of the Lord, even as a serpent to tempt them.

Chapter 5

Revelation on the fall of Lilith received in Ohio on January 12, 2016.

1 Verily, thus saith the Lord unto you my servant, David: I would that ye should know the history of mankind, yea of mankind from the time I brought them into the Garden of Eden.

2 For behold, these truths were kept within the first Book of Remembrance; though they are lost to the world, yet they are not lost unto me;

3 And now ye shall see that these words are restored in this, my Book of Remembrance, kept in these the latter days.

4 And behold, these and more shall I reveal them all unto the world in my due time; for they are also saved up unto me on the record of the house of Joseph; even upon the Plates of Brass.

5 And this is but a small portion given unto thee as revelation to help those of my Church understand the mysteries of God.

6 ¶ Behold, I took unto me, YHVH of Elohim, a man and named him Adam; from the dust of the ground, I made him and placed him in the Garden, eastward in Eden.

7 And there he was not alone.

8 Yea, I had given unto Adam two wives, Lilith for the first and Eve for the second, that they would be helpmates unto one another in the Garden; and given I they Adam unto them, and the one unto the other.

9 But behold, here is wisdom: Lilith had neither love for her husband nor for their wife, Eve, nor for the Lord God; neither YHVH, the Only Begotten, nor Elohim.

10 Yea, and Lilith had a natural affection at the first, but behold, that serpent came unto her and offered her of the fruit of that tree; even the tree of good and evil.

11 And behold, Lilith ate of the fruit of that tree and it made her wise, and she was desirous to share with Adam;

12 Not that he too should gain wisdom; but she sought to make him wise that she might ransom the Lord her God.

13 Behold, she had conspired in her heart to make the man fallen too that she might ransom God to give unto her eternal life, and thus save her in her sins;

14 For she did not know that as God brought Adam into the Garden, so too could he bring forth another man from the world.

15 Yea, and Lilith thought that she came from the head of Adam, yea and that he came from her feet; and not from a rib;

16 And behold, she sought to rule over her husband, and not live in harmony one with another; yea, and she thought also to rule over Eve.

17 ❡ And now it came to pass that the serpent Lucifer did tempt her, and she did partake of the fruit of the tree of good and evil and did become as the gods, to know good from evil.

18 And thus did Lilith go seeking to deceive her husband and their wife.

19 ❡ Yea, and Lilith appeared as a serpent, that is to say a deceiver, first unto Eve, then upon Adam.

20 But behold, Adam was faithful unto his first commandments and said unto her: Nay. I shall not partake, for in the day I do, I shalt surely die.

21 And Lilith said unto him: See ye not that I am still alive?

22 For Lilith understood not my Word, that this death should be a spiritual death;

23 Yet Adam still forbade himself the fruit.

24 And thus, Lilith stole the seed of Adam, as he was still obedient unto the first commandments, yea even to be fruitful and multiply.

25 ¶ And behold, it came to pass that with his seed, bearing fruit, Lilith made to flee from before him, yea even to flee out from the garden.

26 And she sought to flee from before me, the Lord God, as I was in the Garden about the day, and she was not ashamed nor was she afraid.

27 Yea, and she thought there might be a place outside the Garden, even a place to the west wherein which she could hide;

28 But behold, there is no place anywhere upon the earth, nor above it, nor beneath it wherein one might hide from me, the Lord God-even YHVH of Elohim.

29 ¶ And it came to pass that I did send mine angels, Sanvi, Sanzanvi and Semangel; who are known also in the flesh as mine apostles Peter, James, and John; for they had served me from the beginning and thus were they chosen;

30 And these I sent after her to gather her up that I might speak to her;

31 For behold, as she too did try to give the fruit of that tree to Adam, that he too might fall; yet he had rejected her, and thus she fled so as not to be found in her sin.

32 But behold, I know all things, for I am the Lord Omnipotent; and I knew too that she had taken with her the fruit of the tree of life that she should eat and never die.

33 ¶ And behold, it came to pass when she would not return, I had my servants, Sanvi, Sanzanvi and Semangel, cast her out that she may no more return unto the Garden;

34 For she had become perdition, for she too had been from the beginning; and she found for herself a place of rest in the deserts and in the darkness, seeking a place where my Spirit doth not dwell.

35 And behold, Adam's seed did not bear fruit within Lilith, and she did place her blame upon the Lord God;

36 Yea and it came to pass that she could not return unto the Garden to be anymore with her husband and was now alone in the world;

37 And in her anger, she swore vengeance upon the seed of Adam and Eve and their seed.

38 But behold my servants, Sanvi, Sanzanvi and Semangel swore and oath to protect the seed of Adam and Eve from her wrath, should the children of Adam do that which is right by me.

39 ¶ And it was she that tempted Cain, coming unto him in secret; and taught him to love Satan more than me; and she brought much evil unto the hearts of the children of mankind.

40 But behold, his twin, Able; he and his wife were willing to do that which was pleasing before me and thus were they protected by my servants, Sanvi, Sanzanvi and Semangel;

41 And their brother Seth and others were obedient unto the Lord their God and also were protected.

42 ¶ And these things I tell thee that thou shalt know that man had more wives than one from the beginning, and that I knew from the beginning that man would need a state of probation.

43 Yea, and had Lilith returned to me, I would have shown her the path of redemption that she may have rejoiced and dwelt in the forests and in the mountains forever.

44 But behold, she did not return and did not repent;

45 And thus she wasted away her probation, and was alone with none to be an helpmate unto her from me, but gained only what she took and these were the things of the world.

46 Behold, she did partake of the fruit of the tree of life in her wickedness, and thus she shall be sewn down in hell and outer darkness, never to know again her Elohim.

47 Therefore, it is wisdom in me that should a man desire to take another wife, should he put his first wife away, he risks the same as Lilith;

48 And man shall be forbidden from such, even as were the Nephites by my servant Jacob.

49 ¶ And so too, if a woman taketh a husband and putteth herself above him, or leaveth him unto his own, so too shall she be damned unless she repent;

50 But if a man shall love his wife, and keep her, and show unto her affection, and she him;

51 Then if they so desire to take unto them another, and having taken the second with the blessing of the first then all shall be helpmates one unto another;

52 And thus shall they be blessed in me; for behold, I say unto thee, fear not; for all things shall come to pass, even as I will.

Chapter 6

Revelation on hearing and heeding the Lord received in Ohio, January 12, 2016.

1 Verily, thus saith the Lord unto they whom I love:

2 Behold, thou shalt see that I also chasten mankind that their sins may be forgiven, for with the chastisement I prepare a way for their deliverance in all things out of temptation;

3 Wherefore, all mankind must needs be chastened and stand rebuked before my face, for even Adam and Eve did such;

4 For all have sinned against me and fallen short of my glory, and short of the glory of my Father, even the very Father of Heaven;

5 Therefore, I teach ye these things in preparation to prune my vineyard for the last time, that I may pour out my Spirit upon all flesh.

6 Behold, verily I say unto you, that there are many who have been ordained among you before they were in the flesh, whom I have called, but few of these are chosen.

7 For behold, they must hear my call and heed it also;

8 For my paths are straight, and they are known unto me, yet these must know me and hearken unto my voice to harken unto my call.

9 ¶ Behold, I speak these things unto thee that thou might learn wisdom, and that they who read shall also gain wisdom;

10 For as in every man is the story of Adam, and in every woman the story of Eve;

11 So too may every man and woman be saved through my atonement as are Adam and Eve, and stand on the right hand of the Father with me;

12 And behold, even as they, thou might inherit all that the Father hath.

13 But behold, those that keep not their second estate shall be like unto those that kept not their first;

14 And they shall share the fate of Lilith and of Cain, for they are cast out into eternal darkness.

15 Therefore, learn wisdom in these things, and know that ye must practice virtue and holiness before me continually;

16 And behold, I shall tell thee more in my time and in my wisdom; here a little, there a little.

17 But for now, it is enough, watch, therefore, that ye may be ready. Even so. Amen.

Chapter 7

Revelation on the fall of Eve received in Ohio, on January 12, 2016.

1 And behold, that Satan tempted Lilith, as I have before told thee, and she departed.

2 But behold: Lucifer, that Devil, yea even that Satan, he remained in the Garden;

3 And he came again unto Adam saying: Behold this world, modeled after that from whence we came.

4 But Adam had no memory of such; yea he knew of no other world or that he was a son of God, yea even a child of Elohim in the spirit; for he had not tasted of the tree and new not wisdom.

5 ¶ Then Lucifer spake unto him saying: Behold, thine eyes are shut tight, eat of this tree that thou shalt remember and be wise, knowing of who's seed thou art.

6 But he forbade such to come unto himself; and Lucifer came and spake unto the man again, saying: Behold, here is some of the fruit of that tree; and it shall make thee wise.

7 And Adam spake unto him saying, Yea, I shall not partake of that fruit; behold The Lord hath commanded me, saying that in the day I should partake of it, I should surely die.

8 ¶ And Lucifer again came unto him a third time in the Garden and he spake unto him, even with the tongue of a serpent, saying: Behold

the fruit of this tree; thou fearest to taste of it, yet hath thou not been given freely to choose?

9 Therefore, thou shalt not surely die, but shall be as YHVH of Elohim, yea even as the gods, knowing good and evil.

10 But behold, my servant Adam stood firm upon the rock of mine commandments and would not eat, for he knew that Lilith had eaten and she was to be found in the Garden no more; and thus he was blessed.

11 ¶ And it came to pass that Eve too was found in the Garden by that serpent, Lucifer.

12 And he spake unto her saying: Eve, here is some of the fruit of that tree; it shall make thee wise; come and behold, for it is delicious to the taste and very desirable.

13 And Eve did not know who this was that would tempt her to disobey the Lord her God, thus she inquired to know his intent and wherefrom he came.

14 And behold, Lucifer did lie unto her, stating in truth that he was her brother; yet he did not reveal that he had fallen from the grace of God, and kept not his first estate, and was cast out;

15 And he, Lucifer, our common enemy, whom Michael, who is Adam, had thrust out, had been placed in the Garden to tempt man and to try him, that he may know by his own experience the good from the evil.

16 Thus he lied also in stating this; as he is now a brother only to wickedness and darkness, and no longer of the children of Elohim.

17 And thus Eve asked him: Thou say thou art my brother, and come here to persuade me to disobey YHVH the Lord, who is the very Father of my flesh?

18 And with this Lucifer became angry, and said unto the woman, Behold, I have said nothing of the Lord.

19 Yea, I want thee to eat of the fruit of the tree of knowledge of good and evil that thine eyes may be opened, for that is the way our very Father gained his know-ledge.

20 But behold, this was a lie, for Elohim was perfect even in all things, thus being God without beginning or end of days.

21 And Lucifer, being more subtle, said unto her, Behold, ye must eat of this fruit so as to comprehend that everything has its opposite: good and evil, virtue and vice, light and darkness, health and sickness, pleasure and pain:

22 Thus thine eyes shall be opened, and thou shall have knowledge.

23 And thus, being tricked by that serpent, Eve did eat, believing there was no other way.

24 And thus in her innocence, she did lose her inheritance; and thus began the days of her probation upon the earth.

25 ¶ And it came to pass that the woman. having eaten the fruit, her eyes were opened and she feared what she had done;

26 And in her fear believed that devil again when he taught her to go and give the fruit of that same tree unto Adam.

27 ¶ And thus it is forever in the days of man: behold, as one falls so to do they seek to drag another down too that they be not alone in their sin.

28 And behold, even as men do fall, so too might they be saved; and they that are saved desire to bring others unto salvation in Christ.

29 Yea even as one rises in Grace they desire to lift another up unto Christ and salvation.

30 Yea, and even as Lilith sought to gain profit over her husband, Eve sought only to remain with him and to be a helpmate unto him, and for him to be a helpmate unto her;

31 And thus we see that even those with good intent might bring forth destruction on man.

32 And so too shall I show unto thee that I was made a Savior for him, as was counseled in the beginning;

33 That man may be brought forth by the power of the redemption and the resurrection, and come again into my presence, and unto the presence of the Father, and with us partake of eternal life and exaltation. Even so, Amen.

Chapter 8

Revelation on the fall of Adam received in Ohio on January 12, 2016.

1 Behold, I have spoken to thee of the fall of Lilith, and too of the fall of Eve; and now I shall speak unto thee of the fall of Adam.

2 And Eve's eyes were now open, she being as the gods to know good from evil;

3 Thus she knew that she had sinned and broken the first commandments I gave unto mankind in the Garden.

4 ¶ And behold, she came unto Adam, her husband, with some of the fruit of the tree of knowledge of good and evil, saying: Adam, here is some of the fruit of that tree; behold it is delicious to the taste and very desirable.

5 And the man asked of her, Doth thou know of what fruit that is?

6 And the woman she spoke unto him, answering him, saying: Yea, behold it is the fruit of the tree of knowledge of good and evil.

7 And at this the man worried, saying: I cannot partake of it; doth thou not know that the Lord God, yea the very Father of us, by way of placing us here in this garden; he hath commanded us not to partake of the fruit of that tree?

8 And Eve, her eyes being open, asked the man, Doth thou intend to obey all of the commandments of the Lord God?

9 And the man, Adam, answered her, saying: Yea, all of them.

10 Now Eve, her eyes being open was wise, and thinking that this thing Adam had said was foolishness; and she sought to trick him;

11 For she too had become wise after the manner of the serpent from whom she had gained the fruit.

12 ¶ And it came to pass that she spake unto the man, saying: Doth thou not remember that the Lord commanded us that we should multiply and replenish the earth?

13 Yea, I have partaken of this fruit and by so doing shall be cast out, and thou shalt be left a lone man in the Garden of Eden.

14 Now Adam knew not whence Lilith had gone, only that she had eaten of the fruit and was no more to be found among them in the Garden.

15 Thus Adam, not wanting to be alone and not wanting to lose Eve too, his second wife, thus did he think he only had but two choices.

16 Behold, in his innocence, Adam believed that he could on the one hand sin and eat of the fruit or on the other sin and be alone, thus unable to multiply, being a lone man.

17 For Adam did not understand that the Lord God could take Him another man and thus plucking him, place him too in the Garden;

18 Thus Adam did not know that the Lord God could then give unto him a third wife.

19 ¶ And behold, it came to pass that Adam too, in his innocence, did partake of the fruit of that tree, knowing not that there was still a plan for him.

20 For behold, that tree represented the love of God, even Elohim, our Mother in heaven; and to partake of it unworthily, before it was time, was to sin before God.

21 And thus, through Adam and Eve his wife all mankind have a portion of Her spirit that we may be wise, as to know good from evil, yea and this was the plan from the beginning.

22 ¶ And thus ye worship the Father in my name, even Jesus who is the Christ; that they might come again unto that Elohim that brought life to their spirits.

23 And to this end was I born into the world, that my light, even the light of Christ, might shine through the darkness of the probation of man,

24 That all might be born again unto me and have my Holy Spirit to be with them.

25 But Adam knew this not, nor Eve his wife and thus they sought wisdom of the world and of themselves and not from me, the Lord their God.

26 ¶ But behold, there was and is a plan, that man may face the justice of God with the mercy of the Lord and both ends be met that they may regain their inheritance.

27 For behold, Eve too did partake of the fruit of that tree in temptation,

28 Yet she came unto Adam that he should become wise even as her, that they remain equals, for she was born such by his side.

29 ¶ And thus Adam partook of the fruit that they should remain together, as the Lord God commanded them.

30 And this was made possible for I have swallowed up victory over sin and death for all those that would come unto me;

31 Therefore, man should be faithful unto his wife, or even unto their wives, even as Adam was faithful unto Eve, who too was faithful unto him.

32 Yea, and they did journey forth from the garden together and did remain a helpmate unto each other.

33 ¶ And behold, I command those that shall read to give heed to that which is written;

34 And they shall pray always that I may unfold the same to their understanding.

35 And they shall give heed unto these words and trifle not, and I will bless them. Amen.

Chapter 9

The confession of Adam and Eve received in Ohio, January 12, 2016.

1 Yea, and thou hast perceived that Adam fell; in his foolishness he lost his inheritance;

2 But this I knew should be, and so too did he before he was born;

3 And behold, to this end was he born, to be the first man unto God, even as I should be the last.

4 For behold, in my Father's name did I create the Heavens and the Earth, and thus I am the beginning and the end.

5 So too was Adam with me in the beginning, as thou were also with me in the beginning.

6 ¶ But I am before the beginning, the Only Begotten, even before the creation of thy spirit by God who is our Father.

7 For behold, I am the same which spoke, and the world was made, and all things came by me;

8 And I am he which knoweth all things, for all things are present before mine eyes.

9 ¶ And it came to pass that Adam did fall and thus Lucifer thought to thwart the designs of God;

10 But behold he did not account for the righteousness of my servants, Adam and Eve.

11 For, knowing wisdom, Eve said unto Adam, after he is partaking of the fruit: Yea, it is better for us to pass through sorrow that we may know the good from the evil.

12 ¶ And it came to pass that Eve spoke unto Lucifer saying: I know thee now; behold thou art Lucifer, he who was cast out of the presence of God for rebellion.

13 But behold, this Wisdom was from God, for the Spirit had not yet fallen upon Adam and Eve, but the wisdom in them from their Mother had been planted in their hearts from the fruit of that tree;

14 And thus, ye see the Light of Christ is given to every man, that he may know good from evil;

15 Wherefore, I, the Lord, might show unto you the way to judge, and behold this is how she was warned.

16 ¶ And thus did Lucifer say unto her, wisely, as to the wisdom of the world: Yea, and I see that thine eyes are now open, even as I promised.

17 For he sought to keep them trapped and ensnared in his lies, as he had Lilith.

18 ¶ And it came to pass that Adam looked upon the serpent and saw his apron of priestcraft and asked him: Yea, what is this apron that thou hast covered thyself with?

19 For behold, up to this time, man was naked as to the things of the Lord;

20 Yeah, this is not to say that Adam and Eve wore nothing, save it be their skins; yea they were naked as to clothing themselves in righteousness;

21 And, knowing good from evil, Adam saw that Satan was clothed in wickedness.

22 ¶ And it came to pass that Adam asked him again, saying: What is that skin that ye wear?

23 ¶ And twice did Lucifer seek to yield not unto the man an answer, but behold even as he was tempted three times, so too did the man ask

a third time: Behold, what is this apron with which thou hath clothed thyself?

24 And it came to pass that devil, seeking to fool the man, spake unto him upon the third time, saying: It is an emblem of my power and priesthoods.

25 Yeah, and behold; the devil hath no power but unto evil and priestcraft and sorcery and wickedness;

26 Thus the devil called his darkness power, and his priestcraft priesthood to mock that which is holy before me.

27 ¶ At this, the man, Adam, knowing right from wrong by the power given him from the fruit of that tree, which is the spirit of Christ given unto every man, yea even my Light unto them;

28 Thus he did say unto that devil: I am looking for YHVH, my Father, to come down to give us further instructions.

29 And behold, this made the devil angry, and Lucifer said unto him, in much mocking: O! thou art looking for God to come down?

30 But behold, hearing the voice of Adam, calling upon the name of the Lord, Elohim spoke unto me, saying:

31 My beloved Son, we promised the sons and daughters of man that we should visit them and give them further instructions; Come, let us go down.

32 ¶ Thus did the Father send me down, and came I down with the Father, even as we did unto my servant Joseph;

33 And we were then with them, the men and that devil, even in the Garden.

34 And when we entered the Garden, Adam and Eve did hear, and Satan caused that fear should come over him, that the fate of Lilith, unknown to Adam, should fall on him and his wife, Eve.

35 ¶ And it came to pass that, mocking God, Lucifer gave unto Adam to make for themselves aprons of leaves to hide that they were naked in the things of the Lord, saying:

36 See ye art naked; take thee some fig leaves and make unto thee aprons; least Elohim see thy nakedness; Behold, hide yourselves with much speed!

37 And Adam and Eve hid, but unlike Lilith, they did not flee the Garden before us; yea they stood in our presence yet hidden from before us.

38 ¶ And it came to pass that I called out for man, knowing that they had hidden themselves; and the man and his wife called out, confessing their sins, even their nakedness.

39 And though they sought repentance, they did not confess their sins unto themselves;

40 But behold they placed blame one to another and upon that serpent, even that devil, Lucifer.

41 ¶ And it came to pass that I did curse him and cast him out; yea my servants, Sanvi, Sanzanvi, and Semangel commanded him saying unto that serpent: Depart!

42 ¶ And then said I unto Adam: Be not sorrowful, my son Adam, for thou did wish to become a god and yet did thou transgress my command.

43 For behold, knew he not that for this end came he into the world.

44 And I spoke unto him again saying: Behold, I will establish thee, not at this present, but after the days of thy probation, that thou may prove thyself.

45 And thus I prepared them to be sent out of the garden.

Chapter 10

The washing of the Priesthood received in Ohio, January 12 & 16, 2016.

1 And there, in the Garden, said I unto them: I wash thee preparatory to your receiving your anointings, that you may become clean from the blood and sins of this generation.

2 And behold, I did command them to do these things one unto the other, instructed I them by the mouths of my servants; Sanvi, Sanzanvi and Semangel.

3 And thus did Adam wash Eve, and thus did Eve wash Adam.

4 ¶ And thus did I the Lord their God say unto them, by the mouths of my servants:

5 I anoint thy head, that thy brain and thy intellect may be clear and active;

6 Thy ears, that thou mayest hear the Word of the Lord;

7 Thy eyes, that thou mayest see the glory of God;

8 Thy nose, that thou mayest smell of the offerings of the Lord;

9 Thy mouth, that thou mayest speak forth His praise;

10 Thy neck, that it may bear up thine head properly;

11 Thy shoulders, that they may bear the burdens that shall be placed thereon;

12 Thy back, that there may be marrow in the bones and in the spine;

13 Thy breast, that it may be the receptacle of pure and virtuous principles;

14 Thy vitals and bowels, that these may be healthy and perform their proper functions;

15 Thy arms, that thou may be strong to perform His work;

16 Thy hands, that they may be strong and wield the sword of justice in defense of truth and virtue;

17 Thy loins, that thou may be fruitful and multiply and replenish the earth, that thou might have joy in posterity;

18 Thy legs, that thou might run and not be weary, and walk and not faint;

19 Thy feet, that they might be swift in the paths of righteousness and truth.

20 ¶ And thus did I command Adam to say unto Eve, and Eve unto Adam; and behold they were faithful.

21 ¶ And then commanded I them, to place their hands on one another's heads, to seal the washing.

22 But behold, when thou doest as such, behold a High Priest or High Priestess should perform the work, but at such time Adam and Eve were the only living to be ordained unto me.

23 ¶ And thus did I instruct Adam to say unto Eve: Eve, Mother of All Living; having authority, I lay them my hands upon thy head and seal upon thee this washing, that thou may become clean from the blood

and sins of this generation through thy faithfulness. So mote it be. Amen.

24 But behold, these things shall thou seal unto me in my name, yea even the name of Jesus.

25 And thus did I teach them, through the mouths of my servants, Sanvi, Sanzanvi and Semangel.

Chapter 11

The anointings of the Priesthood received in Ohio on January 16, 2016.

1 And behold, whilst still in the Garden did I anoint them also, that they, Adam and Eve, would be properly Initiated;

2 And after their feet were washed, and that washing sealed, thus were they anointed:

3 Behold, I commanded them by the mouths of my servants, Sanvi, Sanzanvi and Semangel, to put consecrated oil upon each other's heads and to bless one another, saying:

4 I pour this holy anointing oil upon thy head and anoint thee preparatory to thy becoming a priest or a priestess unto the Most High God; hereafter to rule and reign in the house of God forever.

5 ¶ And I commanded them to say unto one another thus, and this they did, calling one another by name, and stating the authority that I had given them.

6 ¶ And behold, these were the words which I gave unto them in the Garden to anoint one another:

7 I anoint thy head, that thy brain and thy intellect may be clear and active;

8 Thy ears, that thou may hear the Word of the Lord;

9 Thy eyes, that thou may see the glory of God;

10 Thy nose, that thou may smell of the sweet fragrance offered unto the Lord;

11 Thy mouth, that thou may speak forth His praise;

12 Thy neck, that it may bear up thy head properly;

13 Thy shoulders, that they may bear the burdens that shall be placed thereon;

14 Thy back, that there may be marrow in the bones and in the spine;

15 Thy breast, that it may be the receptacle of pure and virtuous principles;

16 Thy vitals and bowels, that they may be healthy and perform their proper functions;

17 Thy arms, that thou may be strong to perform His work;

18 Thy hands, that they may be strong and wield the sword of justice in defense of truth and virtue;

19 Thy loins, that thou may be fruitful and multiply and replenish the earth, that you might have joy in thy posterity;

20 Thy legs, that thou might run and not be weary, and walk and not faint;

21 Thy feet, that they might be swift in the paths of righteousness and truth.

22 ⸹ And then did they again lay their hands one upon the other, this they did to confirm and seal the anointings.

23 ⸹ And thus did Eve say unto Adam: given authority from the Lord, I lay my hands upon thy head and confirm upon thee this anointing, wherewith thou hast been anointed in the temple of our God, within this Garden; preparatory to becoming a king and a priest unto the most high God; hereafter to rule and reign in the house of God forever, and seal upon thee all the blessings hereunto appertaining, through thy faithfulness; So mote it be, Amen.

24 ⸹ And again, I say unto thee, that thou shall do this in my name, sealing them up in the name of Jesus Christ.

25 And behold, these Initiatories and these Endowments are to prepare thee for service in my kingdom and exaltation in the Celestial worlds,

26 And these should not be seen as a requirement for salvation in the kingdom of God;

27 For the Endowment is given as one dedicates him or herself to a life of service to the Lord their God;

28 And all I require of this generation is a sacrifice unto me of a broken heart and a contrite spirit;

29 For whoso cometh unto me with a broken heart and a contrite spirit, him shall I baptize with fire and with the Holy Ghost.

30 ¶ Behold, the Endowment is an invitation to join the Church of the Firstborn; and this invitation is extended to all.

31 And I say unto thee, O man: Understand that if thou proceed and receive in thyself the full endowment, you will be required to take upon thee sacred obligations in your service to your Lord and Savior, even Jesus Christ;

32 Yea, and the violation of which shall bring upon thee the judgments of God; for I, the Lord your God shall not be mocked.

33 Therefore, all should be given warning that if they so desire to withdraw rather than accept these obligations of their own free will and choice, they may make it known.

34 Yea, and there is no harm in this, for behold not all that come unto me are called to the work;

35 But those that desire to do the work are called, and thus shall these be washed and anointed. Even so, Amen.

Chapter 12

Garments of the Priesthood & the new name received in Ohio, January 16, 2016.

1 And at that day, after receiving their Washing and Anointing, Adam and Eve were ready to leave the Garden, to preach repentance in my name to those outside.

2 But behold, I had clothed them only in spiritual righteousness by my Grace; they had yet to put upon them the robes of my priesthood.

3 ¶ And it came to pass that I set them, even Adam and Eve before the altar, facing eastward, and there gave unto them the Garments of the Holy Priesthood;

4 There I did show unto them the proper wearing of these holy garments; tying it in a bow on the right side for these as they wert new to my works.

5 And this I did to prepare them to leave the Garden.

6 ❡ And it came to pass that they were given new names by my servants, Sanvi, Sanzanvi and Semangel.

7 And there they were then instructed to bless one another as such:

8 Having authority on the name of God, I place this garment upon thee, which thou art to wear in service to the Lord throughout thy life;

9 Inasmuch as thou doth not defile it, but are true and faithful to thy covenants, it will be a shield and a protection to thee against the power of the destroyer until thou hast finished thy work here upon the earth;

10 With this garment, I give thee a new name, which thou should always remember, thy name is Michael for the man and Chavah for the woman, and thus was given unto them a new name.

11 ❡ And further, they blessed one another, as they were moved by the power of the Holy Spirit.

12 And thou too shall do this, for thy garment represents the garments given to Adam and Eve when they were found naked in the Garden of Eden and is called the Garment of the Holy Priesthood;

13 Then shalt thou say: We leave with thee this blessing in the spirit of prophecy and in the name of our Lord and Savior, even Jesus Christ; So Mote It Be. Amen.

14 For behold, all things shall be done in my name, for thou art mine.

15 ❡ And this shall ye say unto the world when they receive these things:

16 Turn thee away from sin as thy father and mother, Adam and Eve, and walk the path of righteousness;

17 Behold, this is the secret mystery of the reverence of the Lord.

18 Those who are worthy, these shall go directly to the secret, for unto them the mystery has been revealed;

19 And I say unto these, look and see, for only unto those filled with the Spirit of God shall be revealed the secret of God.

20 ❡ Thus I say unto thee: Proclaim peace; praise God, the ruler above, in my name; yea preach repentance in my name;

21 And the chosen shall create heaven on earth; the beauty of Israel shall even blossom from their bosoms;

22 For prayers proclaim the glory; by prayer shalt thou stay upon the path of the Lord.

23 Therefore, give praise that thou may grow in grace that the world shall see my perfection in thee.

24 ¶ And thus were Adam and Eve made clean, anointed, and clothed, as thou too have been done;

25 And, as all shall do, just as Adam and Eve when they too prepared to leave the Garden into the world.

26 Let them that hath ears listen, and those that have lips share the secret of the Lord. Even so, Amen.

Chapter 13

Revelation on the "threads of the garments" received in Ohio on January 16, 2016. Compare to the Book of Raziel, verses 26-27.

1 And it came to pass that the Lord called, and another angel came among them; and his name was Raphael;

2 And the Lord introduced the angel to Adam and Eve, commanding them to listen to him as they had Sanvi, Sanzanvi and Semangel.

3 And behold, Raphael was called to be Melchizedek in the flesh and is the king of peace;

4 And he is the angel of mysteries, making known unto man the secrets of God, yea and even the revealer of the Rock of God.

5 And he is an angel of healing, for when he stirs the waters he brings healing to those that do wash in it.

6 And thus he was called upon by the Lord to teach his servants, Adam and Eve, that they might be healed of their sins against the Lord their God.

7 ¶ And unto them he said: The root of the commandments of God is love; and the love of God is the thread of the Garments of the Priesthood.

8 ¶ Behold, thine ears hath been anointed, that thou mayest hear the Word of the Lord;

9 And the first thread of the Garments of the Priesthood harmonizes with the ears; thus do not be deceived by hearing lies, nor hear the ending of the Word.

10 The path to God is straight (Ysrael) and hears the decrees.

11 ¶ Behold, thine eyes have been anointed, that thou mayest behold the glory of God;

12 And the second thread of the Garments of the Priesthood harmonizes with the eyes; thus shalt thou see by raising up the eyes.

13 Do not let thine eyes brim with tears, that after weeping they do not close;

14 Thine eyes are the windows of the soul; speak by the power of the eyes, lest you forget the words seen; yea, cast down thy eyes to salvation.

15 And the eye of revelation is that of understanding, showing unto thee the Crown of God (Keter); and it rests between the eyes.

16 ¶ Behold thy nose hath been anointed, that thou may smell the sweet offerings of the Lord;

17 The third thread of the Garments of the Priesthood harmonizes with the nose.

18 Let thy nose be not irritated or excited by the sweet scent of idolatry, nor desire to keep unto thyself the offerings given unto the Lord, but rather smell the sweet scents of the Sabbath, and other beautiful things of the Lord.

19 ¶ Behold thy mouth hath been anointed, that thou mayest speak forth God's praise;

20 The fourth thread of the Garments of the Priesthood harmonizes with the mouth.

21 Have patience; let the tongue not speak words out of anger;

22 Yea, of all words written, do not labor to make the oath without the intent to keep it, that thy promises be sure.

23 Do not deceive by words or speaking the name of God in vain; do not make the oath and speak falsehoods that thy words be pure.

24 Yea, perfection is of God and the Son of Man alone, all else are made perfect in Him, therefore let the Spirit be thy bridle.

25 ¶ Behold thy neck hath been anointed, that it may bear up thine head;

26 Thus, the fifth thread of the Garments of the Priesthood harmonizes with the throat.

27 Do not swallow any abominations, but maketh to eat unleavened bread, which is to say, only in righteousness and moderation.

28 ¶ Behold, thy hands hath been anointed, that they may be strong and wield the sword of justice in defense of truth and virtue;

29 Thus, the sixth thread of the Garments of the Priesthood harmonizes with the hands.

30 Do not lay the hand in sin and do not steal, but take hold of the Word of God;

31 Yea, open the door of the house of God with the hand and bind the signs and tokens by the means of it.

32 ¶ Behold thy loins hath been anointed, that thou may be fruitful and multiply and replenish the earth, that thou might have joy in posterity;

33 Thus, the seventh thread of the Garments of the Priesthood harmonizes with the loins.

34 Do not commit adultery, but to thy house be true that thou mayest have health in the navel, marrow in the bones, strength in the loins and in the sinews;

35 And that the power in the Priesthood shall be upon thee, and upon thy posterity through all generations of time, and throughout all eternity.

36 Be fruitful and multiply; have joy in thy posterity;

37 Yea, do this and the Lord YHVH your God shall circumcise thy hearts and the hearts of thine descendants.

38 ¶ Behold, thy feet hath been anointed, that they might be swift in the paths of righteousness and truth;

39 And the eighth thread of the Garments of the Priesthood harmonizes with the feet.

40 Thus, do not walk about after strange gods and thou shalt not stumble and fall;

41 Yea, walk after YHVH, the Lord God; journey by all paths, as commanded by the Lord God as spoken unto thee by the Holy Spirit;

42 And watch thy feet as you walk to the house of God, that thou shall do so in supplication before the Lord.

43 ¶ Man is to remember these eight things for all time; let them be written in the heart;

44 Ears first, eyes second, nose third, mouth fourth, neck fifth, hands sixth, loins seventh, and feet eighth.

45 Yea, do not sin by these, for the heart is with each;

46 Yea consider therefore the thoughts of all thou shalt meet:

47 Love thy neighbor as thyself, for to love another is to love the Lord God.

48 Yea, do these and ye shall be blessed. So mote it be, Amen.

Chapter 14

Revelation on the Torah of Sacrifice received in Ohio on January 16, 2016.

1 And behold, knowing I that Adam and Eve should be faithful, I did have my servants Sanvi, Sanzanvi and Semangel give unto them the First Endowment.

2 For behold, the Endowment is given in four parts; two in the lesser or Levitical Priesthood of the administering, and two in the greater or High Priesthood of the ministry.

3 The first is given as one enters back into the world enlightened after meeting the Lord in the Garden, as did Adam and Eve;

4 And I would that thou shall give such to all Deacons and Teachers, as they prepare to bring forth my word out unto the world.

5 And the second is given unto those that shall be my Priests and Priestesses, for these shall give unto mankind my saving ordinances.

6 The last two are given as my servants unto the High Priesthood; one for the Elder and one for the High Priest and High Priestess;

7 For these shall see unto the needs of my vineyard, and these they shall know to assist them, and they do my works of righteousness here upon the earth.

8 And before leaving the Garden, behold Sanvi, Sanzanvi and Semangel did give unto them such.

9 ⁋ And wearing their garments, Adam and Eve came unto Sanvi, Sanzanvi and Semangel, prepared at that time to be dressed in the robes of the priesthood.

10 And they then verified that they did receive a new name unto me at the time they received their garments, and that they did still remember these names.

11 ¶ And thus they, Adam and Eve his wife, approached the altar;

12 The first facing East, the other speaking in the name of the Lord standing on the opposite, the one facing the other.

13 And thus did I command unto them to say: This Endowment is to prepare thee for service unto the Lord, and exaltation in the Celestial Kingdom, and thus are not requirements unto thy salvation in the kingdom of God.

14 The Endowment is given unto thee as thou hast dedicated thyself to a life of service to the Lord;

15 Yea, and thus the full endowment is an invitation to join the Church of the Firstborn and be one with God; and behold, this invitation is extended to all.

16 Understand therefore that if thou proceed and receive thy full endowment, thou will be required to take upon thyself sacred obligations in service to the Lord;

17 Yea, and the violation of which will bring upon thee the judgments of God, for God shall not be mocked.

18 If thou desire to withdraw rather than accept these obligations of thine own free will and accord, thou mayest now make it known.

19 ¶ And behold, it came to pass that each did accept that which they were charged with and given.

20 And thus, each were given a green apron of fig leaves and asked to put this on over their garments.

21 And when thou shall do this, thou shalt first remove thy shoes and thy gartel for these works are holy unto me;

22 Then, putting the apron on over the Garment of the Priesthood the gartel should be returned to the waist in the same fashion as it was when it was removed, with the bow to the right, and the shoes shall then be returned to the feet.

23 ¶ Then taught I unto them, by my servants: This apron represents the Holy Priesthood that thou have been ordained to, and the oaths thou hast made,

24 That thou should remember to repent of thy sins oft before me, and the priesthood and oaths that I did impart unto thee here in the Garden;

25 And this I do give unto thee that thou might worship me, and through me the Father in spirit and in truth, and that through me thou might return to the presence of thy God.

26 ¶ And thus I gave unto them that apron of cloth, spun from leaves, that they should remember to repent of their sins before me and the priesthood and oaths that I did impart unto them in the Garden.

27 And behold, I did teach them by the means of the holy emblems I did placed I upon them;

28 And I made them garments of skins, made holy unto me by the emblems placed I upon them:

29 The square for the justice of Elohim, and the compass for my mercy; for behold in my atonement are both ends met;

30 And the symbol of my Holy Spirit and also a sign unto them and to all generations that every knee shall bow and every tongue confess that I, even Jesus, am the Christ: Son of the Living God.

31 And this I shall give unto all that shall serve me that they may remember that from the beginning they might be saved in me by my name if they are faithful.

32 ¶ Then I commanded them next to say unto the other: Thou art to be given the token of the Law of Sacrifice with its accompanying name, and sign at the altar;

33 Behold, we desire to impress upon thy mind the sacred character of the token of the Law of Sacrifice, and its sign;

34 Yea, and always remember these covenants; to observe and keep the Law of Sacrifice, as contained in my Word.

35 And behold, this was the beginning of the sacrifice of animals unto me.

36 ¶ And then, from across the altar, each was given the Token of the Law of Sacrifice;

37 And to make this token, the individual will clasp the right hand with the right hand of the other presenting the endowment, placing the joint of the thumb directly over the first knuckle of one another's hand.

38 And the name of this token is the new name received with one's garments; each should share their names with the other as they give the token.

39 ¶ And then, from across the altar, each was given the Sign of the Law of Sacrifice;

40 This sign is made by bringing the right arm to the square, the palm of the hand to the front, the fingers close together, and the thumb extended.

41 And thus did they give unto one another the token and the sign of the Law of Sacrifice at the altar;

42 ¶ And I saw that all things which I had made were good.

43 For behold, this I did give them that they might worship me and through me the Father in Spirit and in Truth, and that through me they might return to the presence of God.

44 And by this did that which they had made become that which they sought; even an apron of the holy priesthood that both did have access to, and with this the first signs and tokens of that priesthood;

45 And the Office of the Priesthood that Adam did receive that he might offer sacrifices unto me, in similitude of my sacrifice, yea as I AM, the Only Begotten of the Father, which is full of grace and truth.

46 And the power of the Priesthood after the Order of the Son of God unto Eve did I give, that she might come unto me in prayer, and that she might pray over her seed, even to bless them.

47 ¶ Yet they did not yet know why they should do these things which I, the Lord, did command them.

48 Nevertheless, said Elohim unto me: Behold, these wish to know Good from Evil,

49 Therefore, see that Adam and Eve are driven out of this garden into the lone and dreary world, there these may learn from experience to distinguish good from evil unto themselves.

50 And as it was said, so was it done.

51 ¶ And it came to pass that they did leave the Garden and my presence to bring forth my Gospel unto the world of mankind, to the eternal downfall of Satan, wickedness and evil.

52 And they did wear these and were faithful and became holy through mine atonement unto man.

Chapter 15

Revelation containing the teachings of Raphael on the Torah of Sacrifice received in Ohio on January 16, 2016. Compare to Raziel, verses 1-5.

1 And it came to pass that upon leaving the Garden, I sent my servant Raphael to instruct them further.

2 And Raphael said unto them: Blessed are the wise by the mysteries coming from the wisdom of that tree, given them of the Lord God.

3 Light is given to teach truth unto mankind; the power of the Lower and High Priesthoods is the foundation of the glory of Elohim.

4 This secret word, for it is as yet unknown to the world, is as milk and honey upon the tongues of the righteous;

5 For now, it be to you alone; for behold, these teachings are no longer foreign unto you.

6 ¶ And a commandment I give unto thee, not of my will, but a commandment of YHVH:

7 Stand in the middle of the day, without provocation and without reward, and pray unto God that thou mayest learn the tributes of the reverence of Elohim.

8 ¶ Behold, thou art cast out from the Garden and the face of God, this is but for a time;

9 Turn away thou from evil, journey on the path of righteousness that through Grace thou might see the face of God again while upon the earth.

10 ¶ Behold, I say unto thee: The great secret is reverence to the Lord; for the worthy go directly to the secret.

11 For now, only reveal the secret of God to those that serve the Lord;

12 But the time shall come that all shall know, and at that last day, every knee shall bow, and every tongue confess these secrets.

13 ¶ Yeah, and there are three secrets corresponding to the Law; and all secrets correspond to these three.

14 The first commandment is the first wisdom: Reverence of the Lord.

15 And Reverence of the Lord is the first knowledge;

16 Yea, the beginning of wisdom is reverence of the Lord, corresponding to three wisdoms.

17 And of the outer wisdom, rejoice and build the house of wisdom with the secret of the foundation.

18 Be wise by opening the heart to this secret; for there are but three types of secrets:

19 The secret of the journey, the secret of origins, and the secret of the laws of God;

20 These are made clear by the help of the Almighty God.

21 ¶ There are three kinds of reverence of heaven;

22 They are reverence to the Lord, reverence to the Spirit of God, and reverence to Elohim.

23 ¶ It is made clear that reverence to the Lord is to love God and serve in love;

24 For mankind only receives happiness when they revere the Lord YHVH (Jesus Christ).

25 And it is reverence of Elohim to revere the Lord; and this shall ye do in love.

26 ¶ Desire in thy hearts, yea even write these things upon your hearts, and ye shall keep the commandments;

27 For this is the whole Law: love the Lord thy God in reverence to Elohim; yea revere Elohim, lest you come into the hands of temptation.

28 Mankind is not to serve God in temptation; not rising up by the name of the Messiah (Christ).

29 It is decreed above, and it is written in the heavens: Mankind is beloved;

30 Therefore, to love God is to love thy neighbor.

31 God spoke to you and shall lead thy sons and daughters, even they that shall obey;

32 Thus ye shall know to revere Elohim; thus ye know of love.

33 Know too that mankind is not happy to journey by the counsel of wickedness; yea, mankind is only happy to revere the Lord;

34 Therefore, show ye reverence to the God of heavens and the Earth all of thy days.

35 ¶ Write love in thy hearts, for reverence of the God of the heavens is in thy heart at all times;

36 Yea, and this love is reverence, and this reverence is the purity of the Lord.

37 And those giving reverence are loved by the Lord.

38 Behold, there is much value in living in purity of spirit;

39 Therefore, bathe in the glory of the light of Elohim.

40 Ye that have gone forth from darkness into light, these have been divided from those led astray;

41 And as the light shines down upon the waters of baptism, this is the reverence of Elohim who spoke unto thee in the Garden.

42 From love, understanding was created by the love and reverence; and a thousand generations come after from that love.

Chapter 16

Revelation on the Torah of the Gospel received in Ohio on January 16, 2016.

1 Behold, I say unto thee, here is wisdom, whereby ye may know my mercy unto the meek, yea and unto those that will but humble themselves before me.

2 And it came to pass that Adam and his wife, Eve, did leave the Garden and the presence of the Lord; and they were faithful unto the commands I gave them in the Garden.

3 For behold, I did teach them to keep sacred that which they had learned in the Garden before being cast out;

4 And we commanded them that they should not sell them at any price nor give them unto those that know not the Lord.

5 ¶ And this they did; and they called unto me oft saying: Pe le-El, asking God to hear the words of their mouths.

6 And behold, that devil did try to come among them testing their patience; bringing with him the wizards and sorcerers of the world, and with them that priestcraft.

7 But behold, my servants, Adam and Eve, sought not after idols, nor the whisperings of false spirits; for they had known me in the Garden and would not be fooled.

8 And behold, it came to pass that I sent unto them mine angels, Sanvi, Sanzanvi, and Semangel;

9 And they came unto them appearing as men, to test them about in the world.

10 And behold, Adam and Eve would neither buy nor sell the things of God nor offer to offend the Lord and kept the commandments they were given;

11 Yea, they kept their priesthoods sacred unto me.

12 And thus it came to pass that I sent unto them mine angels, Sanvi, Sanzanvi and Semangel,

13 And they came unto them as themselves; and cast out Satan from their mist and gave unto them mine Everlasting Gospel.

14 And behold, this they did line upon line, and precept upon precept; here a little and there a little.

15 For Adam and Eve had created an altar as they had seen in the temple of the Garden of Eden;

16 And thus, after their own fashion, had created a temple unto the Lord for they, and for their their children, and for all those in the world that learned of the Goodness of God.

17 And thus, at the altar of God, where too these had made their sacrifices of animals, did my servants teach them.

18 After introducing the First Endowment, thus sharing it with their children and their friends as commanded by Sanvi, Sanzanvi, and Semangel, the people of God, led by my prophet Adam and my prophetess Eve, all were given the token and sign of the Law of Sacrifice at the altar.

19 It was then, at the altar, that Adam and Eve were presented with the robe and miznefet of the priesthood;

20 And there too were they instructed to wear them as officers of the Priesthood of the Son of God.

21 Their shoes, apron, and gartel first being removed; then the robe placed over the left shoulder, over the garments;

22 And the miznefet placed upon the head, that the crown of mankind be covered to show reverence to the Lord of prayer.

23 And after this, the Lord instructed that the apron and gartel be put back upon them, over the robes, and their shoes returned to their feet.

24 ¶ Then did the one stand across from the other, they that were receiving facing east, and the other across the altar, facing they that were to receive.

25 And behold, they were instructed to do my works, and they would be blessed and lifted up at the last day.

26 Then were they given the Law of the Gospel, and also a charge to avoid all light mindedness, loud laughter, evil speaking of one another or of the Lord's anointed, the taking of the name of God in vain, and every other unholy and impure practice.

27 And I impressed upon them the sacred character of the token of the Law of Sacrifice, and its sign;

28 And to remind them of their covenants to observe and keep the Law of the Gospel and this charge, as it has been explained to them, in the Garden.

29 And thus were they instructed before the Lord by my servants, Sanvi, Sanzanvi, and Semangel.

30 ¶ And it came to pass that they were then given the token and sign of the Law of the Gospel from across the altar.

31 The token of the Law of the Gospel was given by clasping the right hands and placing the joint of the thumb between the first and second knuckles of each other's hands;

32 And the name of this token is the first given name of the person receiving it, that is their earthly or worldly name.

33 Yea, and too were they given the Sign of the Law of the Gospel from across the altar;

34 This sign being made by bringing the right hand in front, with the hand, palm up, in cupping shape, the right arm forming a square;

35 The left arm raised to the square, the palm of the hand to the front, the fingers close together, and the thumb extended.

36 ¶ And it came to pass that the token and the sign of the Law of the Gospel at the altar were given and received by all that would partake of them from across the altar.

37 And behold, they then prayed as one, they using the sign of the Law of the Gospel;

38 Praying in a circle, placing the elbows of their left arms on the right shoulder of the brother or sister to their right, with their right hand in front, with the hand, palm up, in cupping shape.

39 And thus they did in the name of the Lord, and I saw it was good, and was much pleased.

Chapter 17

Revelation on the types of offering received in Ohio on January 16, 2016.
Compare to the Book of Raziel, verses 6-8.

1 And after being ordained Priest and Priestess, God sent unto them the voice of instruction from Raphael.

2 And the archangel said unto them: There are three kinds of offerings:

3 These are the burnt offering, the peace offering, and the sin offering.

4 So too are there three classes of righteousness; they are love Celestial, petition Terrestrial, and reverence Telestial.

5 The burnt offering corresponds to love; the peace offering corresponds to petition; and the sin offering corresponds to reverence.

6 The burnt offering is a sacrifice to the glory of God alone, and this is to be done as a symbol of the Son of Man who shall come to be put to death by His friends.

7 The peace offering, and sin offering are for the sake of the living body.

8 Proclaim love from the petition and petition ye shall give in reverence.

9 From love, you serve God in righteousness; therefore, give glory and honor to the kingdoms of God: Celestial, Terrestrial, and Telestial, these alone before all things.

10 In his infinite righteousness, the Lord created the universe by the Word, not by the labor of His hands;

11 God the Father, and Jesus the King are strong and wise, good and compassionate.

12 God tolerates all things, filling all the highest and lowest, sustaining in the high places and bringing forth all creatures;

13 He reveals unto men the mysteries of the universe at his pleasure, the knowledge of good and evil he has given unto them that will receive by the fruit of that tree.

14 Yea, the Lord tolerates wickedness now for the sake of the Restoration to come.

15 ¶ Behold, all blessings shall be unto the righteous who love God.

16 Give praise and laud over His works, for they are the greatest works.

17 The burnt offering is sacrifice by petition; serve in the holy place, for blessed is it and as a temple unto the Lord shall it be until the Son of Man shall come.

18 And when thou shall worship the Lord God, fall in supplication and petition, yea and with a broken heart and a contrite spirit;

19 Yea, petition for every measure of goodness, being born again for the sake of the benefit of the body of mankind.

20 This is the foundation of Chokhmah (wisdom), and of Da'at (knowledge), and from wisdom comes Chesed (mercy) and from Da'at comes Gevurah (judgment);

21 Together these bring Binah (understanding); from Binah comes the light of the day to dispel the darkness, for Binah is but Keter (the Crown) to mankind.

22 ¶ And the light shall heal the woman which is the Church of God; and she shall conceive and make sons that shall stand upright before the Lord, for they shall be pierced in the heart.

23 And Raphael blessed them, saying: Thou shall succeed in the works of the Lord;

24 Thou hast forgone wealth, and glory, and worldly treasures, all to the goodness of God.

25 Therefore, as Priest and Priestess thou shall petition the Lord above and sacrifice unto him the peace offering.

26 ¶ Give reverence and serve God in great fear.

27 Be delivered from curses of the land in which thou dwellest.

28 The punishment that came forth from the holy place, Eden, might be a blessing, if thou can see it as it is;

29 Its measure is longer than the Earth and wider than the sea.

30 ¶ Receive salvation from affliction, injury, and suffering;

31 Do not writhe in pain; do not be ruled over by foreign lands or their gods.

32 Do not bring death or speak evil but fill thy days in goodness and blessings in the world.

33 Deliver others from misfortune and affliction and destruction, yea from the fire and burden of sin.

34 The wicked here outside the Garden, without Chesed it shall prepare to burn in flames on the day of the great judgment; So mote it be, Amen.

35 ¶ And the angel of the Lord commended them further: By reverence of the Lord, rise up by sacrifice of the sin offering, teach them the ways of the Lord (YHVH).

36 Make three sacrifices: the burnt offering, the peace offering, and the sin offering.

37 Of sacrifices in the first house through the first priest in the name of the one God, three times in righteousness: by love, by petition, and by reverence.

38 Complete them and be protected by God, protecting and loving you from petition and reverence.

39 ¶ The beginning wisdom is reverence of the Lord and love of heaven, for they that love their neighbors love the Lord their God.

40 The heart of the righteous burns as flames of fire, having been judged by Gevurah and found to possess Chesed; thus keep the commandments in reverence of the Lord.

41 This the Lord requires, not making reward for reverence and love; for reverence and love, the explicit Name was created;

42 Yea all things created by the Word were created of love.

43 Behold, this is the reverence of the Almighty God (El Shaddai); and thou shalt revere God by keeping every commandment, by keeping the Law of Love.

44 ¶ Fall down in supplication and cry out to God; establish the heart and grant the petition at once;

45 Reject wickedness, but condemn not the wicked, yea, ye shall teach them righteousness.

46 Unto those that forsake reverence of the Almighty, know that to withhold mercy for sins is God's judgement; let he who has ears hear.

47 Unto those that forsake the petition, not reverencing the name of the Almighty, teach them not to desire evil, and not to let evil grow in their hearts.

48 In the middle of thy house, behold: The humble show reverence and gather in the house;

49 Stand there, and serve the Lord before God;

50 Show reverence in prayer and receive tranquility therein and the Lord shall deliver thee from all evil.

51 Dwell there in the temple of the Most High, hidden in the light of the knowledge of God Almighty.

52 Pray unto Him that He shall deliver thee from the mouth of the trap of deceivers; petition him in prayer.

53 Yea, speak saying: O God, hear thee the words of my mouth; protect us from the traps of those that would oppose thee!

54 In every petition to God Almighty, be blessed by God the Father and His Queen.

55 By the blessings of God Almighty, I say unto thee: Be fruitful and multiply.

56 ¶ God Almighty sees and turns away the wicked; therefore, be silent unto those that seek not the wisdom of God,

57 And bring forth from the secret place that which the Father reveals to you; So mote it be, Amen.

58 ¶ This Raphael said unto them, and this they taught unto all that the Lord should bring unto them.

59 And Adam and Eve did establish a church unto the Almighty God, of sixty, four hundred, and thirty; and the Lord above counted them as five hundred.

Chapter 18

The prayer of Eve and the Law of Christ received in Ohio on January 17, 2016.

1 And it came to pass that Adam was a humble man, and so too was his wife, Eve, bowing down and rising up before the Lord, making clear the reverence of God.

2 And behold, they served God with love in written the heart, yea and with great reverence and devotion and a prayer in their hearts.

3 And it came to pass that the Lord saw them keeping the commandments, and offering sacrifices to the Lord in reverence;

4 And he too saw them rejoice in supplication serving their creator;

5 And they taught their children too that they should serve the Lord.

6 ¶ And their hearts rejoiced to petition the Lord;

7 And Elohim saw this and blessed them with sons and daughters; one of which was Abel, and the other Cain.

8 And the Lord saw too the suffering and torment of Adam and Eve as Cain fell away from the light he had once received.

9 ¶ And it came to pass that Abel knew the reverence of Elohim; but Cain did not.

10 And Cain slew Abel to get gain, and he was judged and delivered unto retribution;

11 And the Lord was as angered by the sins of man.

12 ¶ And it came to pass that Eve went into the temple of the Lord and there she prayed saying: Pe le-El; my words are difficult to speak, Elohim.

13 I revere you and speak with great difficulty, for my heart is full;

14 Yet I shall not fall but have journeyed to the temple and revere you at the Altar, lest I too be punished.

15 Elohim, O Lord, my God: judge me by my reverence and forsake me not, for now I know good from evil;

16 And I feel as though I too have had my blood spilt, even my heart breaking and broken, spilling blood upon the earth.

17 But still I revere thee O God, speaking only the very word I fear is devouring or consuming my devoted heart.

18 ¶ And it came to pass that after this did I come unto her, and the words that were spoken by the Lord, between she and me, these shall thou not write.

19 Know thou that she was comforted by my Spirit, not to fall from grace;

20 And this because she did in every place revere me, and serve the Lord her God from the reverence of her humility; and thus I did call upon her in secret at this time.

21 ¶ And behold, it came to pass that I charged her to go into her home, that she might fetch her husband, that they should be given the Third Endowment, that they might know the suffering of the Son of Man.

22 And after bringing her husband to me at the altar, my servants Sanvi, Sanzanvi, and Semangel were there before them, waiting to instruct them.

23 ¶ And, there, at the altar, they were instructed how to wear the robes of the High Priesthood.

24 Their shoes, apron, gartel, robe and miznefet were first removed, for the very ground on which they stood was holy.

25 Their robes were placed on the right shoulder over the garments;

26 Their miznefet were returned to their heads, the apron and gartel were put back on over the robes, and the shoes returned to their feet.

27 And I gave unto them a vision, and said I unto them, Look!

28 And they looked, and they beheld the Son of Man, led away bearing His cross;

29 And they saw that I went forth into that place where they crucified me;

30 And they saw, and read the title put upon the cross saying:

JESUS OF NAZARETH
THE KING OF THE JEWS.

31 ¶ And then my servants Sanvi, Sanzanvi, and Semangel said unto them: We shall now give unto thee the Sign of the Nail, in preparation to receive the Law of Consecration;

32 To give unto thee also a charge to avoid all unholy and impure thoughts and practices;

33 And we are required to remind thee of thy covenants before the Lord to observe and keep the Law of the Gospel and this charge, as it has been explained unto thee.

34 Yea, and we desire to impress upon thy minds the sacred character of the token of the Sign of the Nail, and its sign;

35 And to remind thee again of thy covenants, and so to observe and keep these thy covenants and this charge, as it has been explained unto thee.

36 ¶ And thus they gave the token and sign of the Sign of the Nail to one another, as instructed from across the altar.

37 And the token of the Sign of the Nail is received by bringing the right hand vertical, the fingers close together with the thumb extended;

38 The person giving the token placing the tip of the forefinger of the right hand in the center of the palm, and the thumb opposite on the back of the hand of the one receiving it.

39 ¶ And behold, this token represents the nails in my palm when I was crucified for mankind;

40 And the meditation of this token is the Son, which is to say my name, even Jesus Christ; the Son of God, yea the very Son of Man.

41 ¶ And the sign of the Son is made by bringing the left hand in front, with the hand in cupping shape, the left arm forming a square;

42 And this is in reverence to the bitter cup from which I drank.

43 The right hand is then brought forward, with the palm facing down, the fingers close together, the thumb extended, placed over the left hip;

44 And this in reverence of the wound in my side, which was pierced by a spear, that my bones not be broken.

Chapter 19

*Revelation on the call to build a temple and teachings of Raphael received in
Ohio on January 17, 2016. Compare to the Book of Raziel, verses 10-14.*

1 And Adam and Eve were thus given the token of the Sign of the
Nail and the sign of the Son.

2 And upon seeing the death of God for the world, Eve's heart was
pained further, and she said:

3 I shall not see without raising up my eyes unto the salvation of God;

4 I shall not brim with tears, lest I forget all that I have seen.

5 ¶ And it came to pass that the man and woman went out the next
day to teach the sons and daughters of God;

6 And there were five hundred of them; five hundred strong ones, 248
sons and 252 daughters.

7 Yea, there were four more daughters than sons; and the Lord said
unto these: Be fruitful and multiply;

8 Therefore, establish a house of prayer even to petition my name.

9 Thus, the course of the universe is as five hundred years, let he who
has ears hear, for it is treasured by God as the measure of heaven.

10 ¶ And these he commanded to go out into the world and to speak
of heaven;

11 And according to God, there were not enough to serve.

12 ¶ And it came to pass that they did build a house unto the Lord,
and there again, the Lord sent Raphael unto them, to teach them
further instructions.

13 And behold, Raphael did say unto them: Remember the Almighty
God and the Messiah of all the nations sent unto the world by the
Father.

14 Behold the reverence of the Son of Man, he being aided by the
name of God, protected from the evil spirits.

15 Yea, by the protection of God, ye shall lodge and speak prayers of
supplication;

16 Therefore the name of God is written upon the heart of mankind,
or upon all those that serve the Lord.

17 Take hold of the rod of iron, place this the Word, over your hearts;

18 Proclaim and remember the sacred names of God to protect from the evil spirits, that is YHVH.

19 ❡ And when I return I shall reveal the secret of the fourteen signs of the holy name.

20 Thus, until then praise the Lord God in prayer;

21 Yea, proclaim thy praise, and speak saying: Praised is the Ruler above, and the chosen cast down to Earth.

22 For it is written before the earth was formed or even there was dry land for a beast to roam upon,

23 Be ye cast out from heaven to Earth, the beauty of those that shall return straight to the Lord (these are called *Israel*, or the straight path to God).

24 Prayers proclaim the glory; by prayer written with flame upon thy hearts in the letters of glory, stay upon the path of the Lord, which is Israel;

25 Therefore, by the nine Sephirot, thou shalt gain Keter, which is the Crown, in the Holy Temple, the Lord's House of Prayer.

26 Of the days of the Messiah, give praise below the crown, for in these are God's Chesed (Mercy).

27 ❡ Bind to Keter (the crown) and bind therein thy hearts to the heavens;

28 Therefore, fire is the Gevurah (justice) of God in heaven;

29 By the Holy Spirit of God shalt thou create fire and see fire therein, and thou shall feel this fire as it burns within thy bosom.

30 Thus, in the house of the Lord is fire corresponding to the angel of fire, even the Holy Spirit of God.

31 Know also, the Spirit has three branches, corresponding to the three names of God and is over His temples.

32 Go now, and upon the morrow teach unto thy seed all that thou hast learned.

33 And Raphael departed, leaving Adam and Eve alone in the temple.

34 And they wondered what more houses did the Lord have than this.

35 And it came to pass that the next day, they shared the sign and token of the Sign of the Nail with those that wished to receive;

36 But behold, the vision was for them alone, and thus mankind did not yet understand the fullness of my works.

Chapter 20

Revelation on the Torah of Consecration and the teachings of Raphael received in Ohio on January 17, 2016. Compare to Raziel, verse 15.

1 And it came to pass that Adam knew his wife again; and she bare a son, and called his name Seth: For God, said she, hath appointed me another seed instead of Abel, whom Cain slew.

2 And after introducing the third portion of the Endowment, unto Seth did the Lord reveal unto his servants, Adam and Eve, the final Endowment of the High Priesthood.

3 ¶ And it came to pass that I, the Lord, came unto my house and stood before the altar; and there did I give unto my servants Adam and Eve further instructions.

4 And then did I send unto them my servants Sanvi, Sanzanvi, and Semangel,

5 And these gave unto them the final token and sign of the High Priesthood saying unto them:

6 We now give unto thee the Law of Consecration, in connection with the Law of Sacrifice and the Law of the Gospel which thou hast already received,

7 And we remind thee of thy covenants; that thou art the very Children of God.

8 And behold, throughout time thou hast consecrated thyself;

9 Thy time, talents, and everything with which the Lord has blessed thee, or with which he may bless thee, to the service of the Lord and discipleship;

10 And, as a servant of God coming forth from the Garden of Eden, thou hast further dedicated thy services to the building up of the kingdom of God on the earth.

11 ¶ And it came to pass that they, Adam and Eve, were brought before the altar in the temple,

12 And my servants said unto them: The Law of Consecration is represented in the token of the Sure Sign of the Nail;

13 Behold, this token has reference to the crucifixion of our Lord and Savior when he shall be placed upon the cross.

14 Behold, thou hast seen that those that shall crucify him shall drive nails through the palms of his hands:

15 And behold then, that the weight of his body will not cause the nails to tear through the flesh of the hands, they shall also drive nails through his wrists;

16 Hence in the palm is the Sign of the Nail, and in the wrist is the Sure Sign of the Nail, or the Nail in the Sure Place.

17 ¶ And then did I give unto them the token of the Sure Sign of the Nail and the sign of the Law of Consecration.

18 And they did give these to one another from across the altar.

19 And the token is given by clasping the right hands, interlocking the little fingers, and placing the tip of the forefinger upon the center of the wrist, keeping the thumbs parallel with the fingers;

20 And the mediation of this token is Health in the navel, marrow in the bones, strength in the loins and in the sinews, power in the Priesthood be upon me, and upon my posterity through all generations of time, and throughout all eternity.

21 ¶ And behold, the sign of the Law of Consecration shall be made by raising both hands high above the head, and while lowering the hands three times repeating aloud the words Pe le-El each time, with the motion of the hands, which by interpretation means, mouth to God.

22 The hands shall be lowered in three movements, as each word is spoken; Pe: hands above head, le: the arms are dropped to the square, El: the hands lowered to the height of one's chest.

23 And behold at this shall thou come full circle, for thou started with the prayer of thy lips as thou grew the prayer of thy hearts.

24 ¶ And in that day, they did give unto one another the token of the Sure Sign of the Nail and the sign of the Law of Consecration.

25 And this wisdom was passed down orally after the first Book of Remembrance was taken from the earth,

26 And thus this wisdom that was called secret became a mystery because men, in their own wisdom did not understand that this secret was to be revealed by my Holy Spirit, and not of man;

27 For behold, this secret is the wisdom of the soul's awakening unto the understating of God.

28 ¶ And it came to pass that after they received the fourth endowment, I sent forth my servant Raphael to give unto them further light.

29 And my servant said unto them: Behold, the image engraved in the throne of glory resembles the image of a flying cherub.

30 Let thy souls fly over as the cherub takes flight; revere God by the hand of his strength;

31 Yea, revere God by the hand of Adam, the first man to walk with God upon the earth.

32 ¶ And God resembles the Son of Man over the many waters; and thus sing thee a hymn unto God.

33 And the hymn is this: The Lord reigns forever and ever; therefore, reverence to the Son of Man, according to the written truth.

34 Yea, give the children of God the truth of the Lord of Hosts, yea and give the truth to all of mankind.

35 ¶ Do not go forth unto carved images, for the daughter of Lilith was troubled by Eve and the maiden Asherah, who is Eden, the Mother of the Earth.

36 Thus the tribes of man multiply to put forth the Law, yet these do not know the Law; but condemn them not, for they know not what they do.

37 ¶ And ye shall not speak of idolatry in the house of God;

38 Written by the finger of God, the great name and the holy symbols of God shall not be mocked.

39 ¶ The sons of God shall take the daughters of God to wife, and the sons of God shall be their husbands; and ye shall proclaim them to take one another, seeking righteousness.

40 Around them, gather twelve in a circle to pray united, corresponding to the Three as One and Three that spread out as they go forth.

41 ¶ And it came to pass that wisdom was given them, and these were taught the true order of prayer.

42 And Raphael said again unto them: Straighten the back to unite the name of God, for there truth is written;

43 And place the sealing power upon them whilst in the flesh; yea and draw above and below, dwelling in the fourth firmament, the name in the Holy Temple;

44 Thus the holy tabernacle of four coverings: the first covering is spirit; the second veil is of skin; the third is of soul; and the fourth covering is white, as is the purity of the Lord.

45 Let they with ears understand, and these shall be blessed of Wisdom in the name of the Lord; So mote it be, Amen.

46 And the angel of the Lord took leave of them, and they marveled of his words.

Chapter 21

Revelation on receiving the Endowments received in Ohio on January 20, 2016.

1 And it came to pass that Adam and his wife Eve, having proven themselves unto the Lord,

2 And, YHVH, seeing that these had kept their covenants, sent other messengers to teach them further;

3 For behold, Adam and Eve and their sons and their daughters had built altars facing east to worship YHVH, yea unto the Lord their God.

4 ¶ And it came to pass that Seth, to him also there was born a son; and he called his name Enos: then began men to call upon the name of the Lord.

5 ¶ And the Lord sent unto them once again his messengers, Sanvi, Sanzanvi and Semangel, and these taught them many things.

6 And so too did he send others, Gabriel, Raphael, Suriel, Zadkiel, Sarathiel, and Ariel didst he sent unto them.

7 And they were blessed with the wisdom of God, and taught the mysteries of reverence, the Torah was given them to teach unto the sons of men.

8 And to those that would hear, their mouths opened, and from mouth to ear was the strength and glory, the light and power of the highest taught;

9 And such were the works and the foundation of the glory of Elohim.

10 ¶ But only unto the humble were the sacred words as milk and honey to their tongues;

11 From them did the world learn truth, and how to worship and pay tribute to YHVH in reverence of Elohim.

12 Yea, and in that day many were taught to turn away from evil and journey on the path of all righteousness.

13 ¶ And behold, the secret that was taught is thus:

REVERENCE UNTO
THE LORD

yea even this:

HOLINESS UNTO
THE LORD

14 The worthy desire this secret; yea and mankind in righteousness is happy to learn this secret wisdom, even at the last days.

15 ¶ And Sanvi, Sanzanvi and Semangel came unto them and they taught them once they and others had been ordained to the Holy Priesthood after the Order of the Son of God that these should receive a portion of their Endowment.

16 And unto these will they continue to be further Endowed with both light and knowledge as they grow in Grace and in Priesthood.

17 ¶ Behold, for thee in the Fellowship of Christ, the first Endowment is given after being ordained into the priesthood, the second after being ordained a Priest or Priestess, as were Adam and Eve;

18 And the third Endowments are given after one has been ordained an Elder, and the final after being made a High Priest or High Priestess unto the Lord.

19 ¶ And behold, the endowment may be given immediately after an ordination, but should be given no more than seven days from the time one has been ordained;

20 Yea, and none may be ordained to another degree without being properly endowed in the previous degree.

21 ¶ And those receiving an Endowment should wear their garments, and be dressed in the robes of the Priesthood, as they have been given.

22 And two witnesses should come forth and testify that the individual has been washed, anointed, and clothed in the garment of the Holy Priesthood.

23 For behold, in the Garden did the Lord Initiate Adam and his wife, Eve, into the Holy Priesthood;

24 And there they did the Washing of the Feet, and there they were anointed with oil and honey;

25 And thus they were washed clean and could receive of their endowments.

Chapter 22

Revelation on love and perfection received in Ohio on January 20, 2016. Compare to the Book of Raziel, verses 16-18.

1 And it came to pass that Adam and Eve grew old, and the angel of the Lord came to them in the temple.

2 And there Raphael said unto them: In the lowest dwelling, blood is sacrificed upon the altar of degrees, therefore corresponding to the door of selflessness and humility that all must walk through.

3 Teach with selflessness and humility; bind it tight and create mercy.

4 Yea, and this sacrifice shall purify all, it receives the heat of judgement to be dry as fire;

5 And this because of the sacrifice of the Son of Man; therefore, mercy corresponds to giving, the rising of the Son upon the Cross.

6 Judgment too is dry as fire and held overheat, and over anger and wrath;

7 Therefore, when God is angry, remember that He desires that we bestow unto others even as He bestoweth, and that in this God is honored.

8 ❡ And it came to pass that the angel of the Lord commanded them saying: Remove the ashes from the burnt offerings.

9 YHVH has seen that ye were tested by the ten trials, and ye that give these to God in prayer.

10 God, the creator of the Heavens and the Earth reigns;

11 Therefore, bind ye to Keter and He shall create unto thee a delightful throne of glory in the house of the world to come.

12 And God has given unto thee a bride, a virgin; or in other words a pure desire to bestow.

13 ❡ Know ye that the perfection of the Lord is removed at this time from man;

14 Yea, rise over by counsel from God and thou shalt reach the perfection by Christ, who is to come.

15 Yea, rise up to the perfection, but not by thy power, for man canst not do this alone, but by the power of Christ.

16 Do not follow the counsel of men but take instruction from God unto perfection.

17 And perfection is thus: Love thine enemies, bless them that curse you, do good to them that hate you, and pray for them who despitefully use you and persecute you;

18 Do this that ye may be the children of your Father who is in heaven; for He maketh the sun to rise upon the evil and on the good.

19 ❡ As thou art ministers, a High Priest and High Priestess to the Lord God, thou art to give counsel and speak to close friends.

20 Know that perfection is as two fountains or springs of wisdom, and one is justice and the other mercy; for one is to give and the other is to give what they receive, and thou shall abide, binding balance in both.

21 ❡ And God is seen by mankind as to the lifting the hand to the Lord in the first token.

22 Yea, and God desires to reside in the heart; for the faithful reach out with the heart and man is the temple of His Spirit.

23 And thus the Lord desires mankind, as according to our desires to Elohim; and God foresees every man and woman will go through ten trials.

24 And the new name is written of in the heavens and upon the earth when a soul is born unto man;

25 And the new name is given at the altar, and name of the first token is this new name, and this is the name of the soul of man.

26 The ten numbers are as nothing; thus, one and two, three and four, five and six, seven and eight, nine and ten;

27 Then all repeat; begin eleven, twelve, and so on to cleanse the desires of man; yea, nothing is concealed by language when understood by the Spirit.

28 By ten numbers, speak and close the mouth to speak profoundly that thou might grow in grace unto the 125th degree.

Chapter 23

Revelation on the Second Anointing received in Ohio on January 20, 2016. Compare to the Book of Raziel, verses 20-21.

1 And it came to pass that Adam and Eve, after they had heard these, the words from the angel of the Lord, Raphael called them up to the altar, facing east;

2 And there, at the altar, they were instructed as to the Second Anointing.

3 ¶ And it came to pass that they gathered twelve of the Saints, instructing Seth, their son, to lead them.

4 And the twelve they had set apart to lead the Church of God gathered in a circle of prayer;

5 And Adam washed the feet of Eve, his wife, and then she did wash the feet of her husband.

6 ¶ And laying her hands upon the head of her husband, Adam, Eve did bless him and ordain him as the head of the human family, a ruler and High Priest of the Most High God, to rule and reign in the House of Israel forever.

7 And she further blessed her husband, as the Spirit directed, and all those in the circle witnessed angels coming to rejoice;

8 For they knew Adam as Michael, their archangel, he who had led them before he was born;

9 Yea he who, in the name of Jesus Christ, had cast out those that had rebelled against God.

10 ¶ And it came to pass that when it was finished, Adam did bless Eve, his wife, ordaining her a ruler and High Priestess of the Most High God, to rule and reign in the House of Israel with her husband forever.

11 And the angel and the witnesses rejoiced and shouted: Hosanna! to God and the Lamb, glorifying them forever and ever; Saying: So mote it be, and Amen.

12 ¶ And one of the angels stepped forward, and he was Raphael;

13 And the angel of the Lord spoke to Adam and Eve before all in the temple, saying:

14 At the first, Ahman and Shekinah, our Elohim, and the Only Begotten preceded the universe by an eternity;

15 And the glory of the universe is both above and below, deep and profound;

16 It is in the east and west, and in the north and south, and so too is Elohim.

17 How great is the light! It shines forth, to take away the darkness; in darkness, therefore, obscure the firmament.

18 ¶ Here is the name of God: for Elohim is the unity of God;

19 At the end is the creation of the earth and of mankind.

20 As in the heavens above, so too below; as upon the earth, so too in the heavens above; which is to say, as above so below, as below so above.

21 Thus is the sealing power given unto mankind, unto the High Priest and the High Priestess;

22 And blessed is the Patriarch and the Matriarch that use this power.

23 And by constant transformation, change and motion, is man corrected by God through teshuvah to return above.

24 The door is below, here upon the earth; pass through the gates to know the mystery of being and return to the Elohim that sent thee fourth.

25 And the door has a key, and the key is the Holy Priesthood, after the Order of the Son of God.

26 ❡ The God, El Abba, is to the east; listen and heed his voice and revelation shall pour out unto thee.

27 And the sealing power of YHVH is to the west; in the hands of mankind, as the Lord shall give unto thee from time to time.

28 And the Sabbath is to the north; in wisdom rest and renew for Shekinah is with thee.

29 The Holy Ghost is to the south, and from whence come all the spiritual gifts and the fire of purification.

30 The light of all creation reveals light in the air; darkness obscures all things;

31 All is formed; it is in all and it is all; thus, bow down by all, yea rise up and give thanksgiving in the heart.

32 And as ye bow down before God, so too shall thy ancestors go forth.

33 Understand by these teachings, revealed over the Lord;

34 Place this light in thy bosom and kiss the forehead; make thee a covenant unto the Lord in his house.

35 ❡ And much more is revealed in the secret work of the creation with help of El Shaddai.

36 And see too that the powers of God are given in harmony to mankind, as God upholds the second token, the Sign of the Law of the Gospel; yea, from Adam until twenty generations.

37 ❡ The universe was created by God; thus, bring forth small things, as God is diminutive of the true name.

38 God is as a humble man, bowing down and rising up;

39 And thus man too must bow down and rise up to make clear the reverence to his Creator.

40 Yea, man serves God with love in the heart; and great is their reverence and devotion.

41 Establish thy heart; keep the commandments; rejoice in supplication to serve the Creator of the universe.

42 Yea, and by rejoicing and reverence, serve the Lord in reverence and tremble in exaltation; yea, serve the Lord by rejoicing.

43 ❡ The heart rejoices to petition the Lord!

44 Therefore, revere Elohim and serve in fear of Hell and the day of judgment, of the suffering and torment; for this is the reverence of Elohim.

45 YHVH shall judge and deliver retribution, as angered by the sins of mankind.

46 Pray thee: *Of every word, it is difficult to speak, Elohim, I do revere you and speak with great difficulty, very loudly at your feet;*

47 *I shall not fall to rest, but journey to the House of the Lord and revere you, lest I be punished.*

48 *YHVH, judge me by reverence! I revere Elohim, speaking every word devoted in my heart! So mote it be, Amen.*

49 It is spoken, by the YHVH of Elohim: Revere and uphold the reverence of Elohim, not to fall from Grace.

50 Therefore, in every place, revere Elohim and serve from the reverence.

51 ¶ Behold the reverence of the Lord! Serve in love, corresponding to the burnt offering.

52 Be sustained in exaltation by the reverence of the Almighty, for not to revere is not to serve the Lord.

53 Corresponding to the peace offering, fat and blood is consumed; the remainder is to YHVH.

54 The desire of the High Priest and High Priestess is the peace offering, bringing peace in the world.

55 Serve from love and supplication, and strengthen the body; give unto mankind the light of the Law;

56 For of such is wealth and treasures and glory and understanding.

57 Revere Elohim, serving in reverence is the foundation.

58 And of the house of man, do not deprive support corresponding to the sin offering, going over sins;

59 There is great love from the petition and supplication from the reverence.

60 ¶ Yea, verily I say unto you, all those that will fellowship in my name: Listen to the words of my servant, Raphael and if ye will come unto me ye shall have eternal life.

61 Behold, mine arm of mercy is extended towards all, and whosoever will come, these will I receive; and blessed are those who come unto me.

62 Behold, I am Jesus Christ the Son of God, the Great I AM, YHVH; created I the heavens and the earth, and all things that in them are.

63 And I was even with the Father from the beginning; I am the light and the life of the world. I am Alpha and Omega, the beginning and the end.

64 I am in the Father, and the Father in me; and in me hath the Father glorified His name;

65 I came unto my own, and my own received me not.

66 And behold, the scriptures concerning my coming are now fulfilled,

67 Therefore, as many as have received me, to them have I given to become the sons and daughters of God;

68 And even so will I to as many as shall believe on my name, for behold, by me redemption comes, and in me is the Law of Moses fulfilled.

69 And know ye this: Ye shall offer up unto me no more the shedding of blood;

70 Yea, your sacrifices and your burnt offerings shall be done away, for I will accept none of your sacrifices and your burnt offerings.

71 Therefore, when ye shall read these words, and study in this, the Book of Remembrance, know that ye shall offer for a sacrifice unto me a broken heart and a contrite spirit,

72 For this alone do I require, and my Grace shall be enough for thee.

73 And whoso come unto me with a broken heart and a contrite spirit, they shall I baptize with fire and with the Holy Ghost.

74 Behold, I have come into the world to bring redemption unto the world, to save the world from sin;

75 Therefore, shed not any blood upon thine altars for these shall not be acceptable in my name.

Chapter 24

Revelation, teachings given by the angel of the Lord, received in Ohio on January 20, 2016. Compare to the Book of Raziel, verses 22-25.

1 And the angel of the Lord spoke unto them further, saying: At this time, become wise and prosper;

2 Of the love of the blessed, after, write the secret of the mysticism of the Holy Priesthood, after the Order of the Son of God.

3 Let the men and women of the Holy Priesthood, after the Order of the Son of God be wise by reverence of the Lord God forever; and I say unto thee that this is the wisdom of the Lord God unto the world.

4 ¶ And by glory to God, choose thee a High Priest and High Priestess to lead the people of God, for thy days grow long upon the land.

5 And unto those that are chosen I say unto thee: Teach thy people to go and teach the world in the name of the Lord.

6 In prayer, give reverence to the Lord before going out into the world to battle pride and sin;

7 Yea, and if there is not reverence, enemies lay waste, prevailing over the land in every dwelling.

8 The King of all kings, YHVH your God, exalts in reverence before going on all paths.

9 Behold, the Lord is everywhere and, in every place, therefore thou are not alone;

10 He observes both the good and wicked in every place; the worthy revere the Lord in righteousness.

11 Unite the people as one in the Lord in order that the people of God be not divided; yea, work for the sake of the heavens.

12 ¶ Behold, every path is created from the blessings of God; thus, establish the heart, satisfy the Lord; he is eternal, therefore established.

13 Those on the true path shall see that all things which are good come from God;

14 That which is evil comes of that devil that tempted thee in the Garden.

15 And the devil is an enemy unto God: thou shall preach and fighteth against him continually, for he inviteth and enticeth to sin, and to do that which is evil continually.

16 Behold, that which is of the Lord God inviteth and enticeth mankind to do good continually;

17 Therefore, know thou that everything which teacheth mankind to revere the Lord, and to do good, to love God, and to serve him, comes from that God that sent you forth, even the Lord God.

18 ¶ Blessed is the Lord! He commands mankind to bind and set forth in every season.

19 ¶ Of the man who is a sinner or thief or adulterer of women, blind to consider the light of the Lord;

20 Of the wisdom, this man knows not to come near the face of God, disgraced in every dwelling created by the wisdom of Elohim.

21 ¶ Consider the wisdom of God that created the commandments, making reward for love; yea, serve the Lord a little and ye shall serve him much.

22 And mankind considers forever not to forsake the will of Elohim;

23 Yea, bring the Lord of judgment before the earthly judges and their tongues shall be bound.

24 ¶ Reveal unto mankind that the Devil rules over the necromancer and the magician, which is to say those deceivers knowing only the wisdom of this world;

25 For these engage in priestcraft —demoniacal works, or works by the knowledge of the signs of Lilith and Satan.

26 Thus do not be false or deceitful, as it is revealed to those that serve Satan, making them to appear to know all;

27 And shun the works binding with an evil spell, lest you come forth to be judged before those that reject the Lord.

28 ¶ God gives life to man in the heart; by the path of reverence, reveal all thoughts and understanding of all works.

29 God is the Lord over all people, thus know to summon the Lord of judgment;

30 Yea, speak these words to end deceit, and rise up that the words may be true.

31 And those not pure will not rise up to know of the Lord, nor of that Elohim that created them.

32 Guilt makes known when shame is necessary, saying unto these: I will not do acts of iniquity, nor deceive by speaking or writing words, not to establish before the eyes.

33 Do this and in every hour and minute, consider the Lord and search the heart, praying always;

34 Yea, examine the perfection of the Lord and keep the commandments and show reverence over thy lifetime.

35 ¶ Of the root of benevolent acts, measure not what thou hast done previously or thou shalt be judged by every word you write, of favor over all works;

36 Of the root of reverence, the words are difficult; therefore, know that thou revere Elohim and perfection.

37 Of the root of supplication, rejoice in the heart in love of God;

38 Yea, rejoice in the heart from thy petition to the Lord.

39 If ye shall do these things, therefore, ye shall be loved and protected.

40 Of the root of the light and the Law, most profound knowledge of the works of all words, and all that is made by the Lord is good. So mote it be, Amen.

Chapter 25

Revelation on the eight tasks given to Adam and Eve and a few others, received in Ohio on January 23, 2016. Compare to the Book of Raziel, verses 29-31.

1 And behold, Raphael, who is the Keeper of Secrets and the Angel of Mysteries, yeah even the keeper of the great mysteries, did send away all but Adam and Eve and they who were chosen to be the High Priest and High Priestess over the Church of God;

2 ¶ And he said unto them, in the temple of the Lord: Behold eight tasks shall I give unto thee, teach thy people to do these each in their proper order.

3 First, beginning thy rituals in prayer.

4 Second, rehearse unto all the proclamations of the Word of God.

5 Third, open thy hearts to hear and to feel that thou might learn and be blessed.

6 Fourth, place oils and flowers pleasing to the nose to welcome the Lord into thy midst.

7 Fifth, keep thy bodies clean that thy hands might give in righteousness.

8 Sixth, consecrate upon the altar in supplication before God.

9 Seventh, renew thy covenants that the body, mind, and spirit might be renewed therein.

10 Eight, thy feet walk into the temple, yea the house of study and even the house of prayer, therefore complete these that thou mayest return into the world of men in perfection.

11 ¶ Behold, I say again unto thee: The root of the reverence of the Lord is to forsake the pleasures of lust by the path of the reverence of the Lord.

12 Do not revere the Lord for the world's sake, nor for thy eternal glory;

13 Thou shalt revere for the Lord's sake, and the light of God shall spring from thee as from a fountain,

14 And by this thou shall be perfected before God in love, for it is by grace thou art saved, and thy works are as a sign unto the world.

15 As the commandments come into thy hands, thou shall labor in the works, for by thy works shall the grace of God be seen by the eyes of mankind that they too might be converted.

16 ¶ Revere Elohim not so that the secrets of the mystery might be revealed, for was not this knowledge not yet concealed before the womb?

17 Speak truthfully therefore and see that ye are not tempted.

18 Henceforth ye shall be tempted by all temptations, were it not so, how in would thou learn truth?

19 Also, learn the letters that they might reveal unto thee the Word, and teach thy children likewise that they might gain wisdom in their youth.

20 ¶ Thy heart is perfect by all commandments, as it is not necessary to be tempted, but the mind and the body must be overcome;

21 Thus at this time, know this: The Lord is great, yea and the Lord giveth all glory unto to Elohim even as thou give all glory unto the Lord.

22 Therefore go forth and serve in love, believe in love, and teach in love; and by this ye shall be known as the children of God; So mote it be.

23 ¶ And upon hearing these words, Adam and Eve did speak, saying: Elohim, we show reverence to thee;

24 Yea, it is difficult to rise up and go forth to thee by the feet.

25 And Seth and his wife, the chosen High Priest and High Priestess of the Lord, spoke as one, saying: Behold Elohim; I revere thee.

26 And it came to pass that Adam and Eve spoke again saying: Behold, our sons and daughters endured in famine of thy Word; yet now thou, our Lord, art revered.

27 Yea, it is difficult for man to rise up and bow down before God,

28 And also they that fail to rise up and bow down the Lord, His secrets shall not be revealed,

29 Nor shall the Spirit of the Lord dwell with them, and they shall suffer in darkness which is spiritual death.

30 However, thou speaketh of reverence of God with devotion in thy heart;

31 Yea, ye spoke to the Lord, and I, the servant of the Lord, honor thee in thy reverence.

32 Ye that beseech the Lord by the holy words; the weight is upon thy hearts.

33 ¶ Consider therefore the reverence of the Lord, and say in thy hearts: I revere you, O Lord; come not to bind thy Word.

34 And it is difficult to rise up beyond worldly desires to see that the root of love is to cherish the Lord.

35 ¶ The Nephesh is filled with love, yet mankind rejoiceth by passing over the pleasures of the body;

36 Mankind doth desire to reign over the pleasures of the Lord.

37 Love is rejoicing in stren-gth, ye even strengthen the heart;

38 Thus shall thou consider always to create within the desire of God;

39 Then shall mankind bring forth pleasure, walking as the bride unto the bridegroom before the love of Elohim.

40 ¶ From youth and till the passing of days, many do not come before God;

41 Yet the desire of the Lord God, the heart burns to rise up to the Lord;

42 Yea, from much love and desire shall mankind rise up to the Lord.

43 ¶ Behold the lightning of the early rain, how it doth benefit much from all without making desire of the Creator;

44 So too is the body kept in purity and holiness by love.

45 ¶ Yea, place thy hand to the highest when thou art being dragged below;

46 Bind the divisions, that ye be not cast forth to and fro by every gust of wind;

47 Deny not women their priesthood nor their sisterhood.

48 End the bickering words of fools; toil and labor one with another, making favor of the Creator.

49 ¶ The root of humility is to go away from the glory and be praised when returning before the teacher;

50 But thou shall delight not by praises but to fulfill holy desires and rejoice to cherish the Lord.

51 Know when to rest, lie down after hard labors; know when not to toil.

52 Speak thus of labor and desire, for the Lord loves they who are humble before him;

53 Therefore, go before the Lord with the name of thy friend in the house of prayer that thou might give praise to the Lord in the house of heaven together.

54 Great is the glory to revere the name of the Lord; so mote is be, Amen.

55 And Adam and Eve pondered upon what they had heard.

Chapter 26

Revelation on teachings from the angel of the Lord received in Ohio on January 23, 2016. Compare to the Book of Raziel, verses 33-39.

1 And Raphael withdrew from them for a time.

2 And it came to pass that they went out unto the people and taught them all that they had learned;

3 And Seth and his wife Azura did lead the tzaddikim, or the people of God.

4 ¶ And it came to pass that Seth did erect twin pillars, and upon them he did write the words of the Lord that all might know the light and life of the Lord God.

5 And Azura, the wife of Seth, did lead the Sisterhood of God in righteousness;

6 And they taught all that would learn the writings of the Lord that they might read the letters inscribed upon the pillars.

7 And the Sisterhood of God did bless and heal the sick and perform many miracles in the name of the Lord.

8 ¶ And it came to pass that the angel of the Lord came again unto the temple, and upon his return he said unto them: Keep all these commandments in secret;

9 In secret, go with Elohim; when keeping these commandments, may thy obedience be in secret and not by boasting;

10 And YHVH who seeth in secret shall reward thee openly.

11 ¶ In secret shalt thou pray, and when thou prayeth, thou shalt wear the tzitzit in righteousness before the Lord;

12 Thy prayers be in secret; and YHVH who seeth in secret himself shall reward thee openly.

13 ¶ Yea, and thou shalt speak of righteousness, for by the Lord art thou righteous by every commandment; thus, be not occupied by other matters.

14 Place the love of God in thy heart; reverence is necessary before him; thus, shall thou be skillful making thy rules and thy laws.

15 Rejoice before God and speak with honesty and wisdom; in every place and in thy temples, stand in awe before Shekinah; yet establish thy heart only to God;

16 Do not withhold any ordinance from those that are worthy nor passage to the endowments, as there is disgrace before making the covenant.

17 God is angered when mankind is not seen to revere him; thou shall make known to humanity these things so as to not be disgraced.

18 ¶ All passes forth, that which the hands of man make; do not make labor multiply; everyone who toils for the world toils in vain.

19 Let all thy works then be for the sake of the heavens; it is good to possess more from them of the light.

20 When you work for the Lord, be happy in the world; yea, may good things come to thee forever:

21 And they come from the assistance of the Lord who created the heavens and Earth; remember the secret is reverence of the Lord.

22 ¶ All was created in order to know and understand and make wise by the greatest and most wondrous works;

23 Bear witness there is none as, and there is none other than.

24 Write these things in the book to proclaim the secrets and reveal the strength of the creator of the universe;

25 Man is happy to learn the secrets; revere the Lord, shelter him in thy temples.

26 Come and write over the mouth of the gates of all that is above; know of the unity of God;

27 Of the glory, give the heart over to reverence; yea, bow down to Him.

28 He is one and there are not two of him: Blessed is He.

29 ¶ The Lord God is the first and the last; He is king over all the universe; there is no other unto Him.

30 God is first of all.

31 ¶ The first word is El Achad, written of a myriad of myriads before existence.

32 Before the world was, a star was fallen, as he was the first to rebel;

33 Speak sharply, for the morning star fell, as he was at the end of his glory, yea and he tried to rise greater than God: but behold there is none greater.

34 God alone is first and is last; the beginning of days and the end of days:

35 Let it be known that God is in the universe; the Lord that created the universe turned away from the universe; speak in reverence of His power.

36 ❡ Ye do not understand, as foreseen by the destruction of the earth;

37 Speak of the Lord thy God; do not permit destruction in the world; hide thy faces from it.

38 Know that, in the beginning, to create the universe Elohim wrote in the Holy Temple; written therein upon the heavens of the first place of the most holy.

39 ❡ Through the gate of Earth, mankind is falling into chaos;

40 And these kept their first estate, and those serving as angels come here to fall in the second estate, serving in chaos.

41 The Lord God has given mankind two temples; both serving mankind and for mankind to serve God;

42 That is to say, God shall dwell in mankind, and mankind shall dwell in the House of God, Holiness to the Lord.

43 ❡ Remember that to destroy is also to create; they who kept their first estate were destroyed in their second;

44 Yea, all created by God are in pairs; two worlds, heaven and Earth;

45 All enter the Garden of Eden, their path alight by the Sun and the Moon, man and woman.

46 Therefore, by being destroyed mankind is reborn, yea and falls, though is lifted up by the Son of Man;

47 He is one in the kingdom; blessed is he; So mote it be, Amen.

Chapter 27

Revelation on the fire of God received in Ohio on January 23, 2016.
Compare to the Book of Raziel, verses 41-43.

1 And it came to pass that Adam and Eve watched over the church, and the Church was led in righteousness by Seth and Azura.

2 And as the Church of God grew, many men and women were called of God to the ministry, to fulfill the will of God and see to the needs of the people of the church.

3 And those that followed in the path of righteousness were blessed; and the people were one.

4 And because the pride of the people was stilled, yea, and all sought to the needs of the others, none lived in want, and the Lord God blessed them.

5 And those that would not live as one left the church, some to join other peoples, and some formed churches of men;

6 And the people of the Church of God mourned them.

7 And they that rejected the Gospel the people of the church still loved, and they that desired to come back were welcomed with tears of joy and much rejoicing.

8 ¶And it came to pass that Adam and Eve and Seth and Azura were praying alone in the temple,

9 And behold, Raphael came again unto them to give unto them the Word of the Lord.

10 And behold, he said unto them: The Lord has sent me this day to speak unto you, and I say unto thee:

11 The whole of the world, and even the whole of the universe was created by the commandments of Elohim and filled all.

12 And God's creation is united above the seven firmaments.

13 God is the ruler of all, and therefore, He has named the ten sefirot, above to below;

14 The Lord is the end of the ten sephiroth, beginning by Elohim; complete them to see everyone by these, the eyes of God.

15 ¶ Recognize all the most holy names; God begins the chosen name YHVH;

16 Reveal unto mankind that the Lord is one and created all the universe, the highest, middle, and lowest, filling all at the direction of Elohim;

17 There is not a rock placed or the covenant made without Him; blessed is He!

18 Elohim is one dwelling above the seven firmaments, and rules over all.

19 ¶ Consider the one God for many eternities of infinite years;

20 In the beginning of the worlds, mankind sees by them and by them, the splendor and glory.

21 Speak in the heart: Human beings are not to consider the glory of the kingdom.

22 As YHVH commanded and Elohim instructed did ye create the world, and it is to be for a time, yea it is to pass.

23 Therefore, complete the understanding of God in the heart in reverence;

24 Serve in truth with the perfect heart, and goodness to them all thy days.

25 ¶ And when mankind was created, the Lord spoke: All come forth from the breath of the Holy Spirit; it is the first of all the covenants of man.

26 From the Word, this breath comes forth from the mouth; therefore, spirits are not shut up by the worthy in silence.

27 ¶ Here are words of the breath of fire and water: From the Word, man presses the lips; by force, the voice goes forth.

28 Sparks go forth by the breath; therefore, it is spoken, as a hammer smashing rocks;

29 Just as sparks go forth from stones, when in faith thou shall speak, fire comes from the power of the sparks breathed from thy mouth.

30 Therefore, is it not so the power of the Word is as fire?

31 Here is power from the voice of man: the breath of water, which is baptism, to rise from the water as men shall rise from the grave born anew in the Lord;

32 And the heat of the fire consuming the old, making new, in every dwelling as the soul is born and mankind is born again in the Lord.

33 ¶ Behold the Word of God; fire consumes fire;

34 Therefore, speak of how to create new life in the Lord with water and fire.

35 The breath of life is the glory of Elohim, the Word made flesh; from blessings over the days, all exist by the Word.

36 Believers in truth are healing as the light of the Lord flows from them, healing the world to fill the earth and finish the creation in the day after God has rested.

37 Blessed is the Lord God to create all the commandments given unto mankind;

38 The Great Lord: Eternal is His glory and power. So mote it be; Amen.

39 ¶ And it came to pass that this angel of the Lord left them, but they were not alone in the temple;

40 The light of the Lord continued to shine upon them, and their eyes were opened,

41 And they did see many visions, and they did speak many words that shall not be written here.

Chapter 28

Revelation given to Adam from God, received in Ohio on January 23, 2016.

1 And behold, after such was the Gospel preached unto the world, and any of those sons of men that would hear were given wisdom from the seed of that tree in righteousness;

2 And the Holy Spirit fell upon them, yea and they were then counted as the seed of Adam and Eve and as the sons and daughters of God.

3 ¶ And it came to pass that I came to Adam many times, as he was a mighty prophet in my name;

4 And it came to pass that I did speak to him, and teach him of my coming, though he understood not the fullness of it at first.

5 ¶ And I spoke unto him, saying: I am YHVH, that God who made thee to go forth from the Garden of Eden into the world, which does shoot forth thorns and brambles, behold even this part of the earth, this land that thou now dwell in.

6 Behold thy body, it is bent and weakened in age, and yet shall the time come when I shall make thy flesh food for the worms.

7 And after a few days, will I have compassion upon thee and thy seed, and shew thee my mercy in the abundance of my compassion for thee;

8 And I will come down into thy house, and I will dwell in thy flesh, and for thy sake I will be pleased to be born as a man, for thus was the plan, even from the beginning.

9 And for thy sake I will be pleased to endure many sufferings;

10 And for thy sake I will be pleased to hang and to die by the hands of these thy seed.

11 For as one man brought death into the world, so too shall another bring eternal life;

12 Yea and as one man ate of the tree, so shall another be hung upon a tree for all mankind;

13 ¶ Yea, and all these things will I do for thy sake, and the sake of thy seed, O man, that thou and all thy generations may be blessed if they choose to forgo sin and this world and take upon themselves my name.

14 ¶ And behold, many things did I prophesy unto him and unto his wife, the mother of all living;

15 And this was too hard a thing for him to hear, yet he knew it to be true, and thus by my Spirit, the very Spirit of the Lord, did I console him.

16 ¶ And it came to pass that Adam and Eve brought their seed to a rock, yea the very rock where they had first prayed unto me outside of the Garden, even Adam ondi Ahman.

17 And there Adam prayed unto me, and he said unto me: El Shaddai, or God Almighty, yea even the Lord my God;

18 Great is thy name and Holiness is thy name, behold I shall praise thee forever, and forever shall thy works be my works, even the works of God.

19 ¶ And thus was his mouth opened and he did prophesy until the end of the world; and all things were shown unto him, and these were written in a book, which was sealed unto heaven.

20 And behold, every word uttered forth from his mouth has and shall come to pass, for they were said in my name and in my power.

21 ¶ And I tell thee this as a sign that thou should know that this man, Adam, has not yet tasted of the first resurrection;

22 For behold, before I was born, was I AM and I was a spirit, even the spirit of YHVH and He the spirit of Elohim.

23 And it must needs be that I am resurrected, and thus my spirit cannot fall upon man as such, for I am the Second Comforter.

24 ¶ And behold, this man, Adam, was made perfect in me, yea in my atonement;

25 And thus being perfect, I kept my promise unto him, and he is God, even the Holy Ghost, for he was such before the world began.

26 For behold, he is Adam who shall come unto Adam ondi Ahman;

27 He is Michael, the prince, the Archangel, the seventh angel who shall gather together his armies, even the hosts of heaven and shall sound the trump of God.

28 For behold, even as a man is baptized with water unto me, so too is he baptized with fire and the Holy Ghost.

29 ¶ Even as I, the second comforter, sent Raphael, who is Melchizedek, unto you as I did my servant Joseph Smith Jr., to make thee unto me a High priest,

30 So too does Michael or the Holy Ghost send angels unto those in need of comfort and to testify of the truth of my words and my works;

31 For he is the First Comforter, thus he shall send those in spirit, and I am the Second Comforter and I shall send whom I shall send.

32 ¶ And behold, when ye feel of the Spirit, thou dost entertain angels unaware;

33 Therefore, keep thyself holy and teach my people to be a holy people in my name, yea to follow my Word and my Spirit.

34 This men and women shall do that they too may join with thee in the Church of the Firstborn, to be called when Michael shall sound the trump.

35 Behold, he or she that asketh in the Spirit asketh according to my will; wherefore it is done even as he or she asks; So mote it be, Amen.

Chapter 29

Revelation on nonbinary Saints received in Ohio on May 19, 2022.

1 Verily, thus saith the Lord unto my servant, David: Thou hath asked me regarding those that identify as neither male nor female,

2 For as I have said: They that identify as male are they of the Brotherhood of Christ, and they that identify as female are of the Sisterhood of Christ;

3 But what then of those that identify not as male nor female?

4 Behold, this shall I explain unto thee and thou shall add these, my words, unto the Book of Remembrance.

5 ¶ Behold the Tree of life: to the left is the masculine; at the top of the branches is Da'at, representing the Father and below Him, the Left Hand of God, even Gevurah the Holy Ghost.

6 And at the right of the Tree of Life is the feminine; at the top of the branches is Chokhmah, representing the Mother, and below Her, the Right Hand of God, even Chesed, for in Mercy did I, the Son, create all that is.

7 ¶ And in the middle of the tree; at the top, is Keter, the Crown worn by the Father and the Mother, given to the Son in the Holy Spirit;

8 Yet these, Keter, Da'at, and Chokhmah are above the creation; thus is Chesed the first day of the creation, the light separating from the darkness.

9 Gevurah is then the second day of creation, separating the waters from the waters,

10 And in Tif'eret is the third day of creation, for it is the compassion of YHVH and only by the light of Christ can mankind grow desires from the soil.

11 And the fourth day is Netzach and the fifth day Hod, for only through endurance and submission to YHVH can mankind see the stars and read the night sky, and with that knowledge grow the desires that are the birds of the air and the fish of the sea.

12 And the sixth day is Yesod, for mankind is the foundation, and all the desires that mankind doth name.

13 And on the seventh day, I and the gods did rest, and this is Malchut the seventh day, in exaltation.

14 And hidden amongst the branches at the top of the tree, between the five pointed star that is Keter, Da'at, Chokhmah, Chesed, and Gevurah is Binah, where Understanding may be found.

15 ¶ And in all this is En Sof, the Infinite to be found; for before I gave shape to this world, the creation was without form and there was only the Creator.

16 And after the creation the sacred name, YHVH, was formed upon the lips of mankind.

17 ¶ What then does this tell thee of those that identify as neither male nor female, or they that identify as both male and female?

18 These are they of the middle line of the tree, for they are neither right nor left, or they are both right and left.

19 And of this I shall tell thee more, but not yet; for when thou were given the Book of Remembrance it was unknown to thee that I was teaching thee the mysteries of Kabbalah;

20 But now that thine eyes can see, and thy mind comprehend, more shall be unfolded unto thee, and this that Israel shall see, and shall know; for only in this shall Zion be established.

Chapter 30

Revelation on the Saints as Adam and Eve, Cain and Lilith received in Ohio on May 19, 2022.

1 This earth, she is Eden, and as thou has seen, as I have shown thee in vision, there in Eden did I plant a garden, the orchard of YHVH Elohim.

2 And there in did I place Adam, and Lilith, and Eve; and there too did I plant the tree of the knowledge of good and evil, and the tree of life.

3 ¶ But these mankind did eat before their time from the tree, and thus they were cast out;

4 But I did prepare a way back for them into that orchard, the Pardes, that they might see salvation in me; for the Kingdom of God is inside you:

5 The mind, spirit, and body of mankind is that of four people: Adam, the man who desires to bestow good, and Cain the man that desires to bestow in wickedness, so to is Eve, the woman who desires

to receive that which is good and Lilith, the woman that desires to receive in wickedness;

6 And all have these, be they male, female, or any of the other genders.

7 And each Adam and Eve has a part of every gender within them, be they male or female, intersex, nonbinary, or eunuch:

8 And these five types of people are equally represented in the five Sefirot, the five pointed star that is Keter, Da'at, Chokhmah, Chesed, and Gevurah.

9 And they are in each of these genders, and each of these genders are in the five Sefirot; for these were before they were born and shall be everlasting.

10 ¶ Cholem is the soul born in me when, through my everlasting atonement, the spirit and the mortal body until in preparation of the resurrection, and the soul is born to eternal life.

11 When the spirit is born from the waters, by the divine Grace of the Father and of the Mother, in the Shamayim are the elohim born.

12 And they that kept their first estate do come here to be born in the flesh, finite beings;

13 And thus by sin, by the ego, do they keep themselves from me, and thus it shall be until they are born again in me, for the Cholem itself is from Me, and I have made many souls.

14 The white stone given to they that overcome is the Cholem; and the stone is given that mankind may see past jealousy, hatred and contention;

15 Thus it is a seer stone, the great Urim and Thummim that unites mankind and their God.

16 And thus with my mercy is born the Cholem, that through my mercy (Chesed) can mankind survive the fire of judgment that is Gevurah;

17 For all shall burn in that great burning in the Eshmayim, and this that the impurities from this life may be purged away, that only the love and light of Christ shall remain.

18 And thus is the Church a field of the seers, the Sadeh on the Pardes, and at the center, the Tree of Life, and that tree is the Mother.

19 ¶ The voice of YHVH comes in strength, the voice of YHVH comes in majesty, the voice of YHVH draws out flames of fire, and my righteousness stands forever.

20 And all of this and more ye shall read in the Book of Melchizedek, for in its seventy-two chapters are all the secrets of this Book of Remembrance, and this book shall be a key to understanding the mystery that is his teachings.

21 But this book shall only be given to the righteous, and thou, David, shall translate it if I see fit that the Saints are worthy of it, for now they fight in their pride, setting my Gospel to the side for their creeds, and their contention is an abomination to me.

22 I have suffered, died, and been raised again on their third day that my people should live, and I accept them, they that would be my Israel;

23 Yet they forsake me when they war with one another; know ye not that am the Creator, and that thou art my creation?

24 And I love my creation; therefore, it is my will that my creation should love one another, even as I love them;

25 For in this shall the world know that ye are mine: Love one another.

Chapter 31

Revelation, the parable of the garden, received in Ohio on May 19, 2022.

1 And I shall give thee a parable: the Church is like a lord who has a beautiful garden, and in it are thirty-two paths with the tree of life at the very center.

2 And the Lord placed a gardener to watch over his orchard and to look after the thirty-two paths that they not grow wild, and to help guide those that should walk the paths.

3 And it came to pass that the lord said unto the Gardner: Watch over the trees of the orchard and the fields, and walk upon these thirty-two paths daily, for as long as you walk these paths, peace shall be in you.

4 Yet the gardener appointed others in his stead to walk the paths and he spoke unto himself, saying: This task is impossible for me alone,

5 And that the people shall not say: Look there, the lord is walking about in his orchard, I shall assign another gardener for each of the paths.

6 The gardener said: I now fear that the other gardeners shall say: Behold! This orchard and these paths, they do belong to each of us!

7 And thus in fear did he walk the path, and chase the other gardeners about the orchard that none did have peace upon the path.

8 And thus did the weeds come up, and the garden withdrew, that the peace of the thirty-two paths could not be found.

9 ¶ And thus is the kingdom of heaven: for it is so large that it may fit all of the creation within, yet so small that even one of the seed of mankind cannot fit if their ego be too great.

10 ¶ The tree of life is one tree, and it has twelve sides: the northeast and the southeast, the upper East and the lower East, the southwest and the northwest, the upper West and the lower West, the upper South and the lower South, the upper North and the lower North;

11 And these continue on forever and ever for they are the arms of the whole world, for they are a circle and a circle has no beginning, and no ending;

12 And inside the circle is the tree, and these twelve sides are the Twelve Shevet, thus is the number twelve sacred:

13 My twelve tribes with Dinah in the center, my twelve apostles with Mary in the center, and all these with me in their midst;

14 Hear O Israel: YHVH is our Elohim, YHVH is Unity.

15 And this because the white stone is precious, and in it is the sea of wisdom, and thus it is that blue and white are the colors of the Tzitzit; let they that have ears hear, for this is wisdom.

16 ¶ Israel is holy unto me, for they that are Israel do take the Tree into their hearts.

17 And this tree is a pillar that extends from the heavens to the earth, and her name is Righteousness;

18 For it is not of mankind to take the earth into the heavens, but to bring the heavens to the earth;

19 And they that do this are my Church, for the Priest and the Priestess do prepare the earth of the coming of the heavens, and the High Priest and the High Priestess do bring the heavens to the earth,

20 And I am the Great High Priest, and all they that serve the Church, and walk the path, and prune the garden, they are mine.

Chapter 32

Revelation on the nature of God, received in Ohio on May 19, 2022.

1 And I say unto thee, my servant, David, and what I say unto thee I say unto all Israel: Upon the Tree of Life rest Ten Sephiroth and unto these the earth, Eden, is sealed.

2 And what are the Sefirot? These are the divine attributes of mankind, calling down from the heavens declaring the Glory of God.

3 ¶ And they are three from before the creation, they are seven from the days of creation.

4 And even as mankind climbs the tree up towards God they are in sin, but through me, Jesus, who is the Christ, they climb down, bringing the heavens to the earth and in this there is salvation.

5 Holy is the highest Crown (Keter) and holy is the root of the Tree, and holy is the tree; holy, holy, holy,

6 And this because the holiness on high is three, for I am King, and I will be King forever and ever.

7 ¶ Knowledge is the air, and the Father; wisdom is the earth, and the Mother; mercy is the water, and the Son; judgement (strength) is fire, and the Ghost.

8 And the Church, she cries: Where is our mother?

9 And the creeds they sing: You cannot see her now; she is too holy! Let her be hidden from the eyes of Her creation!

10 But She is a woman of valor, of beauty, and She is refined in all Her ways.

11 She cannot come from the Light, for the Light is the Son, which comes from the Mother, and She illuminates the creation through Her deeds;

12 Thus she is the very Presence of Elohim, for it is She that lifts up the prayers of mankind, receiving them into Her bosom:

13 For the Father desireth to bestow, and the Mother to receiveth; and this in the Son may the Father bestow, and the Mother receive and thus are both ends met in me.

14 ¶ Is this not the Glory of God? Did I not show thee thy ministry as a garden and behold the vastness of it!

15 And yet when I took thee up to see my creation, then did thou realize how small thy garden is! And the breath of all the gardens!

16 And would the water be spread throughout all the gardens, that through my mercy knowledge and wisdom might be received,

17 That when the judgment should come thou shall not be found wanting, but understanding should open up, and give unto thee the crown.

18 For behold: The King and the Queen of Heaven did have a Son, and the Son he had sons and daughters, begotten in the flesh as the Cholem is born;

19 And thus are all sons and daughters of the Father and the Mother, and of the Son;

20 And thus is Mercy granted by the Father and the Mother by way of the Son.

21 Let all they who are thirsty come for water, let them drink from my waters, for the fountain is eternal;

22 Yea, without silver nor gold, come all ye and drink from the fountain of eternal mercy, eat of the fruit of the tree of the Mother, for She is Eden; yea, drink and be filled.

Chapter 33

Revelation on the Sefirot and the archangels received in Ohio on May 19, 2022.

1 The first is Keter (Crown), the Highest Crown: Blessed be its name and Israel, its people; let Israel be one.

2 And by the first comes all light before the creation, and all knowledge before the creation, and all wisdom from all of creation.

3 And Keter is not above the Elohim but is All, and thus is Keter the Unity of all they who are unified in All things.

4 And Mitatrun (Metatron) is its herald, and Mitatrun walked the earth as Enoch, until I took him.

5 ¶ The second and the third is Chokhmah (Wisdom), the beginning of the path, before the creation.

6 And by only by Wisdom may knowledge be understood, for the beginning of wisdom is the fear of YHVH.

7 Wisdom is the Right Eye; from Wisdom came the Torah, the treasure of Heaven.

8 And Raphael who is Raziel is its herald, and Raphael walked the earth as Melchizedek until I took him.

9 ¶ The second and the third is Da'at (Knowledge), the Truth of the way, before the creation.

10 And only by Knowledge may wisdom be gained, for the beginning of knowledge is truth.

11 Knowledge is the Left Eye; from Truth came the Torah, the treasure of Heaven.

12 And I, the Great Jehovah, am its herald, but in my place stands Khamael to be its herald, and Khamael walked the earth as Alma, until I took him.

13 ¶ The fourth is Chesed (Mercy) to all the world, the first day of the creation.

14 In my Mercy is mankind washed clean, Mercy is the charity of YHVH, thus is the Right Hand of the Father.

15 And Tzadkiel is its herald, and Tzadkiel walked the earth as John who was known as the Baptist, until he died from the lust of another.

16 ❡ The fifth is Gevurah (Strength) to the repentant, the second day of the creation.

17 Strength is the judgement of YHVH, for all shall look upon themselves and judge, and this is the Holy Ghost, thus is the Left Hand of the Mother.

18 And Michael is its herald, and Michael walked the earth as Adam, and neither he nor Eve, his wife shall taste of the resurrection until the end of the first resurrection.

19 ❡ The sixth is Tif'eret (Beauty), compassion for all the world, the third day of the creation.

20 It is here that the great fire of the soul of mankind is born, and thus it is the Bosom.

21 And Ariel who is Uriel is its herald, and Ariel walked the earth as Joseph Smith Jr. until his blood was spilt.

22 ❡ The seventh is Netzach (Eternity), the victory of YHVH, the fourth day of creation.

23 It is the house of the World to Come, and its place is Wisdom; from the Compassion of YHVH did the Torah enter the world, and thus it is the right foot.

24 And Haniel is its herald, and Haniel walked the earth as Moses, the Law giver, until I took him.

25 ❡ The eighth is Hod (Glory), submission to YHVH for all creation, the fifth day of the creation.

26 In submission all are placed into the Fire of Judgement to be made clean to be burnt asunder, thus it is the left foot.

27 And Qaphsiel who is Moroni is its herald, and Qaphsiel walked the earth as Moroni until I took him.

28 ❡ The ninth is Yesod (Foundation), the bridge between the heavens and the earth, the sixth day of creation.

29 It is the resting place of the Saints, and the path ever forward, and thus it is the reproductive organs, the genitals.

30 And Gabriel is its herald, and Gabriel walked the earth as Noah until his death upon this earth.

31 ¶ The tenth is Malchut (Kingdom), exaltation to all the world, the seventh day of creation.

32 Resting at the bottom of the tree of life, it is Netzach Netzachim, the victory of victories;

33 And thus it is the earth upon which all things rest, and that is my footstool, and it is Eden, as my bride, the Church, my body upon this earth.

34 And Sandalphon is its herald, and Sandalphon was Elijah upon the earth, until I took him.

35 ¶ The eleventh is Binah (Understanding), the reason of creation, the eighth day of creation.

36 Only through it may Keter be found.

37 And Tzaphkiel is its herald, and Tzaphkiel walked the earth as Enoch until I took him.

38 ¶ And the twelfth is the En Sof (Everlasting), the Tree of Life who is before the creation and is the creation.

39 And is all things, and it is apart from all things; and it is the tree in the center of the orchard of the garden of Eden, and the fruit of it makes mankind wise, and grants them eternal life.

40 And Yophiel is its herald, and Yophiel walked the earth as Eve, and neither she nor Adam, her husband, shall taste of the resurrection until the end of the first resurrection.

41 ¶ And Mitatrun is the archangel of the veil, and Raphael who is Raziel is the keeper of the mysteries of YHVH, and Khamael holds the flaming sword to keep mankind out of the garden of Eden.

42 ¶ And Mitatrun is the great teacher, and Raphael who is Raziel is the archangel of healing, and Khamael is the keeper of the chalice, and Tzadkiel holds the blade (athame) of sacrifice, and Michael, the one who was chosen when Lucifer was rejected, is the messenger of YHVH, even the first comforter.

43 ¶ Tzadkiel is the archangel of mercy, and of kindness, and of all benevolence, and Michael, is the watchman over Israel, and Ariel who is Uriel is the altar of YHVH and bringer of the light of the Gospel at the last days.

44 And Haniel is the archangel of life, and he I send to bring unto me they that shall not taste of death, and Qaphsiel who is Moroni is the archangel of caution, and the other guardian of the tree of life keeping mankind away with the flaming sword.

45 And Gabriel is the revealer, and Sandalphon the protector of the righteous, and Tzaphkiel the keeper of understanding.

46 ¶ And Yophiel is the beauty of YHVH, and the watcher of YHVH, and the archangel of wisdom, understanding, and judgment.

47 She is the protector of the Torah, and the keeper of the flaming sword that doth bring illumination unto mankind.

48 She is the protector of the earth, the rib (side) of the tabernacle, she is the Song of Songs, and she is she who did comfort Mary Magdalene in her hour of need.

49 ¶ Thus there are three sefirot above and before the creation, seven that are the creation, and twelve that are after the creation; let they who have ears to hear, hear.

Chapter 34

Revelation on light of God received in Ohio on May 19, 2022.

1 There are two types of light; the pure light of YHVH through which the world and all of creation was made, and the light of Christ that seeps through all they that are born again and glory in my name,

2 All other lights are the illusions of this world, for behold even Lucifer and Lilith may come unto mankind as angels of light, yet they reject the light of the creation and the light of Christ, for they repent not and are perdition.

3 But the illusions of their world are seen through by the true light of YHVH, the very light of Christ; for behold, both the light of the Creator and the light of Christ are one light.

4 But the light of the Creator is hidden away from the creation, not by YHVH but by mankind for they close their eyes to the brightness of it.

5 Yet when they are born again, that light shines forth from the darkness, bringing the light of the Creator back into the creation.

6 The Torah, the scriptures, the Word of God, these are a reflection of the light, but only I, Jesus the Christ, am that light, for I AM the Creator and ye mine creation.

7 And I have sent my chariot unto those that did embrace the light, and these tasted not death, but were changed in a twinkling, brought up unto me to serve me as archangels before my throne.

8 ¶ To sit upon the throne of YHVH Elohim, one must embrace both the man and the woman, the Adam and the Eve, inside themselves:

9 Here is the heart, and the wellspring of wisdom, here are the twelve rods that stand firm and from them flow the clear water from the fountain of righteousness the is before the beginning of the world.

10 And resting above it, the Holy Place, before time, before thought, before all creation: this is the throne of the Creator, in the throne is inside of you.

11 This represents the power of the priesthood, and the blessings and majesty of YHVH, and from all of this grow the tree of life.

12 ¶ Here is wisdom: That the souls of the righteous shall fly forth from the tree of life, and shall partake of the water, for these are the fruits of that tree.

13 Let they that have ears hear, that they might understand, for these are they that shall inherit the earth.

14 These are they that shall stand in the divine Presence of YHVH, these are they that shall be called Tzedek.

15 These are they that shall stand from generation to generation, these are they who do wear the garments without spots.

16 These are they who do stand in holy places, and from who the Holy of Holies shall appear.

17 These are they to whom I have said: I will gather you, these are they whom I have gathered.

18 These are they that wait not for the new world to come, for these are they to whom the new world hath already come unto.

19 These are my good and faithful servants, these are they to whom I have said: Come and be my peace, come and rest in me forever and ever.

20 These are they that shall never lack water, these are they that shall never again hunger.

21 These are they to whom I have come, and who are with me, and to whom I have given al things, even as my Father hath given me all things; blessed be they that are holy.

Chapter 35

Revelation on the temple rituals and a promise of further revelations received in Ohio on May 19, 2022.

1 Behold, my son, my servant David: I have called thee, and I have set thee apart, and I shall tell thee:

2 The ordinances of the ministry begin the moment that a man or a woman is born again, there they enter the garden, and I permit them to eat of the fruit, save it be the tree of knowledge of good and evil.

3 And there, all sin; yet my grace is sufficient to save them, and thus all partake of the sacraments in worthiness.

4 And some have I called to partake in these endowments, even as they have been taught in this book, the Book of Remembrance.

5 But behold, the Initiatories, and the Endowments taught here in are but the beginning, taking thee to the middle of the year, speaking after the manner of mankind.

6 Behold, thy ministry shall take thee out of the garden, and into the world, yet the true path of my temples is back into the garden, back into my presence.

7 And I did give the keys of these endowments to my servant Joseph while he walked this earth, yet he died before the fullness could come, and thus Satan thinks to thwart the things of YHVH.

8 But behold, my will cannot be thwarted, for as thou hast seen, my people were not one, thus they were not ready for my fullness, and so my temple was not finished.

9 ¶ Build my temple, that I may share with my Israel the full endowments, that all may return to the Garden of Eden.

10 And this is not to say that I require it of you for salvation or for exaltation, but I have made these things available to all they that desire it that they may learn the signs and the tokens of the ministry;

11 And these are symbols to help mankind understand my teachings, and to give greater access to my priesthood, which are the power of the Father given unto me, and from me they are given unto you:

12 And these shall help all they called into the ministry, to have power from upon high, and to grant wisdom, and to show my love for mankind, for all these are my creation, and I am the Creator, through the Father and the Mother, and these things are known through the Holy Ghost, and we are one God;

13 Therefore, I say unto thee: Build up my works in my name and set the four pillars straight that those seeking knowledge, wisdom, mercy, and strength shall gain understanding of these things.

14 ¶ There is more to come, therefore wait patiently for more light and knowledge and I shall send thee, and thou shall send it to the world:

15 Worry not that mankind shall not understand these things at the first, for all that is in this book is but an explanation of what shall be read from the Book of Melchizedek,

16 And these things are written as a parable, as a sign, that those with ears may hear and those with eyes shall see.

17 These are not secrets, but plain and precious truths that my Israel shall understand in their own way, and their understanding of it shall increase as they grow closer unto me;

18 Therefore, worry not of the things of this world, but build ye up Israel in my name;

19 Teach teshuvah and unity in my name, and those that hear my voice shall come; even so shall it be, Amen and amen.

Chapter 36

*Revelation on the churches of men and the kingdom of God
received in Ohio on November 28, 2022.*

1 Verily, thus saith the Lord unto my servant, David: I came unto my own, and my own knew me not, and this because they saw only the flesh, and not things as they truly are;

2 And this is the sin of the world, for I, the Creator did not make sin, nor did I make mankind to sin;

3 But mankind, my creation, did create sin when they walked in adultery before me, rejecting teshuvah, and this be the sin of the world.

4 I came into your midst, I walked among you as myself, yet my people did not see me, they saw but a man;

5 And this is why I came: to restore all to the very essence of thy true nature, to restore my creation back to its true form;

6 Therefore, I say unto my Israel: Shalom! My peace be with you, receive thou my peace.

7 ¶ These churches of men, with their creeds, these are an abomination unto me, they cry out saying: Lo here or Lo there!

8 Yet there I am not, for I am with you; follow me therefore from that true source of light in thee, from the broken heart and contrite spirit;

9 Do this and ye shall know me and be my Israel;

10 And they that seek shall find, and they that find shall share my light preaching the gospel of my Kingdom.

11 Wherefore, this instruction shall I give unto thee: Make no laws beyond what I have given thee;

12 And make not any laws as thou should be my lawgiver, lest thou shall be judged by thy own laws and found wanting.

13 ¶ Behold, my passion hath no equal, for love which proceedeth from me is as something contrary to human nature;

14 Yet in me is the Torah fulfilled, and in me is the love and the light of the world;

15 Therefore, do even as I did command my servants, my disciples and my friends:

16 Love one another that the world will know that thou art mine.

17 And if thou love not one another, but build kingdoms and churches unto thyselves, then ye are not mine, but belongeth to they that build up these churches of men.

18 ¶ But there will be those that have been deceived by the churches of men, rejecting my Kingdom for their creeds and abominations;

19 Unto these I say: Ye are mine, for my grace is enough, and will protect you,

20 My atonement is unto thee all powerful and thou shall be restored again unto the Father and the Mother through me.

21 Blessed are all they that do not waver at the sight of me, for they that love me shall know me, and that I am.

22 Behold, I say unto thee: It is not the eyes of man nor the spirit of man that shall see me, but the very soul that is born again in me;

23 Therefore, when the vision comes, they that know me shall see me and not be afraid,

24 They that know me shall see my messengers, and not be afraid,

25 They that know me shall dream dreams, and see visions, and be not afraid.

26 Those that see me but do not recognize me shall learn of me, and be not afraid,

27 But those that see me not, yet fear me; these shall, when they learn of me, they will be afraid, and shall work out their salvation in fear and trembling;

28 But I would that these should know me, and see that my work is sufficient, and when they know me, they will know peace and understand fear and war nor more.

29 ¶ But woe unto they that should know me and commit adultery against me, to pollute themselves before me!

30 Woe unto they that would know me and forsake me, as an old man that would forget the wife of his youth for another!

31 Woe unto these, except they return to me in teshuvah, for they that know me, and yet they that abandoned me, these shall be left alone until they return again to their first love.

32 Wherefore, I say into all ye that shall read this: Judge not, for as thou shall judge another, so too shall thou be judged.

33 For as thou doth grow in my grace, thy soul shall take form as it grows from degree to degree, line upon line and precept upon precept.

Chapter 37

Revelation on casting unclean spirits received in Ohio on November 28, 2022.

1 Go ye and teach my people, that when thou should need to cast out any unclean thing, proclaim thus:

2 I, the Kohen/ Kohanot, in the name of YHVH (or Jesus Christ), mighty be the Name, cast out all destroying spirits, the souls of mamzerim that fled the Lord of Hosts, never to take life in an earthly vessel, the sons of perdition, the daughters of Lilith, they that dwell in the deserts where no life may be found, the whispering spirits that lead mankind astray, any that would lead men and women away from that Spirit of God, of understanding, and all they that would make the hearts of mankind to rot, walking in desolation, to adultery spoiling themselves before YHVH; I cast all thee out, in the name of Jesus who is the Christ, the Living Word, YHVH made flesh: So mote it be; Amen.

3 Then take thee a piece of earth and write or carve upon it a straight line with a circle resting about the middle as the sun risen from the East, and there seal the unclean spirits that they bother mankind no more,

4 Watching over it, least the sign upon it be broken, or the token therein be destroyed, and that evil be freed:

5 And there shall the unclean spirit, that perdition, rest until judgement;

6 For all of nature, and all of the creation, all creatures that exist from before the creation shall be restored again to their true form at the last day,

7 For the nature of these things is resolved in the origins of its true nature, and in its true nature alone through my atonement.

8 ¶ And these are the sins of mankind: first is that of darkness, separated from my light.

9 And the second thy desire, for thyself alone, and not for the creation, for these have already rejected my light.

10 And the third is ignorance, which is to reject things as they are, for all they know is themselves.

11 And the fourth is the love of death and murder, for these do seek to hide in their sins.

12 And the fifth is that church of the devil, the kingdom of pride, for these do make war against Israel.

13 And the sixth is the wisdom of the earth, kesheph, that priestcraft, for these do lead mankind astray.

14 And the seventh is mahan, that great secret and its many combinations that seek to trap mankind in this path of sin.

15 ¶ These are the seven branches of the tree of death, the Qliphoth, the husk, which lay in the shadows of the tree of life for there must be opposition in all things.

16 And this Qliphoth is the great lie, that which would be hidden from the truth, the darkness that must be separated from the light,

17 And there lies Lilith in wait to trap those that would flee from the light to the darkness;

18 Yea, and her name, Lilith, is written upon the sword of death, that taketh the life of mankind, that only through me can be overcome:

19 For like all shadows, the Qliphoth is a shadow, an illusion that fades as the sun reaches its peak in the sky,

20 For sin is but an illusion, yea, and sin is nothing but the rejection of all reality, and like a shadow it disappears in the fullness of the light;

21 Therefore, I say unto thee: Find my light and eat freely from the tree of life.

Chapter 38

Revelation on the five temples received in Ohio on November 28, 2022.

1 There are five temples in the heavens and the earth, and these are: the temple body to house the Holy Spirit,

2 The home temple that all may worship where they are in their homes and synagogues,

3 The temple of the congregation, that communities might gather together in my name,

4 The tabernacles and temples of gathering, that my people might gather from afar off to worship as my Israel,

5 The temple of the heavens that shall descend to the earth when I come, and the city of Zion shall return.

6 And all of these are the same temple, for each temple is a model of the other that all might be one, for I am one.

7 ¶ And the temple altar is a map of the earth, the creation, and upon it rests the Creator, for the earth is my footstool:

8 The Mother to the North, the Father to the East, the Holy Ghost to the South, and the Son to the West;

9 And these are seen as the Earth and the trees, the Wind and the air, the Fire and the incense, the Water and the wine.

10 And in the middle of the altar, as the heart of my temples, lay the scriptures open to my truth:

11 Hear O Israel: YHVH is our Elohim, YHVH is Unity,

12 For I am unity, and in me is the light and the life of the world, and I am thy advocate before the Father and the Mother, in me, the Creator, is peace found.

13 ¶ And verily, the temple and the altar, and these rituals were made for mankind, and not mankind for the temple;

14 Therefore, worry not so much for the temple that thou forsake thy duties to the fields that thy people go hungry,

15 Or to the digging of wells that thy people go thirsty,

16 Or to the raising of thy children, that thy offspring know not me, for I AM YHVH, thy Elohim.

17 ¶ There is no doctrine, no mystery, no secret known or unknown, knowable or unknowable greater than this:

18 Love thy neighbor as thyself, for in love was the Torah written, and in love is the Torah lived;

19 Therefore, keep my holy days in thanksgiving, that thou should know my love by thy love for one another, for I am unity;

20 Therefore, if ye are mine, Israel, thou shall stand united, as one, even as I stand with the Father and the Mother and the Holy Ghost as one.

Chapter 39

Revelation on the holy days received in Ohio on November 28, 2022.

1 I shall speak plainly unto thee on the nature of the sun, the moon, and the stars:

2 These thou shall use to instruct thee all through thy days, for these were given for signs and for seasons, and for the gathering of Israel.

3 And my Israel shall appoint a Chief Priest to watch the skies and to gather my Israel to celebrate Rosh Chodesh, the Sabbath of the New Moon;

4 And this he shall do, that when the new moon appears Israel will gather and give unto me thy sacrifice, that of the broken heart, and the contrite spirit;

5 And this ye shall do that ye may share in testimony, and rejoice one with another, drinking wine in celebration, and remembering to walk in teshuvah:

6 For even as the new moon is in darkness, the light is come, even as Israel grows in my light.

7 And the first of this Sabbath shall be in the spring, before the full moon of the Passover,

8 And six months hence Israel shall gather again at Yom Teruah, and here Israel shall gather locally to prepare to gather my Israel for Sukkot.

9 ¶ And my Israel shall appoint a Chief Priestess to watch the skies and to gather my Israel to celebrate Harah Keseh, the Sabbath of the Pregnant Moon;

10 And this she shall do, that when the pregnant moon appears, Israel will gather and give unto me thy sacrifice, that of the broken heart, and the contrite spirit;

11 And this ye shall do that ye may share in song and in dance and in testimony, pouring out thy libations in celebration, and remembering to walk in teshuvah:

12 For even as the pregnant moon is full of light, so too does my light, the very light of Christ, shine from thee, my Israel.

13 And the first of the Sabbath shall be in the spring, the full moon of the Passover,

14 And six months hence Israel shall gather again at Sukkot, and here Israel will remember that I, YHVH did save her from slavery and sin.

15 ¶ And these are the three times that my Israel shall gather: The Passover or Easter, Shavuot or Pentecost, and Sukkot.

16 And this shall be the season of teshuvah for you, from Passover to Sukkot,

17 And in the winter months, from Sukkot to Passover, this shall be the time of the pain of thy labor, as my Israel is born anew.

18 And the Chief Priest and the Chief Priestess shall give the days, as I have written them for my Israel in the night sky;

19 And all new moons and all pregnant moons ye shall watch and observe that ye not forget, my Israel, that my voice calls thee home.

Chapter 40

Revelation on temple worship received in Ohio on November 28, 2022.

1 And when thou shall build me a tabernacle or a temple, thou shall invite all that should come in, to worship in my name;

2 And then thou shall seal up the place, even as I have revealed unto Israel by my servants, Allen and David:

3 My High Priests and High Priestesses of my temple shall first call upon the Deacons to close my temple doors,

4 And then my High Priests and High Priestesses shall call upon the Elders to prepare my chamber.

5 And then my High Priests and High Priestesses shall call upon the Teachers to prepare the altar and instruct my Israel.

6 And then my High Priests and High Priestesses shall call the ministry to order, and this shall be the Order of the Ministry.

7 And there in my rituals may be performed, that Israel be nourished and enlightened.

8 And when the Ministry has concluded its service, my High Priests and High Priestesses shall cut the binds and permit the Deacons to open the doors that Israel may re-enter the world.

9 ¶ And remember all ye that read this, that in this place, sealed up unto me, that the very ground shall be holy,

10 That Israel shall be open to visions, and revelations, and prophecy, for the very powers of Heaven shall be open unto you;

11 Therefore, mock these things not, yet allow all that would come to do so that these may stand in witness of my sacred works.

12 And worry not that many will not understand at the first, for my grace is sufficient them; therefore, all may enter that all they that seek may find.

13 But know that the darkness cannot see the light;

14 Therefore, I will blind the eyes and the ears of the unworthy that these shall not see that which they cannot comprehend.

15 Yea, all are welcome in the House of the Lord, but not all they that come shall know,

16 But they that have eyes to see shall see and they that have ears to hear shall hear.

Chapter 41

Revelation on David's call and role in working with the Saints, received in Ohio on November 28, 2022.

1 My servant, David, my friend: Thou has asked of me of thy calling, asking if thou are the servant chosen as the successor of my servant, James J. Strang.

2 Behold, I say unto thee: That many have been called as the successors to my servants, Joseph Smith Jr. and James J. Strang,

3 Some were called by me, some by my Saints, and some have called themselves.

4 Know that thou art one of these that have been called by me, and for this reason did I send my servant Raphael to ordain thee—

5 But as I have said unto thee before: The keys of leadership unto any of the branches of the Church of Christ I shall not give thee, except thou be called of them that leadeth these, my churches, within my vineyard, and this that thou not be seen as a usurper.

6 For my Saints to be Israel, and my Kingdom to be built, my people must be a prophetic people, relying not upon the arm of the flesh.

7 ¶ Thou hast been called to move forward the restoration of all things, as my servant Joseph was called to begin this dispensation,

8 But even as my servant James J. Strang was rejected by the many Saints, and thus the progress of this restoration has been slowed, many that I have called have also been rejected.

9 ¶ My Saints of the restoration seek my servants, but know not how to find them;

10 There have been many that cry out: Lo here! and Lo there! But not all that were called have been chosen, and why were they not chosen?

11 Some were called of themselves, and they taught of themselves, and they took for themselves,

12 Some did not have the faith sufficient—they could not see themselves as I see them,

13 And some could not be seen by the Saints for they would not look, therefore these were called but my Saints would not choose them.

14 ¶ But I say unto thee: Worry not on these things, for my servants are born unto every generation until the time shall come that my Saints are ready to be my Israel,

15 And when that time comes, you will have helped lay the foundation even as my servants Joseph Smith Jr. and James J. Strang, for these were truly called of me.

16 ¶ And should my Saints reject the testimony of my servants, and the day come that I appear, and they find their lamps empty, their works shall stand against them,

17 For the oil is offered unto them, but they that take no oil with them, unto these shall I say: Verily I say unto you, I know you not.

18 But worry not, for I say unto thee that my grace is sufficient, even for these,

19 Yet these shall know that I stood ready while they kicked against the pricks.

20 ¶ Least thou misunderstand, I will show unto thee truth:

21 Behold, my Saints were not yet ready when my servant Joseph died,

22 Yet I took him, both that he seal his testimony in blood and because the world was not ready yet for all he had been shown.

23 And as a testimony against my Saints, when I took him, they scattered; yet I had given them the keys to stay organized:

24 James J. Strang, Sidney Rigdon, and Emma Smith as prophets and prophetess in the First Presidency,

25 For did I not send an angel to ordain James J. Strang, after Joseph had sent his letter of appointment and he was taken?

26 And did I not send an angel to my servant Sidney Rigdon to instruct him to be the guardian of the Church?

27 And was not my servant Emma Smith ordained by the hand of her husband, Joseph, as a leader amongst women?

28 And even as I said through my servant Joseph Smith Jr.: All members of the First Presidency are accounted as equal in holding the Keys of this last kingdom;

29 Therefore, my will was made known, but in their pride my Saints warred with one another, for they were not yet ready.

30 ❡ And now I have called thee, my servant David, and others to bring my people home,

31 Yet if my Saints are not yet ready to be Israel, then thou hast not been called in vain,

32 For all that thou hast been instructed to do shall prepare the way when the time shall come that my Saints be ready.

33 Wherefore, again I say unto thee: Worry not, for I am with thee, and in thy works, I am well pleased.

34 ❡ And this counsel shall I give thee: Do not waste thy time with any that would seek to debate or debase thee;

35 Send out emissaries in my name that will represent me and my Fellowship well;

36 Those that I have called to seek out the Saints, and invite them to my Fellowship,

37 Help make them ready, endow them with power from upon high, and send them forth in my name that Israel shall be found and Zion built.

38 Behold, through thee and those that though shall send forth in my name shall Israel be called back home.

39 ❡ Worry not what the world shall say of thee, for just as my servants Joseph Smith Jr. and James J. Strang, thy name shall be had for both good and evil,

40 But find those that would do my works and speak in my name, for I have called others that thou should not do this work alone.

41 Build my temple that I may come unto my house and speak unto my friends; and behold: I come quickly! Even so, Amen.

Chapter 42

Revelation on Israel received in Ohio on November 28, 2022.

1 My children, Israel: Know that I have sent you out into all the world that all may be included in the name Abraham, of whom I call friend.

2 I created you in the flesh in my image, even as the Father and the Mother created you in their image before the foundation of the world,

3 Being created in the image of Elohim, being their offspring, your life proceeds from the middle column of the tree of life, for you are my first born, Israel, even as I am the First Born of the Father and the Mother.

4 It is my light, from that tree from before the creation, through me into the creation, that nourisheth all the world.

5 ¶ And so it is that I have given Israel this book, the beginning of the teachings of my temple, that in prayer and supplication you may once again be in the Presence of YHVH;

6 The Shekinah has been taken from thee, but not from the earth; and why was she taken? Because thou, O man, refused her.

7 With the ten Sefirot in place, and the Father and the Mother sitting upon their thrown, equal in all power and authority, I, the Christ, have been sent out, but will you receive me?

8 My light shineth in the darkness, but will thou see it, O Israel?

9 The Mother stands ready to receive thy prayers, and the Father stands ready to send out the Holy Ghost to fill thee with the Spirit of God.

10 ¶ These gifts of the Holy Spirit have awaited Israel from the time the Book of Mormon was sent out upon the earth, will you receive them?

11 I, YHVH, who is Jesus who is the Christ, yearns to break the yoke and bondage of that old serpent who seeks always to thwart thee, my Israel.

12 In thy prayers, Israel must first seek to unify as Zion with the Divine Presence who is the Shekinah,

13 And use the whole armor of God in combat against that adversary and overcome his temptations of pride, egoism, and doubt.

14 It is the very living consciousness of the Divine spark that has ignited within Israel, in and about all they that have been born again, that is the very same power that endows you with strength and fortitude,

15 It is this power that will set Israel free, allowing her to tread the path of calm in calamity and unperturbed when the world around her falls.

16 Thus it is that Israel is able to achieve the greatest victory in the realization of her destiny, that is the union of the heavens and the earth:

17 Then it shall be that mankind will see the true creation,

18 That throughout the universe, the divine glory of Elohim remains ever the same both in the heavens above and on the earth below; for these are worlds mirrored, that the spiritual and the physical are one.

19 ¶ When mankind understands this secret, the truth shall be known, and this is that truth:

20 Hear, O Israel, YHVH is your Elohim, I AM Unity.

21 Therefore, let the Creator and the creation be one: So mote it be forever and ever; Amen and amen.

Dreams and Visions

Selected dreams and visions given to David.

The First Book of David

A History

The following are selected dreams and visions given to David regarding the history of the Church of Jesus Christ in Christian Fellowship and its founder.

Chapter 1

God, the Devil, and the Freedom to Choose.

1 As a child, my parents decided to find religion; we visited a few churches as my parents were praying on the subject.

2 As my mother has told it, she was making dinner one evening while my sister and I were playing outside.

3 As she was making dinner, my mother heard a voice tell her to call the Church of Jesus Christ of Latter-day Saints.

4 ¶ Presuming there was an unknown male adult in her backyard with her children, she called us into the house, asking who was outside with us.

5 I told her no one and she had me sit with my sister inside, watching television.

6 Once back in the kitchen, my mother again heard the voice, and once again he told her the same thing: Call the Church of Jesus Christ of Latter-day Saints.

7 Presuming there was someone standing outside, my mother shut the window.

8 ¶ A third time, my mother heard the voice, this time inside the house.

9 At this point she did not know what to think but followed her natural instinct to panic.

10 My mother took my sister and I upstairs, telling us we were playing hide-and-go-seek; we hid in my parents' closet until my father arrived home.

11 ¶ My father was upset that my mother had not call the police; however, my mother stated she had not seen anyone, and the voice sounded as if it were right beside her.

12 She stated that the voice did not frighten her, she only hid out of paranoia.

13 After my father searched the house, and a brief discussion, my father told my mother that if she heard the voice again, she should make the phone call and see what happens.

14 ¶ The next day, my mother heard the voice again, around the same time.

15 This time, she got out the phone book, looked up the phone number and made the call.

16 The phone rang for quite some time; just as she was about to hang up, a woman answered, and he gave my mother the address and time of worship.

17 ¶ It should be noted that this woman, it turned out, had also heard a voice in her car, both days.

18 She also did not heed the direction to go to the Church building the first day.

19 The woman listened the second day and heard the phone ringing as she entered the building.

20 She ran to answer, picking up just as my mother was about to give up.

21 ¶ We attended church for the first time with the Latter-day Saints that Sunday.

Chapter 2

God, the Devil, and the Freedom to Choose.

1 As a small child, I was accustomed to playing with my friends on Sundays and getting ice cream from the ice cream truck.

2 When I discovered that we were going to church for the first time and would miss[a] the ice cream truck, I was devastated.

3 My parents had taught me right from wrong and about God and the Devil and had explained we need to go to church to worship God.

4 ¶ That night I threw a tantrum and camped out in the upstairs hall to protest the idea of being at church all day.

5 I had faith that God and the Devil were real based on the word of my parents; In my childish anger, I got on my knees and prayed to the devil.

6 It may have been a dream, but after my prayer, he appeared to me. I remember it vividly because it has haunted me my entire life.

7 ¶ Satan promised me many things if I would just fight against the Church of God.

8 He promised me wealth and fame, but I told him all I wanted was candy.

9 He told me I could use the wealth to buy candy, which I thought at the time sounded good.

10 He gave me questions to ask to make the church look bad, such as Joseph Smith saying he was the author of the Book of Mormon in the original print, and other questions that really only make sense to those without faith.

11 In the end, I would not agree to join him; It did not feel right, and I realized I was being selfish, but I remembered what he told me, in case I thought I needed the information.

12 ¶ The next day, I went to church with my parents; I found it boring, yet decided that rather than ask the devil's questions, I wanted to learn for myself.

13 The people were nice, but I still felt like there was something wrong; it was as if the people were too nice, like they wanted something.

14 What, I did not know, but I really enjoyed the Latter-day Saint missionaries playing with us before their discussions.

15 ¶ Wanting to know the truth, I taught myself to read using the Latter-day Saint Church's child scriptures and cassette tapes.

16 I prayed about what I read but did not really feel anything; I could not tell if this religion was correct or not, but believing that I would receive a vision, I knew I had to discover the truth.

17 ¶ Then one day, we were at an open house at the Latter-day Saint church; my parents had been baptized at this point. I needed to know if God was real for myself.

18 I thought that God must be real, as I had seen the devil; yet, to me, the Latter-day Saint Church seemed so silly: A boy had found gold plates and translated them? This just did not make sense to my child mind.

19 I too—like Joseph Smith Jr.—was a child; a younger one, but still a child; how could Smith do this and I not?

20 I knelt down at the pew and started to pray silently to myself; I told the Lord that if he was real, and Joseph Smith was a prophet, then he, Smith, was no better than me—a human boy.

21 I told the Lord that I did not want my parents to be lied to, and I wanted to know the truth.

22 I asked the Lord, telling him that if He could show Himself to Joseph Smith, a mere boy, He could show Himself to me.

23 ¶ I knew this to be true in a profound way; it was black and white: either God would reveal himself to me, or Smith was a liar, for me, it was that simple.

24 The scriptures teach that we should have the faith of a child, I can honestly say that my faith might never been as pure again as it was that day.

25 I had pure faith in a way I can only describe as that of the brother of Jared when he saw the Lord's finger.

26 ¶ As soon as I finished the prayer, my eyes were opened to a vision.

27 In this vision, I heard the voice of the Lord telling me that Joseph Smith was his servant.

28 The Lord showed me the history of the Latter Day Saint movement, Smith following the Lord, making mistakes, but pressing on as he learned and grew.

29 I then saw Joseph Smith Jr. die; he was murdered and the Church split; I saw that most of the Church went west to Utah.

30 I saw that church grow there and from there throughout the world.

31 I also saw other denominations start, falter, stop, and move on but none with the growth of the Church of Jesus Christ of Latter-day Saints.

32 ¶ I would pause, break out of the vision if you will, every so often to ask my father, who was sitting in the pew next to me while I was kneeling, questions.

33 I had such great faith in my father that when he told me that what I asked was true, I had even greater faith in what I was seeing; if he said he did not know something, I would just go back into the vision to learn more.

34 Eventually, I knew my father could not answer any more of my questions, so I fully enveloped myself into the vision.

35 ¶ Up to that point all I has seen was the past, yet I also saw the future.

36 I saw the Latter-day Saint Church split again; a wickedness had entered the Church from its beginnings and grown over time.

37 The majority of the Saints did not follow the Lord, and I saw that in the wickedness of the Saints, their hearts were hardened against their fellow man.

38 Rather than learn from their time as the underdog, they went from being the oppressed to becoming oppressors.

39 ❡ I saw many more things in this vision, a number of them I've read in the visions of other apostles, but I kept them to myself, as I had been told over and over that what Smith had seen couldn't be seen by others.

40 I did not think anyone would believe me; but I had seen a vision and the Lord told me he had a work for me and asked me if I would like to know more; I said yes.

41 ❡ From that time, for over a year, I was visited by angels that taught me the will of the Lord.

42 All of my life people have said that I have a way of understanding and teaching spiritual truths that amazes them, but this isn't me; it is because of the lessons I learned from angels as a child and my connection to the Holy Spirit.

43 The angels opened my mind to the gifts of the Spirit in a way that causes me to see things the way I do.

44 This is not to say that I am more holy, or better than anyone else—everyone can have these experiences.

45 I am not special in any way, I was merely given a choice and chose to follow a God that promised nothing but information, rather than a devil that promised everything without really telling me anything.

Note:

a.   Back then, the Church of Jesus Christ of Latter-day Saints broke Sunday worship into two parts: starting in the morning, a break for lunch, then back again in the afternoon.

Chapter 3

Meeting the Lord.

1 By the time I was six years of age, I had seen my angel friends numerous times; they had taught me, and answered many of my questions.

2 I told practically no one of my experiences, as the very few people I tried to share my visions with mocked them, thinking they were the imaginations of a child; yet I knew them to be true.

3 ¶ A number of times I had asked to see the Lord but was told I could not; I surmise now it was because I was too young to receive the gift of the Holy Ghost, or simply not ready; but, in truth I do not know why I was not permitted to see Him.

4 I know my faith allowed me to dream dreams, have visions, and visits from angels, but I fear that my lack of understanding as a child may have stood in the way of seeing the Lord for myself.

5 ¶ One day, I was sent up for quiet time, and as usual, I did not sleep; I was playing when the angel of the Lord appeared and asked me if I would like to speak to the Lord.

6 I answered in the affirmative and was told to go to the window, but that I could not open the curtain.

7 My room was on the second story, so I surmised the Lord would be standing on the ground, but his voice was clearly just on the other side.

8 ¶ I asked the Lord if he was flying; He said, with a voice full of joy, that he was, in a manner.

9 I had been told I was forbidden to touch the angels, and wondered if I could touch the Lord, so I asked him if I could give him a hug, to feel Him with my eyes closed;

10 But the Lord saw through me, asking me if I would peek; I admitted that I would, He laughed with a joy I will never forget, and we talked for some time.

11 ¶ He first answered all of my questions and then began to ask me questions; finally, He asked me if I would covenant to serve Him and I told him I would, as he made me happy.

12 After the covenant was made, He left, and as He did, so too did the joy of being in His presence.

13 Wanting the Lord to return, I opened the curtains, expecting to see Him, asking him to come back; but he was gone.

14 ¶ I turned back to the angel who told me that once I was baptized and received the Holy Spirit, I could feel that joy all of the time; it was also explained to me that there would still be pain, trials, and hardships.

15 The angel of the Lord told me that our time together would be over soon.

16 The angel said that I would still receive visions and revelations, particularly after I had received baptism by Fire—the Gift of the Holy Ghost.

Chapter 4

The Creation.

1 As a teenage boy, one night I sat in my room conversing with the voice of the Lord; I was asking Him questions and He was giving me answers.

2 My vision of the creation came this night when I was in bed, pondering the mysteries of the universe.

3 I had been praying and was filled with the spirit. I was pondering the theory of evolution and the creation story, as told by my religious relatives and as I had learned of it at church[a].

4 As a teenager in high school, this seemed very important to me; the Lord had already shown me a few visions that evening, and I was fearful of the answer I would receive.

5 Would God reveal my understanding of the Bible false, or was all the scientific evidence a lie? How could science and what I thought the scriptures taught be in conflict?

6 ¶ I prayed to see the creation, as recorded in the Bible, and a vision unfolded before my eyes.

7 I saw gases and stars; the materials moved, and the sun was formed.

8 Then the earth; it was as if time was on fast forward, the whole of it happened as a series of events, a timeline shown to me with no explanation.

9 At first, I was amazed at how quickly everything transpired; "seven days," as recorded in the scriptures, seemed like mere moments to me.

10 As I asked questions, the events rolled back and played again, like a movie; but things were slowed down so I could see clearer.

11 ¶ Very quickly, I realized the problem with what I was seeing; time was not a factor to the Lord.

12 The Earth was not created in mere moments, nor was it created in seven literal days.

13 Visions are given, not in real time, but in the Lord's time; and, to Him all time is nonexistent.

14 How can one that is eternal measure time in a way comparable to finite beings?

15 ¶ When I asked him about the truth of the battle between evolution and creation, the voice of the Lord spoke to me saying: "What does it matter, know that all things were made by my hand."

16 But I insisted; I wanted to know the truth, and I pointed out that He was a God of truth.

17 The Lord slowed down the vision again, this time I saw the creation of everything, not just of the planet.

18 I saw small cells multiplying and life forming, life growing and changing, evolving right before my eyes.

19 At a quick glance, it was easy to see how one could think things were being created out of nothing; however, at a closer look, it was clear that life was not simply called out of nothing.

20 ¶ I cannot say exactly how everything worked or in what order, but a few things were made very clear to me:

21 First, nothing was an accident; everything was created for a reason, and these reasons are parts of God's plan.

22 Second, Adam and Eve were not alone on the Earth, nor were they the first people; they were the first people in the story of mankind as it

relates to our salvation, the salvation of this human family; not only did spiritual death enter the world through Adam and Eve, but spiritual life as well.

23 Third, revelation is a hard thing to understand, we should not jump to conclusions and sometimes one revelation or vision can have many meanings.

24 Lastly, the Lord does not always tell us what we want to hear, sometimes He gives us the answer we need, even if it is not the answer to the question asked.

25 ¶ At this point the Lord had shown me the creation of the Earth, and enlightened my understanding in many ways, yet I had one other question I was afraid to ask.

26 The Lord eased my mind through the power of the Holy Spirit and knowing it was alright to ask, I inquired as to where He came from.

27 I felt joy from the Lord, knowing he wished for me to ask, and He answered my question with a vision.

28 ¶ I saw, in vision, a pool of what looked like water; there, intelligences were moving on the face of the water. These intelligences began rising up and conversing.

29 Then, they began to glow so bright it was hard to look upon them any longer; these then helped others out of the pool as well.

30 It was then explained to me that what looked like water was in fact "the face of the waters" found in the deep; a great pool of intelligences[b]; this pool was where we all came from, we were a part of it.

31 Whether the first to leave were Gods to our God, as I had been taught by some Latter-day Saints at church, or our Gods, our Heavenly Parents (Elohim) and Jesus Christ, alone was not made known to me.

32 What was made known was that Elohim, our Heavenly Father and Mother, left on their own, creating their own spirit bodies; then they created their own bodies of flesh and bone as they have now, and that YHWH, Jesus Christ, had been with them from the beginning.

33 These then helped other intelligences create their own spirit bodies; the first to create His own Spirit body was Jehovah/Jesus Christ, as he had been with them from the beginning.

34 He, Jesus Christ, was literally the first born of the Father through their help in His spiritual creation; yet He is co-eternal with the Father and a God, just as the Father is a God.

35 From there, other noble and great ones were born to their own created spirit bodies, through the help and instruction of our Heavenly Parents.

36 ¶ It was also clear that the lower the intelligence, the greater they needed help in the creation of their own spirit bodies, yet all humans on this Earth created their spirit bodies themselves.

37 This is why God, in the books of Genesis and Moses, "moved upon the face of the water" but in the book of Abraham, "the Spirits of the gods" were "brooding" or better said, incubating.

38 God the Father and his wife or wives were self-created; as his children we too are self-created, but only through the help of our Heavenly Parents.

39 All that were intelligences understood, to their capacity, what was happening and rejoiced greatly upon leaving the face of the waters in the deep;

40 They understood that this was the first part in creating eternal physical bodies of flesh and bone, as they saw Elohim had.

41 ¶ It should be understood that matter and intelligence are both co-eternal; neither has beginning nor end; the progress of joining these two co-eternal forces is the point of all existence and the end of the first eternity.ᶜ

42 It is the priesthood and the Law that allows this to happen, and only by obedience to the Law can the priesthood work; and, Christ's Grace shows mercy to us that we may use the priesthood though we are imperfect.

43 This helped me to understand the vision I had of the creation, as I was shown in it that we created the Earth, as we are gods; the children of God the Father and a Heavenly Mother;

44 (Whether we are all from the same Heavenly Mother or if Heavenly Father has more than one wife, I do not know);

45 Just as God the Father created His own body, first in spirit then in the flesh, we are now doing the same, with God's help.

46 However, His identity and intelligence are greater than ours, thus we need His divine guidance; we cannot do this on our own.

47 Likewise, our obedience to the Law is too weak; we need a Savior.

48 This is the role of Jesus Christ, to be the Savior of the world; His perfection is so great that His divinity is also eternally greater than ours; we need a way to converse with our Gods, this is the role of the Holy Ghost or Holy Spirit.

49 This is why they are Gods, worthy of our worship; and we are gods, children of the Most High;

50 This is how God is our Father, He and our Heavenly Mother look out for us, lead us guide us and sent their Sons, Jesus Christ and the Holy Spirit, to walk beside us so that we can find our way.

Note:
   a.   The Church of Jesus Christ of Latter-day Saints.
   b.   See Genesis 1:2.
   c.   See DoS 58:30.

Chapter 5

In the Garden.

1 One night the Lord gave me a vision in the form of a dream; in this dream I was at work, watching the news, everyone's eyes were glued to the TV screen, the reporters were stating that the Garden of Eden had been found here in North America.

2 They were talking to experts in religion, philosophy, archaeology, and more, asking: what did this mean for the world? What did it mean for America? What did it mean for religion?

3 Most of the people talking the loudest used this discovery to "prove" their own religions correct;

4 Jews were outside the Garden praying, Protestants were preaching loudly, Catholics were chanting and using hand signs, some waving containers of smoke; Muslims had gathered and were praying and reading the Quran.

5 The Church of Jesus Christ of Latter-day Saints' missionaries in that area were talking to people, pointing out that Joseph Smith Jr. had said that the Garden of Eden was here in America.

6 Other world religions were represented as well, and each gave their point of view on what the Garden really was—from Shangri La to Atlantis and more.

7 There was a fear among many that the unholy would die if they entered the Garden, all of these religions seemed to think this spot should belong only to them and their followers; though the Garden had been found, as of yet no one had entered.

8 ¶ The biggest shock came when the people, archaeologists of no particular religious affiliation, that had made the discovery finally walked in, as when they did, they simply came right back out.

9 These explorers looked just a little younger than when they went in, more refreshed and full of life.

10 Though they had been gone but minutes, they stated they were in the Garden for years—a lifetime!

11 Now reporters were talking to physicists; these scientists were talking about string theory and quantum mechanics, all trying to explain what had happened.

12 Doctors were saying that the men and women that had come out were healthy and strong.

13 ¶ Suddenly the push from people trying to get into the Garden was even greater as everyone wanted the "miracle food" inside that they imagined would cure their ills.

14 Some even thought they would drink from the mythical fountain of youth and live forever.

15 There were also ideas being entertained by some that entering would purify sins and that those that came out were now somehow "holy."

16 These reports went on for days; in my dream, I watched them on my work breaks at work and until I went to sleep at night at home.

17 After the first week, fears of economic collapse due to interest in the Garden had faded, but people all over the world were still making pilgrimages to get to the Garden of Eden.

18 Coworkers kept asking when I was going, shocked to hear that I was waiting until my scheduled time off from work.

19 I felt (in my dream) this was something that should happen at the right time, not just because I wanted it.

20 ¶ Finally, that day came. I drove to Missouri and parked my car; I had to walk for miles from there, due to all the abandoned cars of the people that came before me.

21 As I got closer to the front, I could hear people talking as they came out:

22 "It was really beautiful!" exclaimed one woman, "Yeah, but there wasn't much to do," came a response from the man with her.

23 "I'm getting a tee shirt, to remember the occasion," said yet another.

24 Most of the responses were like this; it seemed that many wanted in, but once there they did not know what to do in the Garden.

25 Besides the religiously fervent, to some this was like an entertainment park, a cool "trick of nature," to others a "scientific curiosity."

26 Yet the religious people that went in expecting to see angels or miracles came out disappointed, some were now even calling it a tourist trap.

27 ¶ As I walked passed them on my way into the Garden, a man tried to stop me from going in.

28 "Excuse me, I need you to fill out this survey before you enter," he said, very politely.

29 "No thank you," I said just as politely.

30 "I apologize for the inconvenience," he said with the utmost courtesy, "but I can't let you in until after you complete the survey."

31 I tried to move him out of the way with my arm, but he put his hands up, asking that I not touch him.

32 "Can't you ask someone else?" I asked, waving my hands towards all the people walking past me.

33 "We are asking everyone," he said.

34 I looked around and saw a few others dressed like him; they too were all asking people to stop, but everyone was just walking past them as if they couldn't even see them.

35 Annoyed that he was focusing on me, but understanding as no one else was listening, I went with him.

36 ¶ After sitting down, the man explained that people were going in freely and free of charge, but that they wanted to see what they learned while in there, among other things too lengthy to go over in this narrative.

37 I thought this rather scientific and was suddenly a little more willing to help.

38 After filling out the forms and listening to his advice, I again started walking towards the Garden.

39 As I walked in, I noticed that some of the others had found a few people to take the survey, though not many; and the people they found seemed to be of the same mindset as myself, annoyed but understanding. I kept going and finally, I went into the Garden of Eden.

40 ¶ Entering the Garden, I was at once in shock and awe of the beauty.

41 There were animals and plants there I had never seen with greens and colors so bright it was impossible not to feel happier just looking at them.

42 The colors of the plants and fruits were so vivid, unlike anything I had ever seen before.

43 The food was so good I felt as though I could eat forever and never feel hungry or full ever again; the wonders and awe that I saw here were too great to describe in written words.

44 I saw many miraculous things, all pointing to the reality of God.

45 I even saw the tree of life at the east of the Garden, guarded by Cherubim and a flaming sword which turned every way.

46 ¶ I noticed that other people did not seem to care to talk to anyone outside the groups they had come in with. As I came in alone, it was as if I were invisible to anyone else.

47 It was clear that some of these people had been there for many years, and out of curiosity I began to study and observe them.

48 I saw people baptizing and being baptized in the waters as I walked around.

49 I saw people trying to teach the people there; some stopped as though they thought they heard something; others walked past them without a thought.

50 Very rarely I would see a few people had stopped and were listening to the teachers; these teachers were dressed in the same manner as the man that had stopped me before entering the garden.

51 There were also merchants selling trinkets, which I found odd as they were selling things that could be easily picked up off the ground; yet people were lining up to buy these items as if there were no other means of obtaining them.

52 Walking around, I also noticed that there were people that would destroy life in the Garden just to watch it grow again; some would cut themselves and pour water over their wounds just to see them heal.

53 The power of the Garden was being used to entertain, not to edify or enlighten; I did not know why, but this made me very sad.

54 ¶ I do not know how long I was in the Garden, but after a time of watching how others were treating this miraculous and wondrous place, and exploring it extensively for myself, I felt the desire to leave.

55 Upon leaving, the man that had stopped me before was there again with his surveys; I was feeling depressed after leaving, trying to process what I saw.

56 I really didn't want to talk to him, but he insisted.

57 I asked if I could come back later, promising that I would return, but he shook his head no; "You will forget," he said. "We must do this now, while it is fresh in your mind."

58 This made sense to me, so I glumly sat down, I went over everything I saw in great detail as he wrote everything down.

59 As my experience poured out, I felt as though the negatives I saw were draining from me, leaving me exhausted but uplifted. It transformed the experience for me.

60 ¶ After I was finished, he looked me in the eyes and asked, "What did you learn from this?"

61 I pondered this for a moment and looked back at him and responded, "It doesn't matter where you are, what matters is who you are."

62 At this he smiled and my understanding of who he was transformed, I instantly recognized him as an angel of the Lord, one I knew from my childhood.

63 As I understood who he was, I warmed up, being filled with the Holy Spirit.

64 Before I could say anything else to him, he responded: "That is correct, now go and tell everyone."

65 ¶ With that, I awoke in my bed, being filled with the Spirit of God and desirous to share this message with the world.

Chapter 6

Ordination.

1 Not realizing I'd ever need to tell my story; I didn't keep the best of records.

2 I was commanded by the Lord to make an appointment to talk to my bishop about being ordained a High Priest as early as 1998, but I didn't heed the command because of my lack of self confidence.

3 This prompting came to me off and on for over a decade.

4 Finally, around 2013 or so, I gave in and followed the Lord's command; at that point I was out of excuses.

5 I spoke to my bishop who told me that to become a High Priest, I would need to either age out of Elders Quorum or receive a Stake calling.

6 He stated that it was really just for the keys of running the Church at that level or to have peers so priesthood meetings would be more relevant.

7 This did not make sense to me both because the Relief Society didn't separate out grandmothers, and it wasn't in line with the teachings of the Joseph Smith version of the Bible:

8 "And thus, having been approved of God, he was ordained a high priest after the order of the covenant which God made with Enoch... to stand in the presence of God, to do all things according to his will, according to his command, subdue principalities and powers; and this by the will of the Son of God which was from before the foundation of the world. And men having this faith, coming up unto this order of God, were translated and taken up into heaven. And now, Melchizedek was a priest of this order" (IV/JST Genesis 14:28, 31-33).

9 ¶ I went home to pray, had I waited too long? Did the Lord have something else for me to do next?

10 I felt peace, knowing I had finally done what the Lord asked me to do, and blessed by His patients with me.

11 When I prayed that night, I felt the peace of the Lord wash over me; I knew there was more to come; what, I did not know.

12 ¶ A few weeks or so later, I was alone, praying when the Lord told me it was time I was ordained a High Priest, as there was a work He had for me.

13 Presuming it was a work in the Church of Jesus Christ of Latter-day Saints, I asked if I should make another appointment with my Bishop, or if I should speak to the Stake President.

14 Rather than answer my question, a light came into the room, in the light was a man, not quite as tall as myself.

15 His skin was dark, like bronze, his hair black; yet he was white— hair and skin, glowing with spiritual power; he identified himself as Raphael, a servant of the Lord.

16 Though startled at first, I was not afraid, I felt a peace wash over me.

17 Not wanting to be deceived, I stuck out my hand to shake his, he grasped my hand in the token of the Law of Sacrifice and I felt a warmth come over me, washing through me with the love and power of God that he had in him.

18 I was immediately reminded of stories in the scriptures, as I shook his hand, of those that had fallen down to worship angels and understood why they had; but I knew he was not a God.

19 ⁋ As I let go of his hand, he told me he had been send by God to ordain me a High Priest and set me apart. His blessing[a] was as follows:

20 David, servant of God, I bless thee and place upon your head all of the keys of the High Priesthood, even as Abraham had.

21 For it was I, Melchizedek, that ordained Abraham; teaching him, blessing and ordaining him with the keys of the Priesthood after the Order of the Son of God.

22 With these keys come the responsibilities of your calling.

23 It was I that taught thee in thy youth, with others in the Lord's name; and, as I told thee then, you will have a hand in completing the restoration of all things.

24 You will see many things and are called to perform a work in preparing the children of men to receive the Lord their God.

25 Even now the horses are chomping at the bits, ready to carry home Christ, our King.

26 Though you are weak, in the Lord you shall be strong; He has prepared you for this day and has prepared others to assist you in this work.

27 And this is your ministry: Unity in the Lord, Holiness to the Lord; to go forward and teach every man, woman, and child to love their neighbors even as they are loved by God; for God loves all.

28 And by this love shall Satan be bound, and Jesus shall reign the one true King over all the earth.

29 Go forward with strength in God, translating the Word of God, and preaching peace in the name of the Most High: Amen.

30 ¶ With this he left, the room seeming dark and bland without the light that had emanated from him.

31 I said a prayer in meditation, repeating his words over and over.

32 I thought now that I should receive a call from someone at church, as I believed the work I was to do was to be in that denomination; it was a call that never came.

Note:

a. This was not the whole blessing, but all I feel prompted to reveal at this time.

Chapter 7

The Store.

1 In May of 2015, I had a dream, it was one in a series of dreams I have had over the course of several years; I know these dreams are not ordinary dreams, but from the Lord; this one made it clearer to me that the Lord had a work for me to do.

2 In this dream, I obtained a small shop in a mall, but this was no ordinary shop, nor was it an ordinary mall.

3 Even before I unlocked the doors, I was told by other shop owners to come and buy from their stores, not to open this shop; and while there were crowds of curious people looking to see the shop that was re-opening, the other shop owners were pushing them to go to their stores.

4 Once inside the shop, my small team and I had to clean the place up, there was a lot of dirt and dust.

5 Worse yet, there was mold on the books and items we were selling in the shop, the mold was so bad it looked like long hair growing on the books.

6 While some were cleaning up the windows, shelves, and signs, I started to clean the books using a thick mold killer and a razor to cut away the age and clean them.

7 ¶ As I cleaned them, I could see they were made of gold and silver, wrapped in leather; the books were beautiful to behold!

8 Upon closer examination I could see what they were, the Scriptures—the Word of God.

9 Even though we were still cleaning, people insisted they be allowed to shop in the store.

10 They would look around, some mocked us for being so small and left.

11 Others, a small few, could see the beauty under the imperfection from what seemed like decades of neglect and stayed to help clean.

12 Meanwhile, the other store owners would come in and tell us the end was coming, that we all needed to get out of this shop and go to their shops for safety.

13 Even in the court yards between the shops, people argued amongst themselves, with every shop owner insisting they had the only safe shop, with various patrons joining in the debate.

14 I asked those working on this shop not to join the debates, and I let everyone know that they were welcome to come and go in this shop as they pleased, and that they were welcome to their shops, but that we would stay and clean.

15 I let them know that they would indeed be safe in their shops, but that this shop was just as safe; it was the mall itself that protected us, not the stores.

16 ¶ It was at this point that a few things happened:

17 First, I realized that this shop I was in was not really a bookstore, as I had imagined, nor were any of the other shops normal stores that sold things like clothing or electronics.

18 All of the stores in this mall sold the same thing: salvation in the Lord Jesus Christ.

19 Some asked for more or less money than others, some were more or less entertaining; but all offered the same service: salvation.

20 It was then that I realized that all of the stores were the various Christian religions; they all claimed to have the only Christ with the saving grace that leads to salvation.

21 Yet those that came to the shop I had reopened were looking for something more.

22 It seemed that the moment I realized this; the sky caught fire.

23 The ceiling of the mall was made of glass windows, how anyone thought their store with glass windows would survive a meteor shower, I did not know;

24 Yet this was their argument, their store was safe while all the other stores had glass windows. In this dream, however, I knew that we would all be just fine.

25 ¶ I was calmly telling another store owner that we in the reopened shop would be fine as the meteor shower started.

26 We both looked up, and he dropped to the ground fearing his own demise as I calmly watched the meteor disintegrate before hitting the roof of the mall.

27 Looking around, I saw many surprised, running for shelter as they were caught unaware in the courtyards. Yet all in the mall were safe, for they all had Christ.

28 The other shop owner that had been trying to argue with me got up and sheepishly scratched his head. He admitted that he had been incorrect, as it was clear that everyone in the mall was safe.

29 ¶ Once the meteor shower ended, the other shop owners and I went out to survey the land, we found it utterly decimated.

30 All life outside the mall had been destroyed but a few stragglers, saved I know not how, the few that were left went to the mall, stunned that it was there.

31 They all stated that they had never seen it, nor knew of it; that if they had known there was a mall they would have entered and warned their friends and family.

32 ¶ This dream was a powerful message and warning to me, Doctrines of the Saints 42:31-46 points out that all that accept Christ will be saved by Christ's Grace; this grace was the glass shield around the mall in my dream.

33 I now knew that it does not matter what "store" or church or denomination we belong to, as long as we are His, that is Christ's.

34 Rather than fighting amongst ourselves, we should be working together to share the Good News of Christ with all; and we read in Doctrines of the Saints 42:31 and 33:

35 ¶ "Yea, verily, the only ones who shall not be redeemed in the due time of the Lord, after the sufferings of His wrath, who shall be brought forth by the resurrection of the dead through the triumph and glory of the Lamb who was slain, who was in the bosom of the Father before the worlds were made...

36 "That through Him all might be saved whom the Father had put unto His power, and made by Him who glorifieth the Father and saveth all the work of His hands, except those sons and daughters of perdition who denyeth the Son after the Father hath revealed Him."

37 ¶ Later in 2015 I was given another dream where I was working in a vast field.

38 Every so often I would bump into a sheet or curtain that got in my way; it was annoying, frustrating.

39 Then the voice of the Lord said: This is as man sees, see as I see, and I was pulled up into the clouds.

40 I saw that the vast field was nothing as compared to the true field that seemed to have no end.

41 There were others working in fields with curtain barriers limiting them to their part of the vineyard.

42 The curtains were easy to pass through, yet people stayed where they were.

43 I felt the Spirit enlighten me to understand the vineyard was the Church of God, and the curtains divided this Church here upon the earth to meet the many needs of mankind through all the various denominations.

Chapter 8

Another Dream.

1 As time moved forward, I pondered my dream from the Lord of the Garden of Eden; what it meant, I did not know; I felt called, but in the Latter-day Saint Church one does not simply start preaching without a call from a Church leader above them.

2 It was after our twins were born that I realized that the dream of the Garden was the Lord's call for me to preach the Gospel, to call others to Christ.

3 I did not fully understand how to go about this and waited for a call from some LdS Church leader, but that call never came.

4 During this time, I was led by the Spirit to learn more about a variety of topics and I gained a number of revelations and insights from the Lord.

5 I kept these to myself, sharing them only with my wife as I did not have the authority to speak on these matters to members of the LdS Church.

6 ¶ During this time, I was saddened often by the rejection of those by the LdS Church that desired to come unto Christ.

7 Why was Christ's Grace powerful enough to cover my sins, but not powerful enough to cover the sins of others, I often pondered?

8 The Lord told me that his Grace was sufficient, but that the Church had yet to learn these truths.

9 ❡ I had felt the Spirit tell me to stop attending the Latter-day Saint Church in the fall of 2014.

10 At this time the Church of Jesus Christ of Latter-day Saints, from my perspective, had started going back to its old ways of exclusion.

11 Just as they had rejected the Lord and had not allowed blacks to receive the Office of the Priesthood, just as they sympathized with Nazis before the U.S. entered WWII, just as they said "no" to women's equality in the workplace, etc. the leaders of the Latter-day Saints now wanted the U.S. government to define marriage for other Churches.

12 The irony in this was that we stopped practicing polygamy for this very reason; the Lord asked us to fight, and when we lost, He asked us to stand down.

13 Now, the Latter-day Saint Church was doing to others the evil that had been done to them.

14 ❡ This meant that my family stopped going to church; my wife was welcome to attend on her own, but did not want to go without me, and I didn't want to go and send a mixed signal to my children that what was happening was correct before the Lord.

15 The Lord had asked me to stop, I do not exactly know why, but in view of my frustration I did not even ask, I just did as the Spirit directed.

16 My anger towards the manmade policies was great, as these policies rejected the Gospel and teachings of the Church as found in the doctrine, the scriptures of the Church.

17 During my time of inactivity from the Church, I prayed daily for revelation from the Lord: Why had he asked me to stop attending? What was my next step? I really didn't know what I should do.

18 The Spirit told me to return only after I was offered a Stake calling, but after Christmas, I returned anyway.

19 I disobeyed the Lord, and I make no excuse for it.

20 ❡ I knew it meant a lot to my wife, and it felt right to go back on a personal, worldly level; yet I still kept receiving revelations from the Lord.

21 I told the Lord that despite the wickedness of the leaders of the Church, from Brigham Young taking the priesthood from blacks to the attacks against religious freedoms in the United States under Thomas S. Monson, I would not leave unless He came to me in the spirit of peace; and I required my wife to be a second witness to me.

22 I feared that my frustration with the evil I was seeing was driving me away, rather than the Lord, and I begged Him to explain to me why He was giving me these revelations.

23 ¶ One night after much prayer and reflection, I had a dream given me of the Lord; this was a dream and not to be taken literally, but there were things taught to me here by the Spirit.

24 In this dream, I was in Utah with my wife, we were at the LdS General Conference.

25 We had been invited there, with a group of about twenty-five or so people, to meet the Brethren between sessions.

26 It was much like a celebrity event, in that there was much hand waving from the Church leaders, and much swooning from the faithful.

27 We, the people there to meet Church leaders, were a part of a PR campaign to make the Church appear more open.

28 ¶ During the first session, I spoke to the others in my small group, asking them what they planned to do or say to the Church leaders when we met them.

29 No one had really thought of anything to ask up to this point; we decided to kneel in prayer and ask the Lord for guidance.

30 The voice of the Lord came to all of us, telling us to ask the brethren if they had ever seen Jesus Christ; after all, this is what it means to be an apostle—a special witness of Christ.

31 ¶ When our time came, we were still on live TV, the speakers were on; those in the crowd and all across the world could see and hear us and our questions.

32 We had voted in unison that this was the question to ask, and it was decided, though I was not keen to do it, that I would be our spokesperson.

33 Once on the stage, with cameras rolling, I asked the Brethren, "Have you seen Jesus Christ?"

34 They all looked at each other, appearing very troubled by this question, then one of them spoke, stating this was not an appropriate thing to ask on live TV.

35 At this point, fearing they would lose control, they broke us up, and there were about two to three people to each of the fifteen Church leaders; I was taken with the group that was now speaking to Elder Ballard.

36 While all of this was going on, my wife went to the microphone and asked the members of the Church what harm it would be for men that claimed apostleship?

37 What would the harm be to state just once, not to brag but to inform, that they had seen God for all the world to know that He lives?

38 At this point, people started calling the Church, and people in the audience wanted to know, had these men seen the Risen Jesus?

39 ¶ Finally, the Brethren went to the stand and stated they would step off stage and pray to know the will of the Lord in this matter; we waited on stage for their return.

40 Time passed, time for the second session came, and they still had not come out; the time for the second session soon too passed.

41 Just as I was about to go backstage to make sure they were okay, my wife asked me if I would go back and see what was taking so long.

42 I went to the pulpit and let the cameras and those in the building know that due to time, I would just step back to see what was going on, and make sure everything was okay.

43 ¶ When I got backstage, I knocked three times, but no one answered; I was concerned I might be interrupting a major spiritual event, then the Lord whispered: Go in.

44 I went in, and the room, at first, appeared empty; then, after closer inspection I saw the room was filled with demons.

45 Using the Priesthood, I commanded the evil creatures to leave and, obedient to the power of the Priesthood and the name of Jesus Christ, they did flee from my presence and from the building.

46 As this was happening, my wife was looking at the equipment in the room, as it happened, the equipment had been on, filming, the whole time.

47 We rewound the tape and watched their discussion, and we didn't want to show the world what we saw.

48 We prayed and an angel of the Lord came to us and told us that the people needed to see the tape, so we connected it to the main feed and played it.

49 On the tape, we saw the Brethren state they were unwilling to answer the question, as in doing so it would appear as though they had given in and lost control of the Church.

50 Very worried about losing power, they opted to leave, and hold a press conference later that would state that after prayer they feared for their safety, and to ignore the question all together.

51 They had decided that they would not outrightly accuse those of us invited to meet them and ask them anything of misdoing, as this may also make them look bad; however, they would plant the seed and let the members point fingers for them.

52 After they left, we saw the evil creatures enter the room, there was no longer anyone there with the keys to stop them, and the deception of the Church leaders had invited them in.

53 I asked my wife to turn the tape off, but she wanted the people to know that the power of the Lord was real, so she forwarded the tape to the part where I exercised out the demons.

54 There was more to the dream, but I feel impressed by the Spirit not to record the whole dream, that the Lord will reveal the rest to others as He sees fit.

55 ¶ When I awoke, I remembered the dream perfectly, and asked the Lord what it meant.

56 The Spirit whispered to me: That they draw near to me with their lips, but their hearts are far from me, they teach for doctrines the

commandments of men, having a form of godliness, but they deny the power thereof.

57 I understood that this dream was not to call out the Brethren, nor was it to glorify myself; this dream was to point out the fear of losing control the leaders of the Church have, and that they are not alone.

58 Every Latter Day Saint denomination shares this fear and has since the death of Joseph Smith Jr.

59 This revelation in the form of a dream was given to point out that when the Lord is ignored, evil enters.

60 And, this dream was to tell me that though many hold the Keys to the Kingdom, these keys are not all or always being used to their full potential;

61 That the fear of men, at times, can outweigh their fear of the Lord, and this was too was a warning to me to fear the Lord above man.

62 ¶ This dream prepared me for further revelations and my call from God to serve the Lord and help build up his kingdom here on the earth.

Chapter 9

In the Temple.

1 At the time all of this was occurring, I was traveling to Washington D.C. to meet with politicians and their staffers on behalf of one of the groups my company was working with.

2 Having trouble focusing, my mind wondered one day to the dreams and revelations I was receiving; I was receiving revelation continuously but did not know what to do with it.

3 For some reason, that day I was reminded of the revelation I had received the first time I went through the Church of Jesus Christ of Latter-day Saints' temple.

4 While in the Washington DC temple back in the 1990's, it was revealed to me that the endowments were meant to be given as we progressed in the offices of the priesthood.

5 The Lord had tried to reveal more to me at that time, but I had pushed the information away as it was not my role or place to receive revelation for this Church.

6 At this point, I knew the Lord had a work for me and in prayer I asked the Lord what I was to do with all the information He was giving me.

7 Rather than answer this prayer, a vision was opened unto me right there in a certain congressman's office.

8 ¶ In the vision, the Lord revealed to me that the temple was never to be secret, this is the dispensation of revelation when mysteries are to be revealed.

9 I saw that the Saints, as they scattered after the death of Joseph Smith Jr., had both added to and used the revealed information without understanding what it meant or what to do with it.

10 I saw Priests preparing the sacrament in their temple clothes, and Bishops sitting on the stand in full temple clothing.

11 I also saw men and women gather in the true order of prayer, and I saw that every congregations' building was a temple of the Lord open to the public.

12 My eyes were opened, and I understood that the temple worship was to be simple worship, there was no need for separate temples and meeting houses.

13 ¶ I did not know what to do with this revelation, I felt the Holy Spirit moving me to tell the world!

14 Yet I feared the Church of Jesus Christ of Latter-day Saints and told the Lord that if it was His will to make these changes, that He should tell his servants, the apostles leading this Church.

15 I shared my visions with my wife, but otherwise kept what I knew in my heart.

Chapter 10

God's Work, A Blueprint.

1 From the time I received the dream of cleaning the store, I knew the Lord was calling me to a mighty work to do in His holy name; I began to receive revelation after revelation of how the Lord had wanted His Fellowship organized.

2 The Lord had shown me where the Latter Day Saint Churches would be today had we not let fear and secrecy take precedence over his will.

3 I was shown the true meaning of the temple rituals, how the Lord had wished for it to be used by this time.

4 The Lord showed me the structure of the Church, as the prophet Joseph Smith Jr. was setting it up, and how it should have been set up by this point.

5 To be clear, however, the Lord did not state that the current or former presidents of the Church are or were evil or that they did not hold the keys to the kingdom.

6 It was and is to me clear that these men still hold the required keys, and are inspired, yet have failings like everyone else.

7 It is also clear that there are flaws in the manmade policies and procedures and we have seen how these have led each Church and its members astray in some areas and have led a number of people away from Christ.

8 ¶ The question in my mind after every revelation was, what do I do with this?

9 As a lay member of the largest Latter Day Saint denomination, I could not just fly to Utah and let the Brethren know that the Lord had revealed these things to me, as this is not how the Latter-day Saint branch of the Church of Christ works.

10 I did not understand why I was getting these visions, for I am no one; I am just Dave.

11 I needed to know why I was receiving these visions and revelations; I had asked repeatedly, but the Lord ignored my questions and just gave me more information.

12 Yet rather than feeling confused, I felt overwhelmed.

13 In my heart I knew what the Lord required of me and that this knowledge was why He was not answering me in the manner I desired.

14 ¶ On November 6, 2015, I learned that the Church would be rejecting children of same-sex couples, and that they had been rejecting the children of polygamists wishing to join the LDS Church.

15 It was at this time that I felt a peace come over me; the Spirit of the Lord whispered to me: It is time.

16 With that, I started a website to hold all of the information the Lord has revealed to me over my lifetime.

17 If it is God's will that something becomes of it, then His will be done; if not, I can at least say I followed the Lord and did as He commanded me.

18 The information is not a perfect record, I am dyslexic and so if there are faults and flaws, they are the mistakes of men;

19 Yet I know that in spite of this, those that read over these revelations and will not reject the Lord but will instead pray to the Lord will know the truth of them.

20 ¶ One thing I have learn through all of this is not to condemn the things of God, that we may be found spotless at the judgment seat of Christ;

21 The Lord is perfect and I, as a flawed human, will do my best to get this information out into the world.

22 The Spirit will guide those that read and pray to know the truth and will testify of the meaning of all things.

23 This work is a Holy work, the Work of the Lord; it is not done to condemn or reject the Latter-day Saint branch or any other Church;

24 We are all able to receive God's Grace if we but ask, salvation is not tied to a church; it is tied to our Savior, even Jesus Christ.

25 The Bible won't save us, the Book of Mormon won't save us; Jesus will save us, if we but accept Him.

26 Regardless of religious denomination, if one has accepted Jesus Christ as their personal Savior this Fellowship is meant to be a place for them.

27 This work is to place to collect revelations and inspiration—the will of the Lord through His servants;

28 A place of hope where those looking to worship Jesus and study the Scriptures without bigotry or rejection can come and find peace.

29 To that end, God bless this work and those that do it; in His name, Jesus Christ, So Mote It Be: Amen.

The Second Book of David

The Fellowship of Christ

A brief history of The Church of Jesus Christ in Christian Fellowship.

Chapter 1

The Church of Jesus Christ in Christian Fellowship, November 6, 2015.

1 On Friday, November 6, 2015, I received a revelation from the Lord.

2 As I read that the Church of Jesus Christ of Latter-day Saints was rejecting children worthy of baptism because the organization disapproved of same-sex couples marrying, I felt a peace wash over me, and I heard the voice of the Lord say: "It is time."

3 ¶ The only way to describe what happened next is to say that the Holy Spirit descended upon me as a dove.

4 I was fully embraced and enveloped in the Spirit of God in a way I cannot describe with human lips or in terms of human understanding.

5 I spoke to the Lord, being in the Presence of God in a way described in the Books of Moses as, when Moses was in God's Presence.

6 ¶ I have been told not to record the full conversation as much of it was for me alone; I will however say this: The understanding I had at that moment was beyond comprehension.

7 I was given access to understanding beyond understanding, and when the moment was over, that understanding was gone as well.

8 I retained the memory of the experience, but that limitless flow of pure knowledge and wisdom was taken from me and I was returned to myself.

9 ¶ That morning, on my drive to work, I prayed to the Lord the entire journey, asking Him about the things I was to do.

10 One of the things I knew I needed to do was create a place to begin this ministry, this journey, the Lord had called me to.

11 My first thought was to build a website, a digital portal to the world, but I had to have a name so I could purchase a URL.

12 ¶ As I drove, I asked God: What should this ministry, this thing you have called me to build, be called?

13 Please Lord, let it be something short that works, like Community of Christ; there are so many churches called 'Church of Jesus Christ' it cannot be that simple, but it does not need to be too long or overly complicated.

14 I am not going to just make something up, I am going to wait for you to give me the name, because this is your work and I wish to do it for your glory not my own.

15 ¶ The prayer was longer than this, but this portion of that prayer is all that is relevant to cover at this time.

16 And, as I went about my day, I listened for the voice of the Lord to come to me, telling me what to name this movement I had been called to create; all day long, nothing.

17 I prayed again on my drive home; I reiterated many of the things the Lord had told me, and things from my prayer that morning.

18 I let the Lord know I could start writing but without a name, I could not start the website.

19 ¶ I ended my prayer after I was in my neighborhood, turning onto the street just before my own.

20 As I was turning onto the circle we lived on, the voice of the Lord spoke to me saying: The name shall be: The Church of Jesus Christ in Christian Fellowship.

21 ¶ When I heard this, my countenance fell; this was not the short name I had ask for or been looking for; however, it was the name given to me from God;

22 I knew I could not go back and tell the Lord He was wrong; I just had to live with it.

23 ¶ Over time, I began to see the wisdom of God in the name given us:

24 We are a Church, a body of religious believers.

25 Faith in Jesus Christ is the core of our different religious beliefs— we are the body of Christ.

26 What we do is gather with fellow Christians of any and all denominations, and with those that do not affiliate with any denominations, to unite as one in Christ.

27 We gather in Christian Fellowship.

28 Thus, we have become exactly what God declared us to be: The Church of Jesus Christ in Christian Fellowship.

Chapter 2

The Book of Remembrance, January 12, 2016.

1 On January 12, 2016 I awoke around 5 am. Knowing the Lord had a revelation for me, I went downstairs to my office and prayed.

2 My prayer ended, I sat at my desk and filled by the Holy Spirit, began to receive a revelation; the revelation I received is now Chapter 4 of the Book of Remembrance.

3 After this revaluation ended, I knelt again in prayer, asking the Lord why I had received this short revelation that seemed completely out of nowhere.

4 After this, I went back upstairs and got ready for work.

5 ¶ Once at the office, I was reading the news for the day and I saw that then Apostle Russel Nelson of the Church of Jesus Christ of Latter-day Saints (Brighamite) had made a statement that the rule his church has made to not to baptize worthy children of same-sex couples was a revelation from God.

6 This had me questioning a number of things, so I took my questions to the Lord.

7 I was then given a revelation telling me to leave it alone, that their policy was not from God but that I was not to war with my fellow Saints.

8 ¶ Later that day, I had finished with my work and was alone in the office, having been asked to stay behind to watch the phones while everyone else was out of the office.

9 I prayed again to the Lord, asking about the revelation I had received that morning.

10 In answer, I was told to put a blessing on the room I was in, to seal it that no evil could enter. While I did not understand, I obeyed.

11 ¶ At this time, I began to receive what is now Chapter 5 of the Book of Remembrance when I saw something move in the hallway outside my office.

12 I called out, asking who was there, but no one answered, I went back to work when I saw again the shadow of a figure in the hallway.

13 I stood up and demanded in the name of Jesus Christ that whoever or whatever was present would manifest themselves.

14 Then, in the doorway stood a woman unlike any I have ever encountered.

15 She had long hair, dirty and matted; so dirty that I could no answer as to what color her hair was.

16 She was naked, her covering her down to her midcalf, like a dress, but open in the middle; again, her skin was to filthy that I could not see the color of it.

17 Her face had a look of rage, and I knew instantly that she was there because she knew I was writing her story, and she had come to stop me.

18 In my mind's eye I could see the illusion she was trying to project of a beautiful woman dressed in fine, seductive purple clothing, yet I could only see her in her filthiness.

19 ¶ At this time I called upon the heavens for assistance and raised my right arm to the square to cast her out.

20 As I opened my mouth, speaking the words to expel her, a light descended from either the window or the ceiling, I do not know which, and Raphael stepped through carrying a drawn sword.

21 Pointing the sword as Lilith, he commanded her to leave as I was uttering the words of her expulsion. I ender my worded in Jesus' name, and Raphael too commanded her to leave in the name of Jesus Christ.

22 And in rage, screaming with utter wrath, she was gone.

23 ¶ I hadn't noticed the darkness that had come in her presence, but with her gone, Raphael too departed and the room was brighter, as if the sun had just broken free from the clouds.

24 Still in the spirit, I went back to my work, receiving chapters 5, 6, and part of 7.

25 ¶ Later that night at home, I felt compelled to go back to my office at home and there, after blessing my home, property, and neighborhood as I has my office at work, I received the remainder of chapters 7, all of chapters 8 and 9, and most of chapter 10.

26 ¶ It should be noted that per inspiration I initially put the revelations I received in 1889 before these, as can be seen in chapters 2 and 3 of the current version of the Book of Remembrance.

27 When preparing the work later, I prayed and was inspired to move parts of the revelations around to make the narrative clearer for the readers.; what is now 8:27-35 was originally part of the revelation that is now chapter 5.

Chapter 3

The Book of Remembrance and Kabbalah, January 16-23, 2016-March 2018.

1 That weekend, I was given the last few verses of chapter 10 and chapters 11-17 on Saturday January 16 and chapters 18-20 on Sunday January 17, 2016 without incident.

2 I was instructed not to put all of the revelations on the Fellowship website, but to hold portion of the revelations back, specifically the teachings of Raphael, from the world for a time.

3 ¶ On Wednesday, January 20, 2016 I was awakened again early in the morning and received chapters 21-24 that morning; I was instructed not to put all of the revelations on the Fellowship website, but to hold portion of the revelations back.

4 On Saturday January 23, 2016 I received chapters 25-28, ending the revelations; I reviewed them as a whole that day and the next, reading

and re-reading both the portions on the website and the portions I was asked not to share.

5 I wondered why I had been given what was clearly the temple drama from the Brighamite tradition.

6 I had received a revelation on January 10, 2016 asking that the Saints of Christ build a temple, was this our temple drams?

7 I was concerned, as if this needed to be acted out, as is done in Brighamite temples and endowment houses, this would be rather lengthy.

8 However, I also knew that these ordinances, the sacraments, were given in stages; line upon line, and precept upon percept so maybe it wouldn't be as lengthy as I was thinking.

9 ¶ In March of 2018 I was praying on the direction of the Church of Jesus Christ in Christian Fellowship and the Lord spoke to me saying: Unite my people in Kabbalah.

10 Not knowing what this meant, I began to study Kabbalah, and after a few months the Lord brought my attention back to the Book of Remembrance.

11 I was told in late July to begin editing the book prayerfully for publication, and re-reading the text with my new found understanding of Kabbalah I realized that this revelation was Kabbalistic teaching, it was a Kabbalistic book.

12 My spirit sank a bit when, while editing, I discovered that the words of Raphael could be found in an ancient Kabbalisitc text known as Sefer Raziel HaMalakh.

13 The portion of the revelation I received that matched the text of Sefer Raziel was not in the same order, nor was it a perfect mirror of it, it was, however, the same portion Raziel had given Adam and Eve.

14 Praying on it, I was told that Raziel was another name for Raphael, and that this was a part of the Book of Melchizedek, thus it is far older than scholars had dated it; this satisfied my concerns, and I went back to work.

15 As I did so the wisdom of the book began to unfold before me, while I was too ignorant to understand when I had received it, this book was the teachings of the ministry of Christ;

16 This was a book given us to help us understand the signs and tokens Joseph Smith Jr. had revealed to us in preparation of the mysteries that would be unlocked when the temple was build.

17 Because of the circumstances in Nauvoo, the temple was not completed, and it was burnt to the ground,

18 I then understood that the Lord was asking us to build a temple that these sacraments would be unlocked for us, for all Latter Day Saints, in these, the last times.

Chapter 4

The Factory, February 17, 2019.

1 Saturday night, I felt very anxious, I had trouble falling asleep; when I woke up around 2:30 in the morning, something was wrong. I could feel it, but I didn't know what it was.

2 I got up; not able to sleep I worked on a manual for the Priesthood for the Fellowship until about 5:30 or 6am; at that point, though still anxious I was finally exhausted enough to sleep.

3 Before I went to bed, I said a prayer; I asked God to help me; I asked for peace and for answers, I needed to know what was wrong and what to do about it.

4 I fell asleep nearly as soon as my head hit the pillow, and I dreamed a dream.

5 ¶ In the dream, I was working in a very clean factory with the members of the Council of Fifty of the Church of Jesus Christ in Christian Fellowship.

6 I was leading, trying to help, but people were arguing, fighting over differences.

7 When we looked at the project, what we were building in the factory, it made no sense; I had no idea what we were even trying to build, and it seemed, neither did anyone else.

8 What was worse, people were placing blame on one another; everyone seemed bent on focusing on their part of what we were building.

9 Each would point at other parts of the project and describe how and why they did not fit; this led to hurt feelings and defensiveness.

10 I asked everyone to stop working and I prayed; then, we all prayed together as one, asking for divine guidance on how to move forward and fix what we thought was clearly broken.

11 ¶ As our prayer ended, an angel of the Lord descended into our midst; he asked us what was wrong and listened as we each in turn explained our views; each seemed to think themselves justified in their own doings.

12 The angel then asked me for my thoughts.

13 I asked why the Lord required this of me when I am not fit to lead, when I couldn't get the project moving as it should.

14 The angel of the Lord told us to come with him and we arose to the highest point of the building, far above what we were building.

15 On the right side of it, he asked us what we saw; it appeared as a puzzle, mismatch and improperly put together.

16 It was as we feared: a mess.

17 He then took us around the backside, to the left side of the building; there he asked us again what we saw.

18 Though it was a different perspective, it appeared the same, though different; it was still a mess, just a different mess, with pieces sticking out as though nothing belonged together.

19 The angel then took us around to above in the front; from there, he stated we could see the project the way God saw it.

20 It was perfect, it was beautiful; everything came together, overlapping to explain rather than hide the overlap—the things we didn't see as fitting together.

21 ¶ The angel of the Lord then told us, it's not about conforming everyone to one will or idea, it's about conforming to one another in spite of our differences.

22 It is about understanding that there are those that need to see the things we saw as ugly or unnecessary or incomplete or even wrong in order to see the whole or bigger picture.

23 He then told us to get back to work and not to be bothered by the things that do not agree, but rather celebrate them, and, build together upon the things we have in common.

24 He then looked at me and said: Now see that this work is completed because it's not your work, but it is required of you.

25 While I do not see issues in the Fellowship at the moment pulling people apart, I do believe this is a warning not to fall for the traps others have in the past;

26 I see this as a reflection not merely of the Fellowship, but of the whole Latter Day Saint restorational movement: the Lord wants us to look past our differences and get His work done.

Other Dreams and Visions

*The following is a collection of dreams and visions of
the First Elder, David, given him of the Lord.*

Chapter 1

The War at the Boarder, February 7, 2021.

1 On the night of Sunday, February 7, 2021, I went to bed as normal; I awoke around 3am on the morning of February 8 and fell asleep again sometime after that; upon falling back asleep, I had the following dream:

2 ¶ In my dream the Mexican crime syndicate, Los Zetas, officially staged a coup, overthrowing the Mexican government.

3 As they began to rebuild their government, the United States officially denounced the new regime, with President Biden sending troops to the boarder to stop all flows of traffic, placing economic sanctions on Mexico, stopping the flow of trade between the two countries.

4 The president demanded Los Zetas step down and return power to the democratically elected Mexican government.

5 With few exceptions, Congress sided with President Biden and gave power to the president to declare war against Mexico, if he decided this was needed.

6 ¶ While this was happening, public opinion was all over the place:

7 Many militia groups sided with Los Zetas as they felt it was the right of the people to overthrow a government, if they felt it was warranted.

8 Others (mostly conspiracy theorists) claimed it didn't matter, as they believed that Los Zetas had secretly held control of the Mexican government for decades.

9 And there were those that supported the president's and Congresses' actions for a variety of reasons.

10 ¶ In the dream, the troops sent to the boarder came mostly out of Texas, Oklahoma, New Mexico, Arizona, Nevada, and California.

11 It soon became clear that the majority of the military sent to the boarder supported the US militias, as they not only allowed Mexican trade to continue, they invited members of the new Mexican government into their camps for private negotiations.

12 By the time US military leaders stepped in, it was too late; the local militias and the troops had joined forces with the states of Texas, Oklahoma, New Mexico, and Arizona seceding to join the newly reorganized Mexican government.

13 ¶ At this point the US was forced to declare war, with the troops from Nevada and California being held prisoner, only to be released if the US would sign a treaty of peace, accepting Mexico's terms.

14 With smaller militia groups all over the US also declaring war against US citizens, the nation began to see bloodshed as we have not seen in modern history.

15 No one was safe; brother turned against brother, sister against sister.

16 ¶ At this, I awoke very calm and at peace; the peace I felt told me that I was in the Spirit of the Lord and this dream was from God.

17 I immediately fell into prayer, asking to understand this dream. Was this was warning? A prophecy of things to come? The Lord spoke to me telling me the following:

18 ¶ Thus sayeth the Lord unto my servant David: Know that all war and all prophecies of war are over economic control; the battles prophesied to come in the end times,

19 If they come, shall be over the flow of goods, power, and man seeking to rule over all other men;

20 And this because mankind hath not the love in their hearts to care for the poor and the needy but take only for themselves.

21 [DoS 65a:11-12] I have said unto my servant Josepha: Behold, this is the way that I, the Lord, have decreed to provide for my Saints: That

the poor shall be exalted, in that the rich are made low; for the earth is full, and there is enough and to spare.

22 [DoS 65a:13-14] Yea, I have prepared all things, and have given unto the children of men to be agents unto themselves; therefore, if anyone shall take of the abundance which I have made and impart not their portion according to the Law of my Gospel unto the poor and the needy, they shall with Divesb lift up their eyes in hell, being in torment.

23 Know ye, that if my people shall give of themselves freely, taking no thought unto themselves, but to give unto their neighbors, and there should be no poor among you; ye shall be made rich as Zion, and I shall come unto thee in peace.

24 But, if ye, my creation, should take for themselves, and care not for the poor among you, and love should wax cold, then ye shall be destroyed by thine own hand, sayeth the Lord.

25 ¶ I understood this to mean that I should not take the dream literally, but as a blessing and a warning, that we, the human race, will not be forced to face or bear the harsh trials prophesied at the end times.

26 If they come, they will be our own undoing: the natural consequences of us refusing to repent of our sins and love one another as God has commanded.

27 We shall be like the Nephites, who through their own pride destroyed themselves, and were only successful as a society when they worked as one, with no poor among them.

Notes:

a. Doctrines of the Saints 65a: 11-14 (Doctrine and Covenants 101:2d-g RLDS/CoC, 104:16-18 CJCLdS).

b. Dives: late Middle English, used to refer to hypothetical greedy rich man.

Chapter 2

On the Appalachian Trail, May 1, 2024.

1 While our family was visiting Virginia, Kristine and I drove to the Appalachian Trail to watch the sunset together.

2 It was a beautiful site in the mountains; that night, I had a dream from the Lord.

3 ¶ In the dream, Kristine and I were hiking the Appalachian Trail.

4 We were not part of a group, but there were many people hiking around us, and we were all friendly with one anther.

5 Eventually, as we walked on, we found ourselves alone.

6 Some had picked up the pace, moving on ahead, while others had slowed down and were no longer in site.

7 At that point, we saw a light from the forest, off the trail.

8 ¶ We stopped as the light moved towards us, in the light was what appeared to be a man.

9 He identified himself as "Moroni, also known as Nephi."

10 He informed us that he had traveled these very mountains on his way to bury the gold plates and other relics.

11 He then took us off the trail to a spot near following water where there was a cave; he invited us to enter.

12 ¶ As we entered the cave, I recognized it immediately.

13 This was the cave I had been traveling to in spirit to translate the plates of brass.

14 The torches were lit, and the plates rested on the table as I had left them in vision.

15 There were other plates, scrolls, and items in the cave, but we were told not to touch them, and we refrained.

16 ¶ Moroni told us that the Lord desired that we take the plate of brass with us.

17 With that, I removed my jacket and we wrapped the plates init, left cave, and began to walk back to our van.

18 But the plates were very large, and very, very heavy., and as we walked, I grew tired.

19 Kristine offered to carry them for a bit to easy my burden.

20 ¶ I want to make clear that this was not an ordinary dream.

21 When I dream, I will understand that there is physical feeling like hunger, exhaustion, physical pain, etc. however, in my dreams I do not feel these.

22 I might run to the point of exhaustion, yet I will not feel tied.

23 My dream self simply cannot run anymore.

24 This dream was different, I could feel the weight of the plates, they were heavy.

25 I could feel my feet hurting as I walked, the heat of the sun, the coolness of the breeze, and my thirst for water as I continued on.

26 ¶ Feeling the weight of the plates, I asked Kristine to stop, and she offered to carry them for a bit.

27 I could feel my burden lift as she took them, and I could see how they weighed her down.

28 After walking for a bit, I took them back and we took turns carrying them until we were back at the van.

29 Once there, we loaded them, and drove away, and right as we started to talk about what happened, I awoke.

30 ¶ There were three things that really stood out to me:

31 The first was that Moroni called himself "Moroni, also known as Nephi."

32 This puzzled me until Kristine reminded me that Nephi was a title for the chieftains of the Nephites.

33 The second part I found interesting was the idea that Moroni had walked a similar path to the Appalachian Trail.

34 Looking up the history of the trail, it appears that it was created from other preexisting routs and paths.

35 I cannot help but wonder if this was literal, or symbolic of the unity of the Saints.

36 We are currently divided into many different paths, some smaller, some larger.

37 And lastly, the idea of Kristine lightening my load by helping to carry the plates.

Revelations

The Revelations of David.

Revelation 1

Blessing & Passing the Sacrament of Holy Communion

Revelation given to David Ferriman in Ohio on November 17, 2015, for the Church of Jesus Christ in Christian Fellowship. This revelation was sustained by the Council of Elders on January 5, 2019, and by the General Assembly of Saints April 6, 2019. This revelation is Section 15d in Doctrines of the Saints.

1 Feeling the Holy Spirit telling me that my family should worship at home, I began to fast and pray on how to do this.

2 After kneeling in prayer and meditation, the Lord gave me the following revelation:

3 Behold, I say unto those numbered with me in my Fellowship, through the mouth of my servant David: Prepare ye the way of the Lord;

4 For I am even Jesus Christ, your Redeemer, the Great I AM; in my great mercy have I atoned for thy sins.

5 Even as a hen gathers her chicks, so shall I gather my people.

6 And I say unto thee, even as I have said before: All ye that come unto me are mine and I shall have claim on them at the last day.

7 Behold, I say unto thee: Be ye perfect, even as I and my Father are perfect, and my Grace shall make whole even these that believeth in my name.

8 And I would tell thee how to be perfect: Love one another; yea strengthen one another in fellowship, for all have sinned and fallen short of the Glory of the Father,

9 Yea, do this and my Grace will carry thee home, if thou are faithful even unto the end.

10 Behold, I would ask thee: Renew thy covenants through the Sacrament of Communion; the bread to represent my flesh, and the wine to represent my blood;

11 Do this too and keep my Spirit with thee that ye may strive to grow in me, even in my Grace.

12 Yea, I have said unto thee: It mattereth not what thou shalt eat or what ye shall drink when ye partake of this sacrament, if it so be that ye do it with an eye single to my glory, in remembrance unto the Father.

13 The kingdom of God is before thee; have patience, for my Spirit is with thee;

14 Therefore, I would that all that wish to fellowship in my name, prepare ye an altar in thy home or place of dwelling facing Eastward;

15 Bless this place, that it will be holy; yea dedicate it unto Elohim in my name.

16 This shall ye do that ye may partake of the Sacraments of bread and wine, that ye shall always remember me;

17 And this place shall be holy by the power of my priesthood, even the Melchizedek Priesthood and the Sisterhood of Magdalene, that my Priests and Priestesses may stand in this holy place to prepare and bless these sacraments.

18 Behold, this shall ye do also: set aside a plate and dedicate it for the bread, and a cup for the wine, and keep them clean.

19 And I say unto thee: When thou shalt dedicate these things unto me, ye shall wear the robes of the High Priesthood, that ye remember that ye do these things in my name.

20 And thou shall use clean plates to pass the bread and clean cups to partake of wine that ye may worship together, one with another;

21 And if there be any sick among you, or there be people too numerous, behold, thou shalt give each a cup unto themselves that all shall partake and be blessed;

22 As it has been taught in plainness: When two or more gather in my name, there shall I be, therefore see that ye do these things in wisdom.

23 And I say unto thee further: When ye bless and pass this sacrament unto these, be it a household or a congregation, ye shall wear the robes of the Levitical Priesthood;

24 For Aaron and his brethren and their offspring did offer sacrifices as such;

25 But I am the last sacrifice required by my Father, no blood shall be spilt for remission of sins.

26 And ye shall do these things in remembrance of my sacrifice that ye may worship the Father in my name and be faithful unto the end;

27 And lo, I am with you; therefore, be faithful until I come; for then ye shall be caught up, that where I am shall ye be also: Amen.

Revelation 2

The Priesthood & the Sacraments

Revelation given to David Ferriman in Ohio on November 25, 2015, for the Church of Jesus Christ in Christian Fellowship. This revelation was sustained by the Council of Elders on January 5, 2019, and by the General Assembly of Saints April 6, 2019. This revelation is Section 15e in Doctrines of the Saints.

1 After receiving previous instructions, I inquired further and upon prayer and meditation, I was given of the Lord the following revelation:

2 Unto my servant David I say to thee: I am well pleased;

3 For thou has sought wisdom in my name, therefore I have more to say unto thee concerning the Sacraments of bread and wine;

4 And I have heard thy prayers inquiring of me as to the vision I gave thee in Washington D.C.

5 Yea, thus saith the Lord unto His people by the mouth of His servant David:

6 Behold, I say into thee that when one is called to be a Deacon, be they male or female, ye shall impart unto them the first token of the Levitical Priesthood, be they of the Aaronic or of Miriam;

7 And they shall receive its name, and its sign, and even the apron and gartel to wear over their garments.

8 And when the Deacons and Teachers gather one with another, they should welcome each other with this, the first token of the Levitical Priesthood, that they may know each other as such.

9 And when one is called as a Priest or Priestess in my name, behold ye shall impart unto them the second token of the Levitical Priesthood; its name, and its sign, and even the robes of the Levitical Priesthood.

10 And when the Priests and Priestesses gather one with another, they should welcome each other with this, the second token of the Levitical Priesthood, that they may know each other as such.

11 Yea, the Levitical Priesthood holds the keys to the preparatory gospel; yea even the gospel of repentance and of baptism, and of the remission of sins; the Law of carnal commandments;

12 And behold, these are but a few of the duties of the Priests and Priestesses that act in my name with my authority:

13 To baptize all they that believe in my name,

14 And to bless the sacraments that all may be born into the Church of God, even the Church of Christ, and washed clean of their sins;

15 Therefore, I would that ye should not only wear the robes of the Levitical Priesthood, but even use the first sign of this, the Levitical Priesthood, when any should baptize and administer these Sacraments.

16 But behold, the second sign ye shall not use; for behold, the first sign of the Levitical Priesthood is the sign of the covenant;

17 Therefore, when blessing the bread and the wine it is pleasing unto me that they who perform these ordinances should raise their right hand to the square,

18 For behold, this is why I revealed the first sign of the Levitical Priesthood to my servant Joseph Smith Jr.: that my people may show unto the world this, the first sign of the Levitical Priesthood when performing these sacred ordinances;

19 And behold, this ye shall do as a witness to the world that these things are sacred, and thus not to mock the things of God;

20 And they in the congregation shall know that these are my servants and act in my name, holding the keys to the office of Priest or Priestess,

21 To perform these duties not by the sign, but by the Spirit that shall accompany them as they do so in righteousness.

22 Therefore go ye and do, even all those that believe in my name that hold these keys, that ye shall be one in my name;

23 For behold, I am Jesus Christ, He who came to redeem the world: Amen.

Revelation 3

Further Instructions

Revelation received in Ohio after leaving a meeting with local Latter-day Saint Church leaders on December 13, 2015. This revelation is Section 13a in Doctrines of the Saints.

1 Behold, I say unto my servant, David: Ye are desirous to know the cause of the Lord in ordaining thee to this ministry;

2 I and my Father, who is your Father, even Elohim, are much pleased in thee for thy faithfulness.

3 Behold, my Spirit was with thee in that room, even when thou preached my Word, and thou remained faithful and true to that which thou hast been called, even though thou didst not fully understand my works.

4 Thou spoke in my name and were honest and true in dealing with the work I, even the Lord Jesus Christ, have called thee to; yet thou still hast questions in thy mind as to the meaning of this work and why thou wast called of me to act in my name.

5 Behold, thy mind may be at ease to thy fears, for I did not call thee to cry repentance to the Church of Jesus Christ of Latter-day Saints, though all men are in need of repentance; even those in the portion of my Church, as formed by the hand of my servant Brigham Young;

6 For they, in this branch of the tree that beareth the fruit of my gospel, have done many works of righteousness, and many grievous things in my name, rejecting my works.

7 Yet I say unto thee: Judge them not; for none are perfect, no not one;

8 And I will call whom I will call, and I will choose they whom I will choose to be leaders of men in these the last days in the many branches of Zion,

9 To cry repentance unto the world, and to carry forth my Word, even the Book of Mormon, to the ends of the Earth that the words of my servant John should be fulfilled.

10 For my servant John said unto the seven churches:

11 [Revelation 14:6] And I saw another angel fly in the midst of heaven, having the everlasting gospel to preach unto them that dwell on the earth, and to every nation, and kindred, and tongue, and people,

12 [Revelation 14:7] Saying with a loud voice: Fear God and give glory to him; for the hour of his judgment is come: and worship him that made heaven, and earth, and the sea, and the fountains of waters.

13 And I say unto thee, and unto the world: No man shall see the gold plates containing the records of my people that were, before the prophet Joseph, hidden unto the world except they be given him of my servant Moroni;

14 And my servant Moroni must return that the work of my servant Joseph might be finished.

15 Therefore, I command unto all my people, even to all those that would call themselves mine, to pray that the world might receive the fullness of the Everlasting Gospel;

16 Even the Book of Lehi that my servant Joseph lost, yea and even the brass plates that the record of the world from Adam unto Moroni may be bound together, that this work may be completed.

17 Behold, the sealed portion shall not be translated until that day when the Gentiles shall repent of their iniquity, and become clean before the Lord, yea it shall be revealed unto the world in mine own due time.

18 And behold, I have called thee, my servant David, to declare my Word and cry repentance unto those that would hear my voice; and for this reason wast thou called of me;

19 For behold, in the days of my servant Brigham there was much diversity, and I called the twelve to lead the larger portion of the branches of my Church,

20 And I had called Brigham Young to lead the twelve through the mouth of my servant, Joseph;

21 And this I did through the voice of my people, as the Holy Spirit moved them to choose for themselves a leader;

22 For behold, did not my servant Sidney Rigdon[a] also have these same keys and more?

23 Did I not come unto him in visions, even as I did unto my servant Joseph Smith Jr.? Did he not also bare witness and testify of my Word?

24 Yet he exalted himself and was cut off from my presence for a time; yea, in treacherous actions he did reject the keys that I, the Lord your God had given him;

25 And thus, I took them, even his keys over the larger portion of the Church, and he was blinded by his own self-worth in leading those that would follow him.

26 But behold, even my Grace is sufficient to save his soul, despite the weakness of his flesh;

27 For he did keep the New Covenant, even his testimony of me and of the Book of Mormon.

28 And behold, when a portion of my Saints went to the far West, to make unto themselves a new home, my servant Brigham began to teach new doctrines that were not of me; yet he continued to do a mighty work for me, and in my name.

29 Yet my servant Brigham took from men their right to the Office of the Priesthood; not for their sins but for the color of their skin.

30 Behold, this work of darkness led to other false doctrines; and priestcraft entered this branch of my Church upon the Earth by these means; yet these works of men could not frustrate the Work of the Lord.

31 And this portion, the Church of Jesus Christ of Latter-day Saints, continues to flourish in my name as a branch of Zion; the keys these men kept, and some did use them, even as they were worthy;

32 But they were not worthy of themselves, but because my Grace was sufficient for them;

33 And these men did speak in my name and preach my Word unto the world.

34 And behold, I, the Lord God, desired that the sins and priestcraft brought into this Church by my servant Brigham be done away; and for this cause did I call many brethren to prepare a way.

35 And my servant David O. McKay saw this wickedness and came to me, desirous to repent the Church of this sin.

36 But behold, the time was not yet right, as there were still those in the twelve of that Church that would not repent nor would they harken unto my Word.

37 Yet for this reason had I set up other churches in my name, even the Reorganized Church of Jesus Christ of Latter Day Saints, or as they are now known unto the world by revelation from me, Community of Christ.

38 Yea, Joseph Smith III did I call, not to condemn my servants in Utah, but to create a place for those that would gather in my holy name that had rejected my doctrine that they kept,

39 And as a refuge for those that rejected the doctrines of men in regard to the segregation by race, and other priestcrafts;

40 For behold: All men are one race unto me, saith the Lord; yea, men are divided by my Word alone.

41 And I divide them as such: Those that have come unto me, or would come unto me, if they knew me; and those that have reject-ed my atonement and forsaken their God, for unto these I died in vain;

42 And those that know me and reject me, these are they that shall be cut off from the presence of the Father; these are they that shall be cast into the eternal fires; for behold, my judgments are just.

43 And for this cause did I prepare men to give keys unto my servant Joseph Smith III; but behold, he did error to condemn the larger branch of my Church, even the Church of Jesus Christ of Latter-day Saints;

44 For do they both not serve the same master, even Jesus Christ? Are they not sisters in Zion, even as the Fellowship is a sister unto both of these and others?

45 And for this cause I did not reunite these two bodies, nor did I give unto any of the branches any more keys.

46 And behold, other men did I prepare and give keys that my works would not be frustrated, and that all might find a place in me with fellow Saints at their level of understanding, as my Grace was and is sufficient for them.

47 And behold, in mine due time did I call another to lead the Church of Jesus Christ of Latter-day Saints, even my servant Spencer W. Kimball, and prepare the path so that the twelve could no longer deny my Word and my voice unto them.

48 And the Church of Jesus Christ of Latter-day Saints did correct this grievous wrong, yet they still have other sins to repent of unto me and unto my people.

49 And this is not all: yea, my servant Brigham brought secret works into my Church;

50 For behold, mine is a Gospel of Truth, yea even a Gospel of Light; yea even to stand on a hill to light the whole of the Earth;

51 But behold, my servant Brigham feared men, and for this cause did he hide my truth behind temple walls and add unto them his own secret doctrines.

52 Know ye not that when my mortal work was completed the veil of the temple was rent in twain even from the top to the bottom?

53 Behold, my servant Brigham made a secret of that which was to be a light unto the world; that all men would know that my works were once again to be found in the temple of the Lord, yea even in my House of Holiness.

54 And behold, even now there are oaths and covenants that are not of me to be found in my house; for behold, where have I taught thee to swear thy allegiances unto a man or even unto a church?

55 Have I not said in mine everlasting covenant that the Law and the commandments of my Father are that ye shall believe in me, and that ye shall repent of your sins, and come unto me with a broken heart and a contrite spirit?

56 Yeah, the endowment and the keys I did give unto my servant Joseph; and yet how to use them I had not fully revealed unto the world, neither did my servant Brigham give heed unto the promptings of my Spirit.

57 Yea, the works that they do in my house are of me, yet not all of them; and even so, these are not all done in the manner that is pleasing unto me;

58 They do these works with the keys of my priesthood, and in my name; but mingled with the doctrines of men;

59 Yet my Grace is sufficient that I shall honor their works; but know ye that I do not require oaths of secrecy, nor do I honor added covenants beyond those what I have asked.

60 And for these and other reasons known unto me have I called thee, my servant David, to establish the Church of Jesus Christ in Christian Fellowship, even that all may come and worship freely;

61 And that my people may worship in my holy temples and receive their endowments and their washing and their anointings, even all those who wish to come to serve me.

62 And this shalt thou ask them: Do you take upon yourself the name of Christ?

63 And, have you been Born Again unto your redeemer, even Jesus Christ?

64 And, do you desire to be baptized in His holy name? (for those desirous of baptism)

65 And will you strive to move forward in Christ, that the Holy Spirit may be in you and with you even unto the end of your life?

66 Are you obedient to the laws of the land in the kingdom of men?

67 And if they say unto thee, yea to all these, and art willing to rejoice with those who rejoice, mourn with those that mourn, and they do not cause that harm come to another, behold, these are my people and are worthy of me and they may partake of mine ordinances as my Spirit so leadeth them.

68 And if they do not, behold thou shalt show mercy on them and teach those that are willing to be taught, until they know me and desire to come unto me, or to reject me;

69 And those that reject me, thou will not teach but thou will also not condemn; for thou shalt love them, as thou hast been commanded to love thy neighbor, and I shall judge them as I see fit.

70 Behold, I say unto my servant David: At this time there is one man to hold and partake of the keys to these works in their fullness,

71 And He is at the head of the Church of Jesus Christ of Latter Day Saints; and so too the Church of the Firstborn, both of which ye are a member,

72 And behold, I am He; even Jesus Christ, the very Son of Man.

73 Yea, and I have given these keys to men, to organize and to bring souls unto me, even in my name, the name of Christ; even as I have given keys to others that all may find hope in my name.

74 And I have given thee keys to perform the Sacraments and sealings.

75 But behold, the time shortly cometh when all keys shall be given thee, and if thou are worthy, even more than this shall be given thee; even the keys that were given my servant Joseph taken from the earth upon his martyrdom;

76 And both of these shall I honor with my priesthood, and both works shall I accept as they are found worthy;

77 For behold, my Grace is sufficient and will wipe clean the doctrines of men from those that know not the pure endowment.

78 But the keys of leadership unto the other branches of the Church of Christ I shall not give thee, except thou be called of them that leadeth these, my Churches, within my vineyard; and they so choose to join with me and thee in fellowship;

79 And this I shall not do that there shall not be confusion amongst those that have come unto me through the keys I have given to others in these, the Last Days.

80 And until such time as more keys are given thee, thou shalt gather my people and work that a temple shall be built and dedicated to me in my holy name; and for this end wast thou called;

81 For behold: It pleaseth me that in every home there should be made a place to serve as a temple, and that ye always do remember to keep your homes holy, that I may find rest within.

82 Yea, the Son of Man wishes yet to bring this, His flock together that they may have a home;

83 Yea prepare ye for this time, for behold I shall come to thee quickly, and with power that my works may not be thwarted; Even so, Amen.

Notes:

a See DoS 86.

Revelation 4

Priesthood Verses Priestcraft

Revelation given to David January 10, 2016, in Westerville, Ohio for the Church of Jesus Christ in Christian Fellowship. This revelation is Section 106 in Doctrines of the Saints.

1 Behold, I am the Lord your God, YHVH of Elohim—yea even Jesus Christ; I AM, the Alpha and Omega, yea I AM the beginning and the end;

2 Therefore, give heed unto my Word, which is quick and powerful, sharper than a two-edged sword, to the dividing asunder of both joints and marrow; therefore, give ye heed unto my Word.

3 ¶ Behold my servant David: Thou hast been doing my work preparing the Holy Scriptures in my name, and I have seen that thou hast questions regarding the words of my prophets, as to their meaning;

4 Yea, I will expound unto thee upon their words, for their words are of me, and testify of me, and were and are spoken in my name.

5 Behold, thou doth wish to increase thy understanding as to the meaning of seer, and sorcerer, yea and of prophet and wizard;

6 And the question hath entered thy mind: How did my servant Aaron have a staff or rod, which seems unto thee to be a wand, yet he not be a sorcerer?

7 How be it that my servant Oliver Cowdery could have the rod of nature, or rod of Aaron, yea even a divining rod, to use in my name if these things are not pleasing unto me?

8 ¶ Yea, this is no great mystery: for behold, all things that delight the Lord your God are mocked of Satan;

9 Yea, even before thy first father, Adam, was cast out of the garden, that serpent, Lucifer, even Satan, beguiled man with priestcraft.

10 And this is what the scriptures mean when they say that the sorcerer and the wizard should be cast out of my presence and into the pits of Hell, for they do mock the things of the Lord, even as did the priests of Egypt.

11 Behold, did Aaron not throw down his rod and it became a serpent? And did not the priests of the pharaoh also throw down their rods and they too become serpents?

12 But behold the power of the Lord, the very power of God: The power of priestcraft was undone by the power of the Lord and his priesthood;

13 Yea, and Aaron's serpent ate the serpents of the pharaoh as a testimony that priestcraft cannot prevail before my holy priesthood, or the priesthood of Elohim; for they are the same holy priesthood.

14 ¶ Behold, even as the moon lights the night sky, so too does priestcraft light the ways for evil men and women;

15 Yea, even as the moon, it waxes and wanes in finite power, and without glory.

16 Yea, and behold as the moon reflects the light of the sun upon the earth, so too is priestcraft but a reflection of the priesthood;

17 And just as the moon has no power to bring life to the creations of God, neither does priestcraft have power to bring salvation unto man.

18 ¶ Yea, here is wisdom: a wizard, as mentioned by my servants the prophets, is but one who is wise in the things of this world.

19 ¶ Behold Nehor, he who slew my servant Gideon by the sword; was he not a wizard and a sorcerer of priestcraft too?

20 Did he not teach for doctrines sorceries, idolatry, idle-ness, babblings, envyings and strife?

21 Did he not teach those who followed him to wear costly apparel being lifted up in the pride of their own eyes?

22 And did he not teach his followers to lie, rob, murder; to commit whoredoms; yea teaching the people not to follow the Lord their God, but to follow the devil in all manner of wickedness?

23 Behold I say unto thee, this was not of me but was priestcraft;

24 Therefore, he was a sorcerer and a wizard, and any works he would do were priestcraft and of that Satan that he did serve.

25 ¶ And also the Zoromites, and their Rameumptom; behold, did they not brag of their own greatness?

26 Did they not brag of their disbelief in my prophets?

27 Did they not cast out the poor for their poverty?

28 Behold, this was a love of the things of the earth; yea this too is priestcraft.

29 ¶ And behold, the sorcerer Simon the Magus; he did try to buy the priesthood from my servant Peter; yea, this too is priestcraft, for my priesthood is a gift of the Spirit, not to be bought nor sold.

30 ¶ And yet behold my servants Moses and Aaron, yea and even Oliver; they didst take the sprout, or even the rod of a tree, and they prayed over it to bless it; thus sanctifying it in my holy name;

31 And this that they did, behold it was pleasing unto me, yea they did use these even in my name for my holy works.

32 ¶ Behold, I say unto thee again: It is no mystery, by their fruits shall ye know,

33 For if they do that which is pleasing unto me and in my name, for my glory and my Father's glory, and for the benefit of their neighbors, and not as a gift unto themselves;

34 By this shall men know that these are of me; for these are they that love one another, even as I love them.

35 Yea, and these are they that serve me, the Lord Jesus Christ, and through me Elohim; and these are they that feed my sheep; and even those that love and serve their neighbors as themselves.

36 ¶ And behold, this is not all; ye also desire to know of my holy garments, yea I see that thou art troubled of the visions that I gave unto thee in Washington D.C.

37 Behold, I say unto thee, the robes of the priesthood and the garments are not given to man for salvation and should not be seen as such.

38 Yea, these things are given as a tool to help others know the works of the Lord, and to remind those that would follow me of their covenants with me, both at baptism and the covenants made entering into my holy priesthood.

39 ¶ Behold I say unto thee: Thou shalt strive at all times and in all places to serve me, the Lord your God;

40 And just as a man putteth on one set of clothing to plow the fields and another to sleep, so too doth man put on another to do the work of the Lord.

41 ¶ Behold, the symbols of my garments were given in the Garden of Eden unto Adam and Eve, as they covenanted with me to take upon themselves my name and to use my holy priesthood;

42 And they wore their garments when they cried unto me without the Garden, and when they did all the works I commanded them to do in my name;

43 In them there was not salvation, yet there was strength given them from me.

44 And thus, I gave these things unto my servant Joseph that the world would once again see and know I AM,

45 And that the world might see and know that my works were once again upon the face of the earth.

46 ¶ But behold, this was made a great secret and a mystery unto many; yet this was not my will;

47 Yea, these things are sacred unto me, yet I will curse who I will curse and bless who I will bless;

48 Therefore, these things were not to be hidden in darkness but brought into the world that those in the world that are of me might see for themselves, and that they not be seen as priestcraft.

49 And if the world shall mock and judge, behold this sin shall be upon their heads; for I am the Lord, and I shall not be mocked.

50 ¶ Behold, I say unto thee: take unto thee a white cloth, be it about the width of thy shoulders and as long as thou art tall; and cut the cloth in the middle of its longest side two thirds inwards and seal up the edges round about;

51 And thou shalt place this upon he or she that shall wear it, and on the right breast place the sign of the square, yea, and on left breast the sign of the compass;

52 For these are signs unto me from before the beginning, yea signs of which are the justice of Elohim and the salvation of the Only Begotten; for in the square is Gevurah, the justice of God, and in the compass is Chesed, His mercy;

53 And place upon this, my holy garment, two lines; one at the bottom on the right about the knee as a reminder that every knee shall bow and tongue confess that Jesus is the Christ,

54 And the other midway upon the front thereof, yea upon the right of the divide, about that of the navel,

55 And this thou shalt do for health in the belly, and as a sign and token of my Holy Spirit, and of temporal salvation;

56 And these shall thou wear when doing my holy works that do not require the robes of the priesthood, and even under the robes of the priesthood.

57 ¶ Yea, and these garments thou shalt wear throughout thy life, at times even as the Spirit directs:

58 To bless the sick, and to preach my Gospel at the pulpit, and to do works in my name as thou art moved to do so by my Spirit.

59 And behold, thou mayest place these symbols upon thy garment by cut or by seam, as thou seest fit;

60 And thou mayest bind this at thy waste with the apron or with the gartel of the robes of the priesthood, as worn about thy waste, or not at all; as thou seest fit to wear them in my name.

61 ¶ And behold, if thou desire to do as the Latter-day Saints and wear these at the day and at the night, hidden beneath the clothing,

thou mayest purchase[a] from them that sell these; this I say unto all that have made the covenant of the priesthood in me;

62 But behold, if they shall keep these things unto themselves, and shall not sell[a] them unto my servants in the Church of Jesus Christ in Christian Fellowship then I say unto you: Condemn them not, for they know not what they have nor what to do with it;

63 Therefore, to keep the peace between my Saints I say that thou should make thine own garments.

64 ¶ This thou may do: purchase cloth and fashioning these of thy own design, or thou may buy garments that were made by the world;

65 And thou shalt make these holy by adding my symbols thyselves and let those with authority bless and sanctify them in my name.

66 ¶ Behold, it mattereth not unto me, as these have not power to save; but act as a reminder of thy covenants in my holy priesthood.

67 And the robes of the priesthood shall be the same, thou may make them as thou pleaseth if thou cannot obtain them from those that maketh them;

68 But behold, the cloth of which should be pure white, as a symbol of my purity and of thy purity in me, except it be the apron of Adam; yea, the apron thou mayest choose a color as thou pleaseth.

69 ¶ Behold, I say unto thee once again; these things thou shalt do as a symbol of my priesthood and thy covenant with me to honor that priesthood.

70 Yea, thou shalt not wear these to place one above another, as all are one in me; but thou shalt wear these as a token and a sign that thou are doing the work of the Lord; even I, Jesus Christ.

71 Behold, I come quickly; therefore, make straight thy paths and prepare ye the way of the Lord, Even so, Amen.

Notes:

a. Members of the Fellowship that are also members of the Latter-day Saint branch, or any other branch that makes and sells garments and temple attire may buy from them to use both in their temples and in Fellowship temples. However, if one leaves or is cast out of the other branch of the Church of Christ, they should stop wearing the garments of that branch. This is because the garments represent the ministry of that body of Christ. If they are removed from that denomination, they no longer have a ministry within that branch. Their baptism, keys, etc. are retained and may be used in the Fellowship. To keep the peace between the Saints, we should respect their rejection and make new garments. They may continue to use the robes of the priesthood or make new robes as the Spirit directs.

Revelation 5

A Temple

Revelation given to David January 10, 2016, in Westerville, Ohio for the Church of Jesus Christ in Christian Fellowship. This revelation is Section 107 in Doctrines of the Saints.

1 Behold, I say unto my servant David: I am well pleased in thy strength, and behold thou have continued to be faithful to me in doing works in my name;

2 And to those who are faithful, I will add unto them as I see fit.

3 Therefore, I say unto my faithful servant: Build a temple unto me that I may come into my house, and that my people shall have a place to worship.

4 ¶ Behold, all things are possible unto me, therefore I will provide a way that this work might be accomplished.

5 Therefore, I say unto thee again: Build unto me a temple that I might come unto the Holy of Holies and converse with thee as a man doth converse with a friend;

6 Let all the works which I have appointed unto you be continued and not cease:

7 Let thy diligence, and perseverance, and patience, and thy works be redoubled, saith the Lord of Hosts;

8 And, I have promised to send my servant Elijah unto thee as I did my servant Joseph.

9 ¶ Behold, he and more shall come unto thee in my holy temple;

10 Therefore, I say unto thee a third time: Build unto me a temple that mine ordinances shall be performed therein;

11 Yea, and keep it holy, that my glory shall be there; for I will not come into unholy temples.

12 Know that I AM, Jesus Christ, the Son of God; wherefore, gird up your loins and continue to do as thou art commanded, and I will come suddenly; Even so, Amen.

Revelation 6

Bring the Children unto Christ

Revelation received in Ohio on January 12, 2016. This revelation is Section 14d in Doctrines of the Saints..

1 After reading that an Apostle for the Church of Jesus Christ of Latter-day Saints, Russell M. Nelson, stated that the Lord had declared by revelation that this denomination was not to baptize children if their parents were in a same-sex relationship, regardless of worthiness, I inquired of the Lord.

2 Was this of God? And if so, what should the Church of Jesus Christ in Christian Fellowship do in light of this supposed revelation?

3 Upon prayer, and peaceful meditation, I received the following:

4 ¶ My servant David, I see that thou are troubled as to the things of the flesh.

5 Behold, mine apostle, even Russell M. Nelson, has stated that I, the Lord his God and your God reject the children of polygamists and homosexuals;

6 But behold, this is not so, and this thing is of man and not of me; for did I not create all flesh?

7 And do I not see all flesh with no respecter of persons?

8 Yea, and did I not say unto my disciples, while in the flesh: Take heed that ye despise not one of these little ones.

9 Yea, and when I visited the Children of Lehi and of Mulek and their peoples, after mine resurrection, I stated unto them: All thy children shall be taught of the Lord; and great shall be the peace of thy children.

10 Therefore, it is not of me, nor of my Father, nor of the Holy Spirit to reject children because of their parents.

11 ¶ Behold, for this cause came I into the world: that all men and women might become as children and worship the Father in my name;

12 Therefore, ye shall teach those of my Fellowship to baptize their children at the age of accountability, even all they that desire to come unto me;

13 For these are the days of the probation of man, and in them shalt all men and women repent and come unto me,

14 And I will save mankind from their sins, even as many as will repent and strive to follow the Holy Spirit of God.

15 ¶ Behold, my grace is sufficient to save all who will come unto me, being in the Church of Latter-day Saints or in the Fellowship of Jesus Christ or any other branch of the Church of Christ: for all these share in my holy priesthood;

16 Therefore, I say unto thee: Baptize all those that come unto me with a broken heart and a contrite spirit; for these are of me.

17 ¶ Go forth and do my works and worry not what other men do; yea, preach mine gospel in my name, and bring those that would come unto me; this shall suffice.

18 Condemn not other branches of the Church of Christ, for contention is not of me; but build bridges that all may come and worship the Father in my name;

19 And this ye shall do, for it is my work, and ye shall do it in my name; So mote it be, Amen.

Revelation 7

Compiling Scripture

Revelation given to David March 18, 2016 in Westerville, Ohio for the Church of Jesus Christ in Christian Fellowship. This revelation is Section 108a in Doctrines of the Saints.

1 Verily, verily thus saith the Lord unto you my servant David: I have heard thy prayers, and the pleading questions of thy brethren, who were chosen to bear testimony in my name;

2 Thus, I shall answer these that my Word might be sent abroad among all nations, kindreds, tongues, and people;

3 And my will too shall be revealed as pertaining to their portion of the grove in which is my vineyard, as it has been assigned by me unto them.

4 ¶ Behold, I say unto thee; art my revelations unto thee for all of my Church or for thine portion of the vineyard alone?

5 Yea, and I ask thee again; of the light and knowledge thou hast received: is it imparted unto thee for all of my kingdom?

6 ¶ Behold, here is wisdom: there is that which is a light unto the world, and there is that which is to govern the affairs of men;

7 Yea, hear my words and I am pleased; do ye my will and I am well pleased;

8 And thou shalt know that which is my will by the voice of my Spirit, even the Holy Ghost.

9 ¶ And behold, it is through this witness, the Holy Spirit, that all shall know their work in the vineyard;

10 Therefore, whosoever will thrust in their sickle and reap, the same is called of God;

11 And therefore, if thou would ask of me, ye shall receive; to those that will knock, it shall be opened unto them.

12 Wherefore, my Spirit shall testify unto thee what is of me for use of my Church in this Fellowship of my people, and that which is for another part of my vineyard.

13 ¶ Yea, bring forth my Word, that ye may be prepared to receive more of my Word, and ye shall be blessed; follow my Spirit and ye shall not be led astray.

14 Be ye therefore a wise servant and be ye without sin; and I will order all things for your good, as fast as ye are able to receive them. Even so, Amen.

Revelation 8

The Sealing Power: Further Keys

Revelation received in Ohio on March 18, 2016. This revelation is Section 17c in Doctrines of the Saints.

1 My servant David, I see thou hast sought after wisdom to gain my council, in this I am much pleased;

2 Thou hast sought to know more of the sealing power and behold more shall I reveal unto you.

3 Behold, there are more powers than one, yet they all bear the power to seal upon heaven and earth.

4 ¶ The keys of the High Priesthood, yea even the keys of an Elder and a High Priest and High Priestess;

5 Behold, these are the keys spoken of by me through my servant Joseph in the first section of my Book of Commandments and Doctrine and Covenants of the branches of my kingdom.

6 [DS 1:10] For I have declared through my servant Joseph: And verily, I say unto you, that they who go forth, bearing these tidings unto the inhabitants of the earth:

7 [DS 1:11] To them is power given to seal, both on earth and in heaven,

8 [DS 1:12] The unbelieving and rebellious; yea, verily, to seal them up unto the day when the wrath of God shall be poured out upon the wicked, without measure,

9 [DS 1:13] Unto the day when the Lord shall come to recompense unto every man according to his work, and measure to every man, according to the measure which he has measure to his fellow man.

10 Behold, this is the sealing power thou hast, as a High Priest sealed unto me; and behold it is this power that my Church, even the Church of Jesus Christ of Latter-day Saints, uses to seal families in my temples;

11 ¶ And behold, this is but one type of the sealing power.

12 Yea, there is another that is given unto them that have their calling and election made sure; yea, and thou hast this gift bestowed unto thee as well, for thy calling and election is sure;

13 And this sealing is to be used for the benefit of the Church of the First Born, of which you are a part.

14 ¶ And there is a third and higher sealing of the priesthood which I was to bestow upon my servant Joseph;

15 Yet he was taken from the earth by wicked men before my temple was finished;

16 And it is this priesthood, and these keys which thou art to receive once my temple is complete, that my house might be in order.

17 ¶ Behold, my servant Joseph taught mine apostles before he was taken, and it was this endowment that they took with them into mine house upon completion;

18 Yea, and no more revelation was given, nor ask to be received; for my servants thought they had the fullness, or that they were not worthy to receive of that fullness;

19 Yet that fullness was and is yet to be revealed.

20 And these men added unto my endowment that which was of men;

21 And over time I have moved my servants, as they would hear me, to remove the portions that were not of me;

22 Yet they still hide my power and my blessings from the world, keeping secret that which is precious unto me;

23 Yea, they understand the sacredness of the ordnance, yet do not know that it is but in preparation for a greater power yet to come.

24 ¶ Therefore, I say unto thee, and unto those with ears to hear: Keep watch and obey my commandments.

25 And I say further unto thee: If this generation shall repent, and seek my face, behold; build my temple and they shall be anointed from on high;

26 And they that enter mine temple and are endowed from on high shall know me, and they shall see and be witnesses of me.

27 ¶ And it is for this cause have I commanded that ye build shall build a temple unto me, and in my name,

28 And I have prepared a way for this thing to be accomplished, should this generation hearken unto my Word.

29 And behold, if they do not, then thou shall be blessed, and they shall be cursed;

30 For damnation follows those that hear my voice and hearken not unto me; Behold, I come quickly, even so; Amen.

Revelation 9

Questions on Marriage

Revelation received in Ohio on April 18, 2016, in answer to questions from the Saints regarding marriage and polygamy. In January of 2018, David was studying the Church of Jesus Christ of Latter-day Saints' Doctrine and Covenants, Section 132 with his wife. Upon reading the last verse he prayed to know when God would reveal more unto us as promised. He was told the two revelations given on this date (Sections 17d & 17e) were answers to this promise. This revelation is Section 17d in Doctrines of the Saints.

1 After numerous inquiries from those both in and outside of the Church of Jesus Christ in Christian Fellowship, I petitioned the Lord on the subject of polygamy.

2 The Lord told me he would answer the question in due time, but at this point He would not enlighten me on the subject.

3 Finally, in April, a family member asked about the topic, and I went again to the Lord.

4 The Lord asked me to prepare myself for a revelation, and after some days of prayer and meditation, the Lord gave us the answers to these much sought-after questions.

5 ¶ Verily, thus saith the Lord unto you, my servants; even the Saints of the Fellowship of Christ:

6 Behold, verily I see that there are many both counted among you as fellows and those outside the Fellowship that have inquired as to my will in regard to marriage;

7 Particularly, there are those that do question my servant Joseph and those that followed the apostles after he was taken from the Earth.

8 ¶ Behold, here is wisdom: The sons and daughters of Elohim will marry and be given of marriage in the flesh;

9 Yet in the resurrection all things shall be restored, and none shall marry nor be given of marriage;

10 For in the resurrection all shall be as one, as it was before the world was; and these shall be brothers and sisters as all are creations of Elohim.

11 Yea, at the first time they are sons and daughters, brothers and sisters, in the creation of Elohim; yea and these are even the Sons and Daughters of God;

12 And at the end of the final resurrection, they that shall rise in righteousness shall all be sealed as one, to restore that which was taken in the flesh to its purest form.

13 ¶ And these shall not be sons nor daughters, nor husbands nor wives; yet all shall be brothers and sisters in me;

14 Yea, and these shall be counted as my children, even the Children of Christ;

15 And in this they too shall be Sons and Daughters of God, and shall stand with me on the right hand of the Father;

16 For behold, I am not a God of the dead, but of the living, this and my Father also; who is my God and thy Father, and also thy God; and I am the Father and the Son;

17 And there shall be bodies of telestial, terrestrial, and celestial; given even as my grace shall suffice all that will come unto me.

18 Therefore, what doth it matter provided the children of Zion are raised in love and in righteousness?

19 ¶ Behold, my servant Joseph did take unto himself many wives, even wives that had been promised to another;

20 Did I not say into him that if a man receiveth a wife in the new and everlasting covenant, and if she be with another man, and I have not appointed unto her by the holy anointing, she hath committed adultery and shall be destroyed?

21 And ye see that my neither servant nor his wives were destroyed; and thus these were of me.

22 ¶ But behold, not all of his wives were sought in a manner pleasing unto me; for behold, his wife, Emma, knew of these things, yet she suffered greatly in her heart.

23 And some that he sought to take to wife he took with impatience, and these were not full grown into maturity;

24 Yea, and there was deceit among my Saints, thinking that a woman being sealed to one of my servants would place their family higher unto me.

25 Behold, it is I and I alone that have provided the grace sufficient for saving the souls of man;

26 And this sealing power was given unto my servant to make that which is on earth as it is in heaven, that the Father's will be done on the earth as it is in Heaven.

27 ¶ Behold, this is my will and commandment to my Saints in the Fellowship of Zion:

28 That ye love one another, and that ye teach that my grace be sufficient to save the souls of man, and that anything more or less than this is not of me.

29 For verily I say unto you, the keys of the dispensation, which ye have received by the hands of righteous men of my Church of Latter-day Saints have come down from their fathers;

30 And the keys from Raphael, who is and was Melchizedek; by the hands of this angel thou hast received, and my Saints may receive by the hands of my servant David, keys having been sent down from heaven unto you through him.

31 ¶ Verily I say unto you, and unto all those that are mine: Cleanse your hearts and your garments, lest the blood of this generation be required at your hands.

32 Be faithful until I come, for behold I come quickly; and my reward is with me to recompense every man according as his work; so shall it be, for I am the lamb slain for the sins of the world; Even so, Amen.

33 After receiving this revelation, it was impressed upon my mind that this, plural marriage, was not something that the Lord thought on as much as man, except to say that the Lord is not pleased when men use plural marriage to indulge their lusts.

Revelation 10

Given in Marriage

Revelation received in Ohio on April 18, 2016, in answer to questions from the Saints regarding marriage and polygamy. In January of 2018 David was studying the Church of Jesus Christ of Latter-day Saints' Doctrine and Covenants, Section 132 with his wife. Upon reading the last verse he prayed to know when God would reveal more unto us as promised. He was told the two revelations given on this date (Sections 17d & 17e) were answers to this promise. This revelation is Section 17e in Doctrines of the Saints.

1 Verily, thus saith the Lord unto the Saints of the Fellowship of Christ: Hearken, and lo, prepare ye the way of the Lord, make his paths straight;

2 For the keys of the kingdom of God are committed unto man on the earth, and from thence shall the Gospel roll forth and fill the whole earth.

3 Therefore, I say unto you: Blessed are they that receive mine everlasting covenant; even the fullness of my Gospel, sent forth unto the children of men, as it was written by the prophets and apostles in days of old.

4 ¶ Behold, if a man taketh unto himself a wife, so too doth a woman take the man as a husband unto her; yea and these are one flesh to grow together in my Grace.

5 And if these two, as one, decide as one to bring another into their hearts, they too shall become one;

6 Yea, the man and woman are one, and as they add another unto these, all art one in the sealing covenant, and there for one in me.

7 ¶ Yea, and I shall speak unto my people plainly: If any take unto themselves another husband or another wife they are one in me; and these are to raise all of their children unto me.

8 Behold, I say unto thee: that which is not of me is to take another as two, or in other words for a man or a woman to leave their spouse to cleave unto another.

9 ¶ And behold, I shall speak plainly unto my people: If a man is to take another wife, or a wife take another husband, and not cleave unto his first wife or her the first husband, and one puts the other away; behold, this is not of me.

10 ¶ And also know this: a man may have one wife or one hundred wives; this does nothing to bring them closer unto me or to unto my Father.

11 But behold, it is their unity that gives them strength and shows that they are of me: that my Grace is in them through the work that is the gift and sacrament of the sealing power;

12 For the natural man is full of pride and lust, but he that is of me is filled with love for one another; and these are not prone to jealousy or hardheartedness.

13 Therefore, I say unto thee: One man and one woman in the Lord, or if they are naturally drawn like unto like, then one man unto one man and one woman unto one woman in the Lord;

Revelations

14 And these should be of age; which is to say, consenting adults in the eyes of both the laws of the land and the Lord your God;

15 For it is wisdom in me that those that wish to marry should wait to be eighteen years of age;

16 And if they seek to be joined of the Fellowship, these should be sealed by the sealing power given unto my servant David and given unto others as he sees fit by my Spirit; and these shall be one flesh:

17 For behold, all that hold the Keys to the High Priesthood hold these sealing powers, but to maintain peace and unity among my people only those holding the office of Pastor or Bishop, Patriarch or Matriarch, Seventy, or Apostle should perform such ordinances;

18 Or if they prefer, they may assign or give consent for another with the Key to perform the ordnance.

19 ¶ And if they as one desire to be sealed to another, be it a man or a woman, and they be found righteous, then behold: let them be sealed by my servant as one flesh, thus the three become one;

20 And if these, as one, desire to take another, it shall be as the Spirit shall moveth them;

21 But behold, those that wish to be sealed as a family of more adults than two, that is to be polygamous or polyandrous, should wait until twenty-one years of age;

22 And if they cannot legally marry let them be sealed by my Holy Priesthood that they are one in me.

23 ¶ And if the law of the land states they may not be bigamous, or share the same residence, then the law of man shall be obeyed as it was established;

24 And all shall be of age that none be found guilty of crimes against me or against the laws of their land.

25 Behold, if any breaketh the laws of their land they shall be sent away unless they repent.

26 ¶ And behold I say unto thee: He or she that taketh another spouse in my name shall be given them of the first spouse, every time; for this is the Law of Sarah.

27 And if the first spouse be sent away, the sealing shall be broken of all other spouses, except it be that the spouse flees in sin;

28 And if one wishes to leave a union formed by the law of Sarah, as the burden upon their hearts is too great, behold the Fellowship is to care for them even until they shall find another spouse in righteousness.

29 ¶ Behold: Man should not take such things lightly; be mindful of Adam, and Lilith, and Eve; yea and be mindful of Abraham, and Sarah, and Hagar;

30 For these were given in righteousness, yet sin made man abandon that which the Lord provided them.

31 ¶ And thou shalt ask of those wishing to marry:

32 Do you take upon yourself the name of Christ, being born again unto your redeemer?

33 And, do you desire to be sealed unto (person or persons) by the sealing power of the Holy Priesthood and in covenant to God?

34 And will you strive to move forward as one in Christ that the Holy Spirit may be in you and with you that you might be seal for all time and eternity?

35 Art thou obedient to the laws of thy land in this, yea even the kingdom of men?

36 And if they say unto thee, "yea" to all these, and art willing to rejoice and mourn with one with the others, and none do cause that any harm come to another;

37 Behold, these are my people and are worthy of me; they may partake of mine ordinances as my Spirit so leadeth them.

38 Yea, and those that are to be joined in marriage shall, at this time, do so according to the laws of their lands before being sealed by one with authority.

39 ⸿ And if it so be that these desire to be sealed unto another, in the Law of Sarah, yet it is not lawful for them to be wed, yet it is lawful for them to be sealed to one another by the power of my Holy Priesthood, then these shall be seal, but not wed as to the laws of man.

40 And behold, when these shall be joined there shall be two witnesses; one at the right and one at the left of the one that holds the sealing keys to stand at the altar;

41 And they that are to be joined shall kneel one before the other at the altar; and if any desire to be given another, behold their first shall be asked:

42 Do you give your spouse unto this person to live in harmony within the Law of Sarah?

43 And if they say thee "nay," then behold; their spouse shall not take another;

44 But if they say thee "yea," then behold these shall be joined and become one in my name.

45 ⸿ And all those sealed unto these shall too gather around the altar, kneeling with their hands upon the altar;

46 And those to be joined shall be asked to rest their hands upon the hands of the current spouse or spouses, as a sign or covenant of support as they too shall be sealed; and all these shall be one in me.

47 And then they may be sealed, by the power of my Holy Priesthood, for time and all eternity;

48 And then ye may seal upon them the blessings of the holy resurrection, with power to come forth in the morning of the first resurrection, clothed in glory, and immortality;

49 Then shall ye seal upon them the blessings of Abraham, Isaac, and Jacob; and say unto them: Have joy and rejoicing in the day of our Lord, Jesus Christ!

50 And all these blessings, together with all the blessings of the new and everlasting covenant, shall ye seal upon them by virtue of my Holy Priesthood, through their faithfulness;

51 And this shall ye do in the name of the Father, and of the Son, and of the Holy Ghost.

52 ¶ And behold, if any with children desire to be sealed too one to another, that the hearts of the fathers be turned to the children and the hearts of the children be turned to their fathers;

53 And these are they which were not before sealed when these children were born;

54 Yea, these shall ye gather around the altar with their parents;

55 And my servant, with authority to seal one to another shall, by the authority of my Holy Priesthood, seal them as one in me, calling each by name;

56 And this they shall do for time and all eternity, as an heir or heirs as though they had been born in the new and everlasting covenant;

57 And this they too shall do in the name of the Father, and of the Son, and of the Holy Ghost.

58 ¶ And by this shall my people covenant one with another;

59 But behold, thou shalt not make such covenants lightly; for I am the Lord thy God, and I shall not be mocked.

60 Commit not adultery, but be true to thine covenants; and all art to keep these sayings, for they are true and faithful;

61 Continue in these things even unto the end, that thou may be crowned in eternal life at the right hand of my Father, who is full of grace and truth;

62 Thus saith the Lord your God who is the Alpha and Omega; your Redeemer, even Jesus Christ; Amen.

Revelation 11

The Gift of Translation

Revelation given to David May 4, 2016, in Enon, Ohio for the Church of Jesus

Revelations

> *Christ in Christian Fellowship. This revelation is Section 108b in Doctrines of the Saints.*

1 Having started a new job, and stuck living with very limited access to the internet, I wanted to know what the Lord expected of me at this point.

2 Living away from my family as my wife prepared to move, was I to rest or continue the work?

3 After prayer and meditation, the Lord came to me and said: Behold, blessed art thou, my servant David in this Work that thou doth do in my name; and for speaking my words which I have given thee according to my commandments.

4 And now, behold, I say unto you: the thing which will be of the most worth unto me will be to declare teshuvah (repentance) unto this people,

5 Yea, and thou shalt do this that thou might bring souls unto me, and that thou shall rest with them in the kingdom of Elohim.

6 And behold, I say unto thee: I know this work is hard, yet it is my will that it be done; therefore, go and do my will, for I shall provide thee a way.

7 And behold, I say unto thee: Prepare thyself to translate the Holy Scriptures;

8 For behold, I say unto thee, that night that I spoke to thee in thy dream, did I not show unto thee thy task?

9 Was thou not cleaning that part of my store that housed my Word, yea even the Holy Scriptures?

10 And I say unto thee, did I not speak to you through the voice of my Holy Spirit, commanding you to translate the plates of brass?

11 And did not my servant Raphael give unto thee the command when he ordained thee a High Priest in my name to prepare thyself to receive and to translate my Word?

12 Therefore, I say unto thee: Study and prepare, for the time shall soon come that the plates of brass shall be made manifest unto you;

13 And these plates were compiled for me, and in my name, and kept safe from the world to be brought forth in the last days;

14 That the light of my Word, yea and the truth of my Word, shall stand forth out of darkness.

15 Behold, many of the works contained in the plates of brass are still yet among the children of men;

16 Yet they have been hidden up, and changed by the whims of man and held in the shadows of darkness by those that do not understand them;

17 Yea, and now is the time that they are to be brought from darkness into light, and my wisdom shall pour out and shine as a beacon unto all those that shall hear my call.

18 And behold, this is not all; for thou shall compile all of the Holy Scriptures for me;

19 And they that shall use them shall be blessed by hidden wisdom;

20 And they that shall use them not shall remain in darkness and ignorance.

21 And now, behold, I say unto you: Thou shall use my Word to declare teshuvah unto this people;

22 And those that thou bringeth unto me, these shall rest with thee in the kingdom of Elohim. Amen.

Revelation 12

The Sisterhood of Christ

The following revelation was given to David in Ohio on August 21, 2016. The Lord speaks on the organization of the Fellowship. After it was decided by the Sisters before organization that the name may change, references to a "Relief Society" were changed in the revelation to "the Sisterhood of Christ" or "Sisterhood." This revelation is Section 10f in Doctrines of the Saints.

1 Unto my servant, David, I say: I am Alpha and Omega, Christ the Lord; yea, even I AM, YHWH; the beginning and the end, the Redeemer of the world;

2 Behold, I see that thou once again desire to know concerning the organization of the *Sisterhood of Christ*.

3 Yea, as I have said unto thee before, the High Priestess and Elect Lady that shall be called in my name as prophetess, seer, and revelator; she shall do this work in my name.

4 I have told thee the formation, and thou hast set it forth; but thou are of Melchizedek and these are my High Priestesses after the Order of the Sisterhood of Magdalene;

5 Yea, after mine ascension into heaven, behold the flock was scattered and those that followed my servants Peter, James, and John were overtaken by those that followed my servant Paul;

6 And these drown out the voice of my servant Mary; yeah even the wife of the Son of Man;

7 Yet these could not be hid fully from the world, as her title, Magdalene[a], was a sign unto those with eyes to see and ears to hear that she too was a fisher of men.

8 And even when my servant Joseph sought to restore this Sisterhood, behold his wife Emma tied to raise her status before it was time;

9 Yea, and she fought with her husband over his interpretation of my doctrine;

10 And though both were far astray from my views on this, my doctrine, for neither fully understood the ways of the Lord in this matter;

11 And neither would come together in my name and thus the Church was scattered.

12 And my servant, Brigham Young, took from his branch of my church the Sisterhood of Magdalene, and reinstated as Relief Society after the order of men;

13 And my servant Wallace B. Smith did restore that which my servants Joseph and Brigham took away, yet did not allow them their

own space in my Church; thus were these merged with Aaronic and Melchizedek priesthoods in my Reorganized Church[b].

14 And behold, what thou hast compiled pleaseth me, and I give unto thee a commandment to publish this work.

15 And I, Jesus Christ, your Lord and your God, have given this command unto you that I might bring about my righteous purposes unto the children of men; Even so, Amen.

Notes:

a   Magdalene is in reference to the city Magdala, which is from the Aramaic מגדלא meaning "tower." Magdala was a fishing city. Putting these tow facts together may imply that "Magdalene" is in reference that Mary was both a fisher of mankind (an apostle) and a leader, a head of the Church in ancient times.

b   The Reorganized Church of Jesus Christ of Latter Day Saints, now Community of Christ.

Revelation 13

The Law of Sarah

Revelation received in Ohio on January 11, 2018. David was studying the Church of Jesus Christ of Latter-day Saints' Doctrine and Covenants, Section 132 with his wife. Upon reading the last verse he prayed to know when the Lord would reveal more unto us as promised. The following day he was given this revelation. This revelation is Section 19a in Doctrines of the Saints.

1 One evening in January of 2018, I felt compelled to sit down with my wife, Kristine, and go over Latter-day Saint Doctrine and Covenants Section 132;

2 I was inspired that the revelations given me in April of 2016 were some of the promised additional information the Lord said He would share with the Saints.

3 We sat down together and poured over the Section a little at a time, going over together what we each understood it to say.

4 We then went over the two revelations given to me and saw that our eyes were opened to greater understanding of this Section.

5 The following day, I went to the Lord in prayer to inquire more on the Law of Sarah.

6 And the Lord came to me, saying: Hearken, O ye people of my Fellowship; my servants and my friends; even the Saints of the Fellowship of Christ, I say unto thee: Hearken unto my voice!

7 The Keys of the Law of Sarah, named after Abraham's first wife, are given to those that are called to and accepted by revelation, and by my Word for the woman to heed my voice;

8 And these Keys are not given unto the husband; yet they are one flesh, and they shall go forth as one flesh in acceptance of this, my Law.

9 ¶ As I have said unto thee, my servant Joseph did not fully obey my voice, for he did not listen to the voice of my handmaiden, Emma;

10 And thus, I sent and angel with a flaming sword, commanding him in the name of the Lord to repent;

11 And it was because of this that the Church that he had organized in my name fell into disarray and was divided, torn asunder, when I took him.

12 ¶ Behold, I say unto thee: The Law of Sarah is the keys of the Priesthood, as given unto women as equal partners with their husbands.

13 Yea, and it is the Spirit of Revelation given them of discernment for those that are married in the Lord, which is to say Sealed for time and eternity by the Holy Priesthood, which is the High Priesthood.

14 For behold, a Priest may marry one unto another for time, but with the High Priesthood lies the Keys of the Sealing Power,

15 Yea up unto the Keys of the Holy Spirit of Promise, which are given unto only one at a time upon the face of the earth; and this is done that there be no confusion among the children of men.

16 And the Law of Sarah is given that the man does not overstep his authority, as he and his wife are one flesh in my name, whether they be married for time or sealed for eternity;

17 Thus, the woman is no longer given or taken in marriage, for this was a lesser Law given from Moses that taught a stiffnecked people that would not harken unto my Higher Law.

18 For were they not taught that Eve came from Adam's rib? Yea, even from the side of man?

19 Yet they understood not the meaning of this saying; and thus they put the woman just below man, as are the angels; but behold, men and women are equal in me.

20 ¶ And behold, I, even I: Jesus who is the Christ, did teach unto they that could not hear when I walked as man upon the earth:

21 The children of this world marry and are given in marriage; but they which shall be accounted worthy to obtain heaven, and the resurrection of the dead, neither marry, nor are given in marriage (see Luke 20:34-35).

22 And they understood not the higher Law, for I said unto them, those that follow the higher Law give unto one another, and these are not given, nor are they taken but allow themselves to join one with the other.

23 And this too I say unto those that are attracted like unto like, for I am One God, and what I say unto one people, I say unto all.

24 ¶ Behold, I have more to say unto thee, my Fellowship, regarding the Law of Sarah, yet at this time this shall suffice; I shall come unto thee again when ye have need;

25 For line upon line, precept upon precept shall I teach my people; yea here a little, and there a little; milk before meat.

26 For now, here is wisdom: Do all things in me, in my name; love one another in righteousness; worry not about what is past, but what is to come. Even so, Amen.

27 ¶ As the revelation ended, it was clear that the Lord had more to reveal to His Saints, but that at this point in the organization of the Fellowship, that information is not yet needed.

28 ⁋ The following year, on January 2, 2019 I ordained my wife a High Priestess to the Most High God, giving her the keys and authority to help find and set apart the Elect Lady of the Fellowship.

29 The next day, the Lord instructed me to lay my hands upon her head again give to her the keys of the Law of Sarah.

30 These, I was told, were given me when I was ordained by the angel Raphael, and she may now pass them on to the Sisterhood of Christ.

Revelation 14

Council of Fifty

The following revelation was given to Allen through the prophet David on November 15, 2018 in Miamisburg, Ohio. In this revelation, the prophet David is told to start the Council of Fifty for the Church of Jesus Christ in Christian Fellowship, in preparation to organize the Fellowship. The Lord calls Allen to be the first member of the Council. This revelation was voted and accepted as scripture by the General Assembly of Saints April 6, 2019. This revelation is Section 50a in Doctrines of the Saints.

1 After meeting for the second time with Allen, I inquired of the Lord to see if he had been called to help organize the Fellowship;

2 After praying on this the voice of the Lord came to me saying: Verily, thus saith the Lord unto you, my servant David: I am well pleased with your offering and service to my cause which you have made;

3 For unto this end have I raised you up and set you apart, that I might show forth my wisdom through the weak things of the earth after they have been humbled.

4 Your prayers are acceptable before me, and in answer to them I say unto thee: You have been called to make a solemn proclamation of my

gospel, and to teach all they that will hear my voice and heed the direction of my Spirit.

5 You have come unto me seeking direction for my servant Allan and for the Fellowship and behold I shall give you both.

6 ¶ Verily, verily, I say unto you my servant Allen: Listen to the voice of him who speaketh, to the Word of the Lord your God, and hearken ye unto the calling wherewith you are called,

7 For behold, I have called you in the past and I am calling you even now to be a High Priest in my Fellowship, and to give counsel unto my servant David.

8 As I have said in the past: if you have desires to serve God you are called to the work; and the field is white already to harvest;

9 Therefore, thrust in your sickle with all your might, and I will bless you, and you will perish not, but bring salvation to your soul and unto many others.

10 And I say unto you: Labor in my vineyard; call upon the inhabitants of the earth, and bear testimony, and prepare the way for the commandments and revelations which are to come.

11 But behold, as I have said before, faith, hope, charity and love, with an eye single to the glory of God, will qualify you for this work; and if you have not these you will strive in darkness and in vain;

12 Have faith, therefore, and I shall be with you, and my Spirit shall go before you to prepare the way for all those you would teach my Gospel.

13 ¶ And behold, you did feel my Spirit give the call to the Quorum of Seventy within the Offices of the Priesthood, and as a Seventy you will be called to preach my Gospel and help organize those that would fellowship in my name.

14 But this is not all; at the first you will be called to the Council of Fifty within the Order of the Ministry to help organize the Church of Jesus Christ in Christian Fellowship.

15 And these roles you shall fill until others are called that you may focus fully on your role both in the Offices of the Priesthood and in the Order of the Ministry as a Seventy in my name.

16 And this command I give to you, and this shall be your charge: Desire this ministry with all your heart; for if you have this desire you are called of God to go into the world and preach my gospel.

17 Therefore, never cease striving until you have seen me face to face; strengthen your faith casting off all doubts, repent of your sins and all your unbelief;

18 I say unto you, do this and nothing can prevent you from coming unto me;

19 Your ordination will not be full and complete until both God and man have laid hands upon you.

20 ⁋ And unto my servant David I say: You shall lay hands upon my servant Allen and set him apart as soon as you are able;

21 Be faithful, doubting not but believing, and I shall make a straight path for you that my will shall be done.

22 ⁋ And this I say unto you: All that are called shall be called to the Council of Fifty within the Order of the Ministry until my Church, the Fellowship, is established.

23 Therefore, go thee unto the world crying repentance in my name;

24 And this commandment I give unto all the Elders of the Fellowship, that everyone that will embrace their call with singleness of heart may be ordained and sent forth, even as I have spoken.

25 I am Jesus Christ, the Son of God; be clean ye that bear the vessels of the Lord. So mote it be: Amen.

Revelation 15

For the Benefit of the Church

Revelation given to David Ferriman December 5, 2018, in Long Beach, California for the Church of Jesus Christ in Christian Fellowship. This revelation is Section 112 in Doctrines of the Saints.

1 Having read, pondered and studied the Sections of the Community of Christ's Book of Doctrine and Covenants, I prayed to the Lord, asking Him what His will was concerning them for the Church of Jesus Christ in Christian Fellowship.

2 After prayer and contemplation, the Lord spoke to me saying: Verily I say unto you, my servant and my friend David, I give unto you counsel, and a commandment, concerning all the revelations and guidance I have given unto the Reorganized Church of Jesus Christ of Latter Day Saints, and unto Community of Christ;

3 These I gave unto them for the benefit of my Church, and for the salvation of men until I come; and some were given as counsel unto them, and some gave I unto the whole Church.

4 Therefore, I say into thee: Read them, ponder their words in your mind and you shall know;

5 You have inquired of me as you read, and you know they are true and of me as I did enlighten your mind; and now I tell you these things that you may know that you have been enlightened by the Spirit of Truth.

6 And now, behold, this is the spirit of revelation, therefore this is thy gift; use your gift, and be blessed; doubt not, for it is the gift of God.

7 And I say again unto thee, that which was given them from me for them they shall retain unto them, and my Fellowship shall pursue it not; but this does not make these words untrue, or not of me.

8 And that which I said unto them that is for the whole earth and all of my Saints, this shall thou use, and it will be pleasing unto me.

9 And again, I say unto you: Use your gift and you will know, and all will be well with they that learn from it;

10 And not just of this branch of the faith but use this gift to find my words to thee and

11 my Fellowship throughout my Churches throughout all times.

12 Therefore, continue in my goodness, that my Fellowship may be a light unto all, and by the power of my priesthood my people, even Israel; So mote it be: Amen.

Revelation 16

Of Lehi and Korihor

Revelation given to David Ferriman December 8, 2018, in Long Beach, California for the Church of Jesus Christ in Christian Fellowship. This revelation is Section 113 in Doctrines of the Saints.

1 Having read Christopher Nemelka's "Sealed Portion," and Bzhishk Nizak's "Book of Lehi," I prayed on both to know the truth.

2 The Lord had told me to study them out in my mind.

3 I met Bzhishk Nizak and learned more about him and where the Book of Lehi came from as I got to know him.

4 I also met and got to know a disciple of Christopher Nemelka's, asking him what he got out of Nemelka's teachings, etc.

5 Both appeared to be good people, and I wondered, was Christopher Nemelka's book a way to bring atheists to God?

6 However, the more I learned, the more I felt I needed guidance from the Lord;

7 The Spirit whispered to me the purpose of both books, and in time I received the following revelation:

8 ¶ Thus saith the Lord unto you my servants, concerning the Sealed Portion:

9 Behold, the Gold Plates shall not come forth by deception nor by force.

10 Yea, these things were hid from the world because of the wickedness of the Jaredite people;

11 And yet it has come to pass that secret combinations and wickedness from those that seek to gain is again upon the face of the Earth.

12 Behold, it is always so with man, and as they fall into the trappings of Satan, their wickedness and secret combinations grow.

13 Yet in the days of the Jaredites, their wickedness rivaled that of the days of Noah before the flood,

14 And thus I took them from the face of the Earth by the sword of their own hands; and by their own greed were they slaughtered.

15 And so too are the combinations of man today; they are not yet as wicked as before the flood, but as their wickedness grows mankind suffers.

16 Yea, there are those that make combinations to take from the poor, to feed them foods without nourishment, to teach their minds to be weak, and to keep their fellow man in poverty by deception.

17 ¶ And behold, I say unto you, and unto the world: Be not deceived, for Christopher Nemelka is an Antichrist, a false prophet sent to lead the hearts of the children of man away from me and to the devil;

18 Like Korihor and others of his kind, he had truth but set out to deceive.

19 And behold, he is a Korihor, which is to say and Antichrist, unto this day;

20 Yea, and I shall say no more on this wise unto you except this: As thou gather the sacred books of the Restoration, behold these two thou shall not gather—the Sealed Portion of Christopher Nemelka and the Book of Onias.

21 Behold, that Book of Onias has a portion of truth, for the Devil will tell an hundred truths to persuade men to believe one lie.

22 Yea, but no man neither woman shall bear the cursing of their fathers and mothers by the color of their skins;

23 Yea, and the color of a person's skin is a blessing from me, and not a curse,

24 And there is not one above another for all are one in me.

25 Yea, and all mankind has fallen short, and through mine atonement all mankind may be saved.

26 ¶ And behold, as to the Book of Lehi, behold ye shall call it Sepher Lehi, and ye shall include it in collecting the works of this restoration.

27 Behold I say unto thee and unto the world: This book is a work of fiction, yet it is of me; for it is a parable.

28 Behold, the daughters and sons of perdition cannot repent.

29 This is not because I am not a merciful God, but because it is against their nature to do so.

30 Yea, and I say unto thee: the demons converted to the Lord in Sefer Lehi are not perdition but are the weaknesses and vices of mankind.

31 And when thou shall take a weakness and give it unto the Lord, behold I shall make thee strong with it;

32 And Even as I took Enoch and his weaknesses, turning his weaknesses to strength, so too shall I do with thee.

33 For this have I done with all my servants, even thee; and thou are still weak, yet I give thee strength and bless thee with wisdom as ye use my works.

34 Therefore, this book, Sepher Lehi, ye shall use to teach wisdom in me with this parable;

35 For behold, they who wrote it did so in weakness, and I the Lord made them strong in this thing.

36 Yea, and I shall bless them and strengthen their words.

37 ¶ Go forth and hearken ye to these words; be sober and treasure these things up in your hearts.

38 Behold, I am Jesus Christ, the Savior of the world; keep all my commandments, endure to the end. So mote it be; even so. Amen.

Revelation 17

Robes of the Priesthood: The Head Covering

Revelation given to David Ferriman December 22, 2018, in Miamisburg, Ohio for the Church of Jesus Christ in Christian Fellowship. This revelation is Section 114 in Doctrines of the Saints.

1 After working for some time with my wife to design the temple clothing for the Fellowship, based on both the revelations we had

received and what is taught in the Law as found in the Torah, I became stuck.

2 As much as I searched, pondered, and prayed I could not, of my own accord, determine what to do about the head covering;

3 Particularly, the idea of the headwear was most troubling as I searched for a way to place the words: Holiness to the Lord upon it, as required in Exodus 28:36-38:

4 And thou shalt make a plate of pure gold, and grave upon it, like the engravings of a signet, HOLINESS TO YHVH.

5 And thou shalt put it on a blue lace, that it may be upon the mitre; upon the forefront of the mitre it shall be.

6 And it shall be upon Aaron's forehead, that Aaron may bear the iniquity of the holy things, which the children of Israel shall hallow in all their holy gifts; and it shall be always upon his forehead, that they may be accepted before the Lord.

7 I looked into a number of things, including stencils and cloth markers, putting gold leaf of the fabric, having gold engraved with the words, etc.

8 Not sure which direction to move forward with, I took the options I had gathered up to the Lord, to see which, if any, He would find pleasing;

9 No sooner had I asked than the Lord answered filling me with the Holy Spirit, enwrapping me with such joy that I could not hold back my tears.

10 And the Lord spoke to me, filling my whole body with the sound of His voice, saying:

11 ¶ Thus saith the Lord unto my servant David: I am well pleased with your offering and the work which you and my handmaiden Kristine have done to make the Holy Garments and Robes of the Holy Priesthood.

12 You have searched and you have prayed, and your efforts are acceptable before me; and in answer to prayers unto me I say unto you: Here is wisdom:

13 I have seen your struggles and your desire to find a way to fulfill the Law as it is written, and this is pleasing unto me;

14 But behold, the Law of Moses was but a symbol of my Higher Law, and all the Law and the words of the Prophets are fulfilled in me.

15 Therefore, ye shall look to me to know the meaning of the Law, and I shall instruct and teach thee all the days of thy life;

16 For it was I that sent the angels that taught thee in thy youth;

17 Yea, and it was I that spoke to thee from beyond the veil;

18 And it is I, even Jesus Christ, that speaks to thee now;

19 And I say unto thee: Peace, be still.

20 ¶ And Behold, I have seen your struggles to find and to make a plate of gold and to write upon it 'HOLINESS TO YHVH,' that my servants might place this upon their foreheads, as was required by my Law;

21 And you have come now, seeking with faith even as did the Brother of Jared seeking came he before me looking to light their way across the great waters.

22 But behold, this was done at a time before, and have I not said all I require of this generation is a broken heart and contrite spirit?

23 Yet so too have I said ye shall make clothing to wear when ye shall labor in my name;

24 And I say unto you now, the symbols I require of this generation are written upon the Holy Garments.

25 And 'HOLINESS TO THE LORD' does not need to be written upon your foreheads, for behold these words shall be written in that which is purer than gold:

26 And I say unto thee that my name shall be written upon your hearts.

27 ¶ And the Levitical Priesthood, the Priests and the Priestesses, these shall cover their heads with miznefet, which is to say a hat that does not cover the face or ears.

28 And the Deacons and the Teachers shall neither cover their heads nor their faces, neither the males nor the females.

29 ¶ And of the High Priesthood, the Elders shall wear a miter upon their heads, both male and female; which is to say a loose hat,

wrapped, tied, or bound to the head neither covering the face nor the ears.

30 And the High Priests and High Priestesses, these shall wear a tallit, which is to say a prayer shawl with tzitzit, or fringe;

31 And they shall cover their heads as moved by the Spirit, but they shall not make to cover the face, neither the High Priest nor the High Priestess;

32 And the High Priests and the High Priestesses may wear a hat covering their heads as do the Priests and Elders in addition to this as they desire but know thee that it is not required of me.

33 ¶ And behold, these ye shall wear to show humility before me, and not of status, nor out of pride;

34 For in the day one shall hold their calling from me in pride shall they hold that call in vain.

35 ¶ Remember, remember the words of my servant Paul to the Corinthians:

36 The head of all mankind is Christ, yet the man and the woman; and the head of Christ is God.

37 And every person that prays or prophesies against the head is disgracing his head, who is Christ;

38 And as the woman comes from the man, so too does the man come from the woman; yet all come from God (see 1 Corinthians 3-4, 12).

39 And I say further unto thee that to disgrace the Son is to disgrace the Father, therefore let thy hearts be pure that thy works be done in the name of the Lord.

40 ¶ These words I give unto the true and faithful; wherefore, transgress them not, neither take therefrom;

41 Do ye these things with a oneness of heart and mind and I, the Lord, will bless thee, and all those that do them shall enter into the joy of my service; Even so, Amen.

42 ¶ And when the vision closed, I understood and wrote down the words that they would not be forgotten.

Revelation 18

Organizing the Peaceful Kingdom

Revelation given to David January 15, 2019, San Diego, California for the Church of Jesus Christ in Christian Fellowship based on Community of Christ Doctrine and Covenants Section 120. The second half of verse 10 was added February 10, 2019, based on inspiration and revelation given the previous week that caused David to return to the Lord before finalizing this Section. This revelation is Section 6b in Doctrines of the Saints.

1 In organizing Synagogues and Congregations for and on behalf of the Church of Jesus Christ in Christian Fellowship, thus saith the Lord:

2 I say unto thee, it is written in my Law that whosoever repenteth and cometh unto me, the same is my Church; and again, as I have said: When three gather in my name, Behold: I am with them.

3 My vineyard is wide, even encompassing the whole earth, yet my Church does not yet cover the earth;

4 And that my people may find solace and comfort, I have set apart many in the vineyard that they might bring souls into me;

5 That these may grow in my Grace, feel of my Spirit, and fellowship in my name; that good works may be done and all might be edified.

6 ⸿ And for this reason have I called thee and set thee part, and sent my servants unto thee, that ye may grow the kingdom and those that seek may find.

7 And as hidden things are revealed, it is wisdom in me that ye study together in me; that ye learn to be one, even as the Father and I are one.

8 ⸿ And behold the Word of my Law has been established to carry out the work of the ministry in caring for the membership of the Church and Kingdom.

9 And behold, to relieve the Twelve and Seventy from the task overseeing the direction of each congregation, ye shall have these find those called of me and set them apart.

10 ¶ And each Congregation shall have a Bishopric to preside over the ministry with their congregation, but a Synagogue shall be lead by a Pastor whos is a sole Bishop;

11 And the Bishopric shall be led by a High Priest and a High Priestess, and these shall call a counselor, even a First Deacon to assist and to watch over the Church within their Congregation and surrounding communities.

12 ¶ And the First Deacon too shall be called from among my High Priests or High Priestesses, and these shall have the keys to lead and preside within this, the order of their ministry; and this according to my Law[a].

13 And the First Deacon shall be the President of the Quorum of Deacons and Teachers within their congregation, presiding over these in righteousness and humility, serving with another High Priest or High Priestess called as the Second Deacon, and with a Teacher called to the Levitical Priesthood as their councilor, as in the Bishopric.

14 And the Deacons and Teachers shall perform their duties as given in my Law.

15 ¶ And the Bishopric shall oversee the quorum of Priests and Priestesses, and these shall see to the ordinances and needs of the congregation, performing their duties as given in my Law.

16 ¶ And the Elders and High Priests and High Priestess shall see to the spiritual matters of the Church, working with the Levitical Priesthoods, training them up in the Lord to do my works.

17 And these will seek out and teach all those seeking my name, not to build up a kingdom unto men, but unto me;

18 Therefore, it matereth not if these should join my Fellowship, so long as they find their home in me they are a part of my vineyard and my Church shall be with them as they gather with others in my name.

19 ¶ And these shall form a High Council of Evangelists, and the High Priests and High Priestesses of this quorum shall be traveling Bishops;

20 And these shall follow my Law, being sent out in twos to teach in my name, yea traveling locally with and Elder, Priest or Priestess, or Teacher to do my works for the glory of the Father.

21 And this High Council shall be led by a Patriarch and a Matriarch, a High Priest and High Priestess, in my name;

22 For these shall be Evangelists to watch over the congregations of my Fellowship and shall do their duty as assigned in my Law, and as needed to assist relieve the duties of the Seventy and the Apostles called to watch over the flock.

23 ¶ And the Seventy *Elders* are called forth and sent out to assist the Twelve, and the Twelve to assist the First Presidency, and the Evangelists, and the Bishopric, and the Council of Elders as they watch over my Church and the Fellowship.

24 And all these shall be filled in mine own time, saith the Lord: for now, call those I send to fill roles as needed in my peaceable Kingdom;

25 And the first shall be last and the last shall be first; therefore, serve one another in brotherly and sisterly love:

26 ¶ And behold, the Kingdom of God is as a man that builds a house;

27 And behold the house hath four pillars, and the pillars work as one to hold up the roof.

28 Yea, and when the first pillar says: Behold my strength, that I might uphold this wall alone.

29 And a second pillar says: Nay, but behold my strength that I uphold the walls and the roof also.

30 And the third and fourth pillar bragging too of their own strength until, divided these part ways and house does fall, and the man is left cold.

31 And the man whips the pillars, and they bear the strikes, and do they learn to love the man

32 And the man whips the pillars, and they bear the strikes, and do they learn to love the man?

33 I say thee, nay; but they learn to hate the man; and as one they shun him and protect him not from the winds and rains: and thus the man is destroyed.

34 But the Lord of Hosts comes unto the pillars, and these he loves, and these he commands to be as one;

35 Yea and they love the Lord and stand as one, no more divided, and no more boasting of their own strength, for each has their place in the House of the Lord.

36 And the man is the church of men, or the church of the devil; and he builds with discord and pride;

37 But the Lord of Hosts may use the same and build with patience and peace:

38 ¶ Therefore, ye too shall build with patience and peace.

39 I say unto thee, what is past is past, what is now is now;

40 Therefore, go ye and build up my kingdom, not of pride but with love, and this ye shall do in my name; and if ye do so in my name ye shall not fail.

41 ¶ Behold I am with thee, be ye one with another and ye are one in me; my mission is thy mission, and my ministry thine;

42 Therefore, go forward in faith, endure to the end, and do all things in my name that thy works shall be Holy. So mote it be; Amen.

Notes:

a   see 5b:50

Revelation 19

Feed My Sheep

Revelation received in Miamisburg, Ohio January 24, 2019. Though this revelation was to Brother Alexei Christopher Mattanovich, the first Apostle called to the Fellowship of Christ, this revelation should be read and studied by all called to the Apostleship. This revelation is Section 12f in Doctrines of the Saints.

1 My mind being in reflection on the evening of January 24, 2019, on the Church of Jesus Christ in Christian Fellowship, its direction and in particular the action or future actions of the Council of Elders and the Apostles, I was given a vision and a revelation.

2 In the vision I saw Apostle co-president Alexei Christopher Mattanovich standing in the doorway of a temple, dressed in the Robes of the Priesthood as a High Priest.

3 There, standing as the overseer or guardian of the temple as it were, he was feeding the poor, giving shelter to those in need with great joy in his heart;

4 All around bout the temple were people in tents, finding rest and sanctuary there on the temple grounds, others were lined up to receive the food being brought out from within.

5 Whether this was literal or figurative, I know not—though it felt to be both.

6 And then, just as suddenly, the voice of the Lord came to me saying: Behold, thus saith the Lord unto my servant and my friend, Alexei:

7 I have seen thy works and been with thee as thou hast opened thy mouth in proclaiming my gospel, teaching the things of the kingdom, expounding mysteries from out of the scriptures, even according to that portion of Spirit and power which I have given unto thee.

8 And now, I have a few words to say unto thee.

9 Behold, in that moment thou came to me, meekly and in submission, it was then that I forgave thee of all thy sins.

10 And as many times as thou shall come unto me and seek forgiveness thou shall be forgiven, therefore feed my sheep;

11 For I know thee, and I knew thee before thou wast born in the flesh; and before thou wast born I blessed thee and set thee apart.

12 Yet there is a gap between thee and me, and it is thus: even as I have forgiven thee, thou too shall forgive thyself of all thy wrong doing.

13 For behold, it is not meet that thou shall run faster than thou are able, nor to walk further than it is given thee to walk.

14 But behold, all things are given thee to teach thee patience and long suffering, and thou hast endured these well;

15 Not perfectly, no—for none are perfect, not one; yet all may be perfected in me, as thou hast been.

16 Behold, I God am thy judge, therefor thou shalt not judge thyself too harshly; for behold thou art a special witness in my name and a judge in Israel;

17 And for this reason, in thee is given the gift and power of discernment, not to place blame, but to take it from those that grieve in shame and will humble themselves in my name.

18 And behold, it is given thee to see and converse with angels, and to work miracles in my name, therefore feed thee my sheep;

19 But to do this thou must forgive thyself, and forgive others;

20 Behold my Church, even the Church of Jesus Christ of Latter-day Saints; yea many have they wronged and for many they have been their undoing;

21 But behold, these still do a mighty work in my name, therefore they are still mine, though they are flawed and seek not my ways at first.

22 But behold, by my strong hand do I guide them, and I have prepared many other servants to build a house or houses in my name that all may find rest;

23 And this is why I, the Son of Man, have no house to rest my head—for no church, sect, or denomination is perfect; no, not one;

24 Yet men and women do I still call to speak in my name, and these do, here a little and there a little, that all might be edified.

25 And I have called thee, and I have set thee apart for this work, to build a home for those that will come seeking shelter,

26 Therefore I say unto thee even as I said unto the Apostles of old: Feed my sheep.

27 But I say unto thee, for thou too to do this, thou must first forgive thyself even as I, the Lord thy God, have forgiven thee;

28 And thou must forgive those that have wronged you, and those you have seen to do wrong—even the Church of Jesus Christ of Latter-day Saints.

29 And behold, many servants did I call by the mouths of my people when my servant Joseph was taken—and I took him;

30 For behold, dost thou thinkest that man can thwart the will of God? I say thee no.

31 Dost thou thinkest that my servant Joseph, who was betrayed by his friends, could be killed by the hands of men before his time? I say thee no.

32 But behold, I had told my servant Joseph to change the errors of his ways, for he had set in motion both that which I love and things that I hate, and thus it was his time.

33 Yea, and he died too that his testimony might be sealed by blood, even as the prophets of old.

34 Yea, here is wisdom: there are more sides than one and I the Lord God see all sides; therefore worry not what was, but what is to come;

35 For though thou cannot change the past, thou shall be an instrument in my hands to make a way for the future of my work;

36 Therefore, forgive thyself, and this too, forgive others, even as I have done the same.

37 And behold, I say unto thee also, all things that have come to pass shall gather momentum at this time, that the works of my servants shall be known for good as well as evil;

38 But thou shall focus only on the good and that which shall unite my people;

39 For those that are mine are Israel, for these are the straight path to God.

40 Seek to soften thy anger, walk the path of teshuvah daily, teach others that thou too shall learn, grant forgiveness to those that seek forgiveness, and bless those that seek my face;

41 For thou art of the Church of the Firstborn, worthy and receiving of the Second Comforter, and ye shall receive my face and handle my wounds when thou hast found peace in thy heart;

42 Until then, know I am with thee, and thou art with me; I am thy comfort and thy guide, walk with me the remainder of thy days and by thy works and thy example shall thou bring souls unto me.

43 Wherefore, be faithful, praying always, that thou might be ready at the day of my coming, and behold, verily, verily, I say unto thee, that I come quickly; even so: Amen.

Revelation 20

Remote Ordinances

Revelation given to David Ferriman May 16, 2019, in Miamisburg, Ohio for the Church of Jesus Christ in Christian Fellowship. This revelation is Section 116 in Doctrines of the Saints.

1 While putting together the plan with the Council of Elders on worship services, I felt impressed by the Spirit that the Orders of Prayer should be done in some manner, and we had been asking how to do temple ordinances and other sacred practices that require the laying on of hands for some time.

2 Going to the Lord on the matter, I asked everyone to pray that I would receive instructions on how the Lord desires we in the Fellowship to perform these sacred tasks, and the Lord came to me, giving me the following revelation:

3 Verily, thus saith the Lord unto those whom He loves, yea speaking unto my servants and my friends; those of my Church, even the Church of Jesus Christ in Christian Fellowship: Hearken, O ye people of my Church;

4 Yea and verily I say unto thee that many things have been given of me, things given unto thee and those that dwell upon the earth for both profit and learning;

5 And all things have and shall be given to the Elders of my Church from the beginning even up to this day and forward, if my people shall but ask of me.

6 And behold I say unto thee: Conduct all thy meetings as ye are directed and guided by the Holy Spirit, for by this shall ye know and shall all things be profitable unto all, speaking spirit to spirit.

7 But more than this, ye seek and desire instructions on how to be one as my Saints with such great distances between one another;

8 And behold I have prepared a way unto thee, but some of ye fear and doubt because of the habits of men; and I say unto thee: Fear not!

9 Behold, I have given thee the means, greater now than in days past; yea, ye have the ways placed before thee, and I will instruct thee in my ways in this matter.

10 I say unto thee that it is by both the spirit and the flesh that all things are done, for the spirit and the flesh are one in me, and this is my purpose: to make on earth that which is in heaven that all are one in me and in the Father; yea to bring to pass the immortality and eternal life of mankind.

11 Thus I say unto thee: If one needeth the laying on of hands, bless a cloth, and sent it to them, be it a napkin or a tallit, let the Spirit guide;

12 And behold, when they that require the laying on of hands receive this blessed cloth, they shall lay it upon their head, and it shall take the place of the hands of they that shall bless them in my name.

13 And if temple ordinances are to be done, behold ye shall do this by means of technologies in that ye shall see one another to instruct and to bless,

14 And ye shall place the tallit or the napkin upon the head of they that are to receive their Initiatories or their Endowments, and another shall act in thy stead, as proxy for those performing the Initiatories or the Endowments,

15 And they that shall give unto they that shall receive shall instruct them from afar, watching that all things done in my name shall be done correctly,

16 And there shall be two witnesses that all things done in my name are performed correctly, and these shall sign as witness as such.

17 And behold, as to the Order of Prayer, as given by me unto the world; these ye shall do when ye gather to worship; and it shall be led by one in authority that has been endowed unto the proper order of things.

18 And I say unto thee, they that are afar off in their homes or synagogues, or wherever they might be; these shall stand with those in

attendance in their order of the prayer which is to be given, shoulder to shoulder if they are with other or alone if they be alone;

19 And these shall not close the circle as they shall be connected to those in my Fellowship that are with them in spirit by my Holy Spirit; and thus ye shall be one in me, the Lord your God.

20 And behold, my servant David, I have more to say unto thee as to thy condition and thy roll in my Fellowship: get first thy own house in order.

21 Behold, I said unto thee that I should send others to help thee prepare a way, and behold: this thing hath been fulfilled and there shall be more to come still;

22 Yet thou hast not swallowed thy pride and given unto all of these opportunities to do my works, yea thou hast taken to task all things and this pleaseth me not.

23 For behold, the ship with many oars and rowers shall go far upon the face of the waters, yet if only one shall row all shall go slowly or not at all;

24 And behold, there are many among you that can do these things, and all things shall be done in time as it is pleasing unto me;

25 Therefore, worry not if these things cannot be done in thy time, which is to say the time thou thinkest thing should be accomplished, but rather let all things be done in my time.

26 Wherefore it is pleasing unto thee that thou shall be there for thy wife and thy children, and those I have sent unto thee, and divine the labors of my vineyard unto those willing to do the work;

27 And if there are not those that are willing to do the work, behold all things shall be done in my time, therefore worry not if these things cannot be done right away;

28 And all things shall be done for thy benefit and the benefit for my people, even the Saints of Zion, for all things done in my name are done in my time, sayeth the Lord.

29 Yea, and these things too I say unto all of the Council of Elders, and all those in the Council of Fifty: worry not, for all things shall be done in my time;

30 And unto those helping now with the work, and those willing to help with this my works I say unto thee, I am well pleased.

31 And now I say unto thee and unto all of my people in the Fellowship and in every one of my vineyards, go and do all things in my name, and remember that that which is done for another is done for me, therefore do all things in my name. Even so shall it be; Amen.

Revelation 21

Revelation to the Levites

Revelation given to David Ferriman on August 13, 2019, in Miamisburg, Ohio for the tribe of Levi throughout the world. This revelation is Section 117 in Doctrines of the Saints.

1 On the evening of the thirteenth of August, I was engaged in conversation about the week from Sukkot to Shmini Atzeret, the Feast of Tabernacles to the Eighth Day of Assembly and the event being organized by the Levites;

2 While talking I felt the need for a revelation as to the role of the Levites in this dispensation, and as I did so I felt the Spirit of the Lord preparing me to receive this revelation.

3 Later that night, the Lord spoke to me, saying: Hearken, unto me, O ye of the tribes of Levi, saith the Lord, your God, and give ear to my Word;

4 Unto those in the land of Missouri, yea even the land which I have appointed and consecrated for the gathering of the Saints, and unto all they of the tribes of Lehi in this generation shall I speak this day.

5 And I say into thee: In times past thou were chosen to act as the Priests of my Covenant Peoples, yea and it was thy fathers that were commanded to watch over and keep thy traditions;

6 And as time passed thy fathers began to sleep a mighty sleep, forgetting why they were given these things.

7 And behold, when I, the Lord thy God, hung upon the Cross and freely gave up the ghost, the temple veil was rent in twain, torn in two, from the top to the bottom, even as the keys of the priesthood had been divided into the Levitical and the High Priesthood.

8 But behold, these Keys are still yet one Priesthood in my name, and shall work together as one, in my name:

9 For the Levitical is the Keys to ordinances, Holy Days, feasts, and fasting, and of the months and days in the year, as keepers and guardians of the temples, singers of the Psalms, and to perform all other duties given in my name; and the High Priesthood that of miracle working, and organizing:

10 Thus shall the Levites keep the days alone, and lead not? I say thee nay; but these shall be mine holy Kohanim and judges in Israel and assist Ephraim in gathering my people back into the straight path in remembrance of my Law and thy covenants with me.

11 And behold, here is wisdom: this is the last generation of mankind, thus saith the Lord thy God; and this after the generations of mankind after the reckoning of Elohim:

12 For this last generation are all those that have lived and all they that shall live from the time of my servant Joseph Smith Jr. until Zion is gathered and I have returned to the Earth.

13 And there shall be a number of generations, after the counting as to the manner of mankind, in this the last generation, and unto each of these I give this command:

14 Pray unto me upon thy Sabbaths, asking for thy share of light; thy share of wisdom and knowledge: that is shall be given, and received in humility.

15 Yea, and unto the Levites I give this charge: teach all that come unto me the Law of Sacrifice, which is the Law of the Broken Heart and the Contrite Spirit; teach all that accept the renewed covenant, even the Book of Mormon, to pray as such in my name.

16 For behold: this is the last generation, and it is the fullness of time; yet did my servant Joseph Smith Jr. restore all things? I say thee nay.

17 And I have sent out and given unto the world others from the time of his death even until now, that this generation might grow line upon line and precept upon precept.

18 What then of the Levites? Behold, I see many asking this day about things that have been done away;

19 And what of Miriam, the sister of Arron? For as it was Moses that taught the priests, and Aaron that took charge of then, and Aaron from that a portion of the Levitical Priesthood was named; yea, and it is Miriam that taught the priestesses, and Miriam from that a portion of the Levitical Priesthood is named.

20 Therefore, I say unto the Levites: at the head of thy council shall be a High Priest and a High Priestess: and these shall teach the Law and the Covenants to my people; and my Law is this: Love God, love thy neighbors, keep my commandments:

21 Do this and ye shall be purified and behold all thy offerings unto me shall be made in righteousness.

22 And it has been asked, what of the Law? Was not the Law put away in Christ? Behold, I say unto thee: I AM the Law: I AM he who gave it, and I AM he who fulfilled it: and behold I never dieth and so to shall my Law never die.

23 And what of the sacrifices? O fool! Know ye not that the sacrifices never did wash away sins? But it was I, the Son of Man, that forgave and that forgive; for I AM Chesed, I AM Mercy, I AM YHVH, I AM the Lord thy God;

24 Therefore, I say unto thee: observe the covenant, return to my covenant in teshuvah and in righteousness; not that thy works shall bring thee salvation, but that salvation hath led to my works; for ye are my covenant people: ye are the People of the Law.

25 And again, it has been asked: who whom doth the Levites belong? And I say thee: the Levites belong to the Lord thy God, YHVH Elohim, and should come from every walk of life, and from every branch of the tree, every garden of the vineyard not only of the Latter Day Saints, but from every branch and vineyard of the Jews, and of every church of the Gentiles as is their birthright.

26 And these shall sit in council: and all things shall be done in order; and the heads of their councils shall on the Council of Israel, when the heads of the tribes shall meet, and more shall be given on this as I gather the tribes, for this work has already begun.

27 And the Levites are to assist every branch of my kingdom, as they are asked and so moved by my Spirit to do so, loving all my people as one, and serving them as one.

28 Therefore, I say unto my people, even the Saints of Zion: listen to the Levites and return to my Holy Days and remember the covenants of thy fathers and mothers, for their covenants are thy covenants.

29 And as to the sacrificing of animals, do this only as written in the Law only for feasts and festivals; and do so in humility and in remembrance of times past; and see to it that no part is wasted.

30 For this thing that thou do is in remembrance of the covenant, to feed the poor, and to remember that as my covenant people thou hast died to the world to live in my name.

31 Therefore, go, my Levites, and do they part in the gathering of Zion; for behold, this is the restoration of all things: So mote it be; Amen.

Revelation 22

Revelation to the Elect Lady

Revelation given to Kristine Ferriman through her husband, and co-president, David Ferriman October 13, 2019 in Chillicothe, Missouri. This revelation is Section 8b in Doctrines of the Saints.

1 My beloved daughter, Kristine, Harken ye to the voice of the Lord; I the Lord thy God say unto thee:

2 ¶ Behold, thou hast been called and set apart before thou wast born, yeah and even before the world was I called thee;

3 And this was and is thy call: to come forth in these, the last days; to help restore unto mankind that which they have discarded and thrown away;

4 For behold, thou art an Elect Lady, and a helpmeet to thy husband, both in the things of this world and in the ministry.

5 And I have called thee, and set thee apart to do a great and marvelous work in my name,

6 And thou were called to come forth at this time to help restore balance.

7 ⸿ Yeah, there are three pillars, with one on the right hand and one on the left, but the seed of men have sought to tear down the right pillar;

8 And thus thou hast been called to restore my right hand amongst the children of men; for the daughters of God have cried out unto me, even the Lord their God, seeking to gain their birthright.

9 ⸿ And to this end wast thou born; to help build my kingdom, to restore the pillars, to raise up righteous seed before me;

10 And for this reason did I command my servant David to lay hands upon thee, giving thee the keys to the presidency of the Sisterhood and to the Law of Sarah, even before thou understood thy calling;

11 For behold, unto thee has been given the royal birthright, and thou are the High Priestess in my name of this royal generation;

12 And a High Priestess and queen shall thou be for time and all eternity to the Most High God, should thou keep thy Covenants and remain faithful unto me.

13 ⸿ Behold, I send thee this revelation as a means of instruction, therefore I say unto thee: Feed my sheep! for thou hast been called to minister in my name.

14 Fear not, for I shall give thee strength; and lean upon me, for I shall provide unto thee all that thou shall need for thyself and thine family.

15 Yeah, and behold; harken unto my voice, for I AM the good shepherd;

16 And when thou shall hear my voice by way of revelation, know that I shall speak unto thee in a voice that thou shalt recognize;

17 Worry not that my Word shall sound different to thee than that of thy husband, for behold: I speak unto all in a language they shall understand;

18 But search thy heart, and when it is of me I shall tell thee in thy mind, and thou shall feel it in thy heart.

19 ¶ And know this: thou hast been given the gift of discernment, and this shall tell thee what is of me and what is not; and thou shall feel it to thy very core;

20 For the Spirit if God is the Spirit of Pure truth and Pure knowledge; and in wisdom shall thou be given my Word to be received by my people.

21 ¶ Therefore, go and do as I have commanded, and I shall bring peace to thy heart; worry not of the things of this world, for in me shall thou and thy family be provided for:

22 And the blessings of heaven shall pour out in abundance in so much that thou shall not know what to do save it be to bless others temporally with that which ye shall be given.

23 ¶ Therefore, I say unto thee: raise thy children in righteousness; continue to counsel with thy husband in all things; seek to restore that which has been lost to mankind that women may be restored to their rightful place upon the throne in my kingdom;

24 And know too that I have sent others to help thee in this task;

25 Therefore I say unto thee to find these women; ordain them and prophesy over them, lead and guide them, that all may be restored to its proper order.

26 Behold, I have called thee to gather my daughters, and to gather my Saints;

27 To build a home for those seeking my shelter, and to teach and ordain those that I have called to this work.

28 ¶ Kristine, thou art a leader amongst women, and with thy husband ye shall together be leaders of mankind;

29 Therefore, fear not; for I am with thee, all the days of thy life.

30 Many are called, but few are chosen:

31 And behold, thou hast been called and are chosen unto me after the order of Eve, and of Sarah, and of Miriam; and Deborah, and Phoebe, and Junia, and Salome, and Emma; and many other women: prophetesses, apostle, ministers, and elect ladies all called in my name;

32 And in the order of Magdalene shall thou surpass many of those that came before thee, and all those that did not harken unto my call.

33 Therefore my daughter, go forth and serve, for behold, in thee rests the strength to overcome and endure to the end.

34 I the Lord, have spoken it, thus shall it be: Amen.

Revelation 23

YHVH

Revelation received by David Ferriman November 12, 2019. People had been debating the correct pronunciation of "YHVH." David had been pronouncing it "Yahweh," while others were pronouncing it "Jehovah." After this revelation was received David began to pronounce it "Yahvah," (Yah-VAH) placing an "a" after the "Y" and the "V" consonants. This was by inspiration, but not revelation as not to take sides in the debate. In this revelation the meaning of YHVH is given, but not the pronunciation. This revelation is Section 45e in Doctrines of the Saints

1 **Question:** What is the name of God in Hebrew?

Answer: YHVH

2 **Question**: How is this name pronounced?

Answer: This will be shown unto you in the Holy of Holies after my temple is built.

3 **Question**: What does this name mean?

Answer: It is the I AM that I AM, Ahyeh Asher Ahyeh (אֶהְיֶה אֲשֶׁר אֶהְיֶה, ʼehyeh ʼăšer ʼehyeh): "I AM the One that Creates," the Creator.

4 **Question**: Who is YHVH?

Answer: Jesus who is the very Christ, the Great Jehovah.

5 **Question**: What is the meaning of YHVH?

Answer: In me is that Father and the Mother, and I in them, and in us is the Holy Ghost; and we are in Spirit, and we are One God: י Y, Yod representing the Father, and ה Hei representing the Mother and the very Presence of God, ו Vav representing the Son, and the very condescension of God, ה representing the Spirit; and I am YHVH, for all things are done in me by the will of the Father, and the will of the Father and of the Mother are One.

6 **Question**: Why do we not know how to pronounce YHVH?

Answer: Because of the fears of men this knowledge was lost, but fear not to say the name, neither squabble over how to pronounce it.

7 **Question**: Why is the Mother hidden, why don't we pray to Her?

Answer: The Father and the Mother are One, when the Father is called upon, the Mother also is called upon; when the Mother is called upon, so also is the Father called upon: but all things are done in me, for I AM Jesus Christ, and ye are my Church: therefore, be ye one in me even as the Father and the Mother one and the Holy Spirit shall abound and ye shall be comforted by me.

Revelation 24

Come Ye Israel

The Word of the Lord given to all the world, both to the descendants of Abraham and all that would be Israel, through His servant David on the morning of November 30, 2019. This revelation was voted on and sustained as canon for use in the Church of Jesus Christ in Christian Fellowship by the Assembly of Saints on April 6, 2020. This revelation is Section 2g in Doctrines of the Saints

1 On November 30, 2019, the Word of the Lord came to me saying: Hearken O Israel to the voice of the Lord, thy God;

2 For the hour is near, and the time is nigh; and what I say unto thee this day, I say unto the whole earth!

3 Behold, thus sayeth the Lord of Hosts: the Hour of the Gentiles[a] has come and gone; the Gospel has been sent forth, and shall continue to be sent forth until it fills the whole earth;

4 But the days of the Gentiles are now passed, and I shall once again remember my Covenant, which I have made unto my people, O house of Israel:

5 And who is the House of Israel? Who are my Covenant Peoples?

6 ¶ Behold, I came unto my own, and these rejected me; and my Word was not taken from them, but these rejected it;

7 For they studied not my Law, but added unto it the precepts of man; and they sought the favor of man, and recognition for their genealogies, and for their studies, and their knowledge of the Law;

8 But these took not the time to live the Law, and to learn my ways; and so it was as naught;

9 For these cared more for their vain obligations, and their Sabbaths, and their meetings, allowing the love of many to wax cold.

10 ¶ And were there no good among them? I say to thee: nay, not none; for if the hearts of all had waxed cold, they should have been destroyed for forgetting my Covenant;

11 But the children of Abraham, Isaac, and Jacob now cover the whole earth, and their blood fills many veins; and these are still mine covenant people, and I forget them not.

12 And the Gospel went forth and has gone forth for many, many hundreds of years, by the reckoning of time by men; a Renewed Covenant being given unto the Gentiles;

13 And these, the Gentiles, have forsaken my Law, and forgotten my Holy Days, and my Sabbaths, and used my Word to divide, rather than to unite, and to control rather than to enlighten and to teach.

14 ¶ Behold, it is as I have said: My ways are not thy ways, neither are my thoughts thy thoughts.

15 And thus I have sent the Restored Covenant unto the world by my servant Joseph Smith Jr., and what thanks did ye show unto me? Ye slayed him, my faithful servant.

16 Was this man perfect? I say to thee, nay; no man nor woman is, but in me; for I AM the Rock of thy Salvation;

17 Yet he gave to thee my Word, and when I took him ye sought for me no longer, but broke apart by thy vanities;

18 And did ye observe my Holy Days? And my Law? I say unto thee that, yea some did—but not all, and not many.

19 And thus we have a people of submission in observations, and a people of submission in prayer, and a people of submission in the Cross; but my people are not one people.

20 ¶ And thus, I shall ask of thee once again: Who is the House of Israel? Who are my Covenant Peoples?

21 And behold, I say unto thee that theses are the people of Israel: these are those of Yashar-El, the path Straight to God;

22 These are those that shall seek my face, and turn not from me;

23 These are they that shall taste the fruit of the Tree of Life, and it shall taste sweet, and these shall not turn away;

24 These are they who shall love the Lord their God with all their hearts, minds, and strength, and this they shall show by their love for their fellow man, and their care for the Earth and her creatures.

25 These are they that shall do my works, and shall bring to pass the oneness of the Heavens and the Earth;

26 These are they that to whom I shall say: Well done, my good and faithful servants.

27 ¶ Therefore I say unto thee, my Israel: Quarrel not amongst thyselves in vain repetitions; but love one another as I love thee;

28 For there is but one priesthood, of the earth and of the heavens; and there is but one Gospel, of the earth and of the heavens;

29 And there is but one people of God; and these are my Israel, these are my covenant peoples; these are they that live my Law.

30 And this is my Law: to Love the Lord thy God and to love thy neighbor, for to love me is to love thy neighbor;

31 For I AM thy Creator, and thou art my creation, therefore to love me is to love all the good things that I hath made upon the earth as in heaven.

32 ¶ Therefore, I say unto these: Come before me in love of observations, and in love of prayer, and in love in the Cross;

33 For the observance of my Holy Days are not made for the Sabbaths, but these my Shabbat for all mankind.

34 Yea, these are the times of my festivals that ye might worship together as one in my name, no longer to be tossed to and fro, but united as my Israel.

35 And the prayers are not for submission nor supplication, but that thou might know me, the Lord thy God, and to learn my ways, and for to teach thee to grow in my Grace.

36 And the Cross was not given thee to suffer, but to be lifted up; for I have atoned for thy sins, and I have made thy ways straight; therefore I AM the very Lord God of Israel.

37 And thus I say unto thee that the days of the Gentiles have ended, and the trump has sounded, and I prepare to return to the earth;

38 And this is not to say that I know the day or the hour, for none know but the Father; but I say unto thee as I have said unto all in this generation: the time is nigh, even at the door;

39 And this I say unto thee because I shall come as a thief in the night, and quickly shall I return:

40 Therefore make thy ways the ways of peace, even now and the very ground thou shall walk upon shall be holy, for I AM holy, and ye are mine.

41 ¶ Therefore, go forth and contend with one another no longer, but unite in my name; cease to find fault, but build upon that which ye love;

42 Wonder not why I have revealed myself unto thee in many ways, but know ye that I shall reveal myself unto all they that seek my face and desireth to know my name:

43 Therefore, I have created many mansions that all might return unto the Presence of the Father and know me always.

44 ¶ And remember ye this: That ye are mine, and I am your God; therefore go now and take this message to the four corners of the Earth,

45 Tell ye the world that the Kingdom of God is at hand, and that the laborers in my vineyard have been called to gather themselves as one, as Israel, in teshuvah in my holy name; Even so, Amen.

Notes:

    a   See DoS Section 26c:34-40

    b   "from on high" crossed out in RB1 pg. 68, returned to the revelation by inspiration.

    c   1 Corinthians 15:52

    d   DoS 21a:29

Revelation 25

Make Ready the New Jerusalem

The Word of the Lord given to the Churches of Christ through His servant David February 18, 2020. Words in italics were added by the Elect Lady by inspiration from the Holy Spirit. This revelation was voted on and sustained as canon for use in the Church of Jesus Christ in Christian Fellowship by the Assembly of Saints on April 6, 2020. This revelation is Section 2h in Doctrines of the Saints

1 Behold, and hearken to the voice of the Lord unto thee, all those of my Church in the last days;

2 Yea, listen to the voice of He who has all power, for I AM from everlasting to everlasting, the Aleph-Tav, even Alpha and Omega, the beginning and the end.

3 Thus saith the Lord unto all they who are assembled in their many congregations, in their meeting houses, their temples, and their synagogues;

4 Yea, unto all they whose sins are forgiven, for I, the Lord, forgive sins and am merciful unto those who come unto me with humbled and broken hearts and contrite spirits.

5 And I ask thee now, all they who have come unto me with an eye single to my glory, and according to my commandments: Are ye one? Behold, I say unto thee: Nay.

6 And for many years, as to the reckoning of man, have I looked down upon my people with a broken heart, for thou draweth near unto thy husband, for I AM the bridegroom and thou my bride, with thy lips, but thy hearts are far from me.

7 And how art thy hearts so far away? Behold, thou doest many great works in my name, but thy pride and thy vanities are unto thy churches, making them like unto the churches of men.

8 And have ye remembered my new covenant, even the Book of Mormon?

9 Behold I say unto thee, thy testimonies and the testimonies of this work rest not upon the hands of men!

10 And I say unto thee again, the Book of Mormon was not given unto thee by men, but of prophecy and revelation, and is to be given and received in the spirit of prophecy and revelation;

11 If thou wishest to know all things, look not to the hands of men, but come to me *through your study and prayer*, together in my name, and ye shall find me; ask of me and ye shall receive, knock and it shall be opened unto you.

12 Behold, I say unto thee that I have sent forth many men and women, out into the world, to gather Mine Elect and chosen people, and ye see with thine own eyes that I have indeed created for thee many mansions;

13 Yet thou hast forsaken thy brethren and thy sistren in the ministry, thou forget that there is one ministry and one baptizing in my name in rejecting the baptisms of thy sisters in Zion.

14 And yet my grace hath been sufficient for thee, and I have not rejected thee, for my mercy and grace are with thee, and I am slow to anger, and my mercy is from everlasting to everlasting.

15 But now is the time for teshuvah, my children and my friends, for these are the last days and this is the restoration of all things;

16 Therefore, I say unto thee: Be ye one in Zion.

17 And how shall ye be one? Build unto me a temple in my name, a common place for all of my Saints, in these the latter days.

18 Behold, I have given charge unto the Church of Christ, and called my servant Granville Hedrick and blessed these, my people, to hold the land dedicated by the hand of my servant Sidney Rigdon for the building of my house.

19 And ye see that I have blessed the Church of Jesus Christ of Latter-day Saints with much worldly wealth, that they might uplift and sustain their sisters with the precious things of this world,

20 And so too that they might provide the funding to build my temple that all of my people may worship together as one in my name.

21 And the Church of Jesus Christ, as organized by my servant John Alpheus Cutler, they have been awaiting this day that they might impart upon my people the treasures I have given them to watch over.

22 And unto Community of Christ, and the other Reorganized branches of my vineyard, in these have I preserved many gifts, and these shall be a bridge between my peoples.

23 And more have I gathered, and more have I preserved, but in me ye are not yet; even as the lot of mine temple, ye circle about me and place stakes in the corners, but ye have yet to build.

24 And what is this that ye should build? Are all to gather to one church in my name? I say thee nay, for all are my Church, even the Churches of Christ, therefore be ye one in my name.

25 And I say unto thee: Build a council and send delegates from as many of my Churches as will be a part of my kingdom, and these shall lay the foundations of Zion,

26 For I say unto thee that all art called, but few shall be chosen, and why shall they not be chosen? For the pride of their hearts.

27 Therefore, I say unto thee, forgo thy pride and thy Egos, and the theologies of man, and unite in me, for I AM, the Savior of the world unto all they who shall believe in HaShem, my name, and seek my Shalom, for I AM, the prince of peace.

28 Remember the Law, and the New and Everlasting Covenant, for the days grow shorter, and the nights longer;

29 Therefore, go now and take the talents I have given thee and be ye one in my name, be ye Israel, and build my Zion, make ready for the New Jerusalem;

30 For I have given unto all of these oil for thy lamps, that ye might see, and not go seeking oil from another and miss the wedding party, but work together and be my light unto the world, that all may know of my coming;

31 Therefore, be ye ever watchful, be ye ever ready, for behold, I come quickly; Even so, Amen.

Revelation 26

A Revelation to David

Revelation given to David Ferriman February 2020 in Miamisburg Ohio. This revelation is Section 118a in Doctrines of the Saints.

1 Verily thus Saith the Lord unto you my Servant David: It is wisdom in me that thou shalt finish the translation of the First Book of Moses from the plates of brass and set aside the Doctrines of the Saints at present.

2 Yea, and thou shalt translate the words of my servant Zenos from these plates, for his words have been preserved to be given to the world at this time, and to prepare my Saints for my coming;

3 And this that my people might better understand the words of my servants Nephi and John, for unto these have I given the vision of my Creation, of things that have come to pass and that are soon to come to pass.

4 And thou shalt not be taken from the earth until this work is done, for this is the work I have called thee to do, and I have all power, even over life and death;

5 Therefore, worry not as to the things of the flesh for I AM, thy God, looketh down upon thee and watcheth over thee, and what greater protection can any have than this?

6 As I have told thee before, if this work is to be done by this generation, that is the work of the Church of Jesus Christ in Christian Fellowship, then it must be done by they whom I have called, for thou has thy duties, and other duties have I given unto thy brothers and thy sisters;

7 Thus I say unto thee: Learn patience, for all things shall be done in my way and in my time, and the work that thou doest is to prepare the way for my coming, for my people are not yet ready;

8 Yea, thou hast seen the pride of their hearts, and felt my pain in my peoples, and thou hast not walked away, this in spite of thy weakness;

9 But behold, it is in thy weakness that thou hast been strong, for thou doest not these things for thine own glory, nor for reward, but for my glory, and because I have asked it of thee,

10 Yea thou have been faithful to our covenant made in thy youth, and for this I am well pleased, and thy sins are forgiven thee;

11 I have seen thy deeds and found thee worthy, worry not therefore upon the opinions of mankind, for the darkness cannot comprehend the light, no not at all.

12 Go forth and continue in this, my labor, and build up mine vineyard in my name, and fulfill thy calling in faith, steadfastly and be thou my rock, unmovable, Even so, Amen.

Revelation 27

A Revelation to Kristine

Revelation given to Kristine Ferriman, February 2020 in Miamisburg Ohio. This revelation is Section 118b in Doctrines of the Saints.

1 And unto my servant Kristine, my Elect Lady: What more can I say unto thee than that which I have already[a] said?

2 The time is now at hand to restore all things, and the keys of the kingdom have been given thee, thou art called and thou hast heeded my call,

3 Yet the things of this world way heavy upon thee, and time is fleeting; therefore I say unto thee that this duty is not given unto thee alone.

4 Yea, others too have I called and set apart to help thee, yet thou must take the lead, thou must call forth the daughters of Zion and oversee this, my work.

5 And this thou shall do, for thou art faithful; yea thou wast faithful in thy first estate, and thou shall be faithful here as well;

6 Therefore, seek my council in prayer, seek the council of thy husband, for he shall support thee, and seek they that have been called; yea, call unto thee two councilors to assist thee in this work, and seek too their wisdom;

7 Yea, do this and all things shall be done even as I will, Even so, Amen.

Notes:

a   See DoS 8b.

Revelation 28

A Revelation to Alexei

Revelation given to Alexei Christopher Mattanovich February 2020 in Miamisburg Ohio. This revelation is Section 118c in Doctrines of the Saints.

1 Unto my servant Alexei I say: As I told[a] thee before, thou art a shepherd in my name and in my vineyard, and I have called thee as a talmidim, a disciple, my shaliaḥ, an Apostle in my name,

2 For thou art an emissary, a teacher, a messenger, and a special witness of HaShem; but in this task thou are not to be alone, for many are called though few are chosen.

3 And I say unto thee: I have called many apostles in these, the last days, for the benefit of my Churches,

4 And thou shall seek and thou shall find, and thou shall call eleven brethren to assist thee, for thou art the chief apostle of the Brotherhood in my Fellowship, and the co-president of the twelve for the Order of the Ministry in this, my vineyard;

5 And ye shall behold that these shall come to thee, sent from me, from all walks of life, and from all corners of the earth, and from different parts of my vineyard,

6 And these shall raise their voices with thee, and ye, as one, shall cry teshuvah unto my people.

7 And now I say unto thee: My work has been placed before thy feet, and thou hast been given thy mitzvah; therefore go forth unto thy duty; Even so, Amen.

Notes:

a   See DoS 12c.

Revelation 29

A Revelation to Victoria

Revelation given to Victoria Ramirez February 2020 in Miamisburg Ohio. This revelation is Section 118d in Doctrines of the Saints.

1 Unto my servant Victoria I say: thou art a shepherd in my name and in my vineyard, and I have called thee as a talmidim, a disciple, my shaliaḥ, even an Apostle in my name,

2 For thou art an emissary, a teacher, a messenger, and a special witness of HaShem; yea and thou art a diamond in my crown, yea even a diamond with a thousand facets.

3 And I say unto thee: I have called many Apostles in these, the last days, for the benefit of my Churches; yet in this day not many that I have called have been chosen from the daughters of Zion, yet I have called them;

4 And thou shall seek them out, they whom I have called, and thou shall find them, and thou shall call ten more of my daughters,

5 For thou art the chief apostle of the Sisterhood in my Fellowship, and the co-president of the twelve for the Order of the Ministry in this, my vineyard:

6 And ye shall behold that these shall come to thee, sent from me, from all walks of life, and from all corners of the earth, and from different parts of my vineyard,

7 And these shall raise their voices with thee, and ye, as one, shall cry teshuvah unto my people;

8 And thou shalt work with the Elect Lady to help organize my daughters, they too shall be one in me, yea even the daughters of Zion.

9 And now I say unto thee: Go fourth, O my Daughter of Zion; for thou hast been given thy mitzvah and it is thy duty; Even so, Amen.

Revelation 30

A Revelation to FayEllen

Revelation given to Fayellen Kraig Ely February 2020 in Miamisburg Ohio. This revelation is Section 118e in Doctrines of the Saints.

1 Unto my servant FayEllen I say: thou art a shepherd in my name and in my vineyard, and I have called thee as a talmidim, a disciple, my shaliaḥ, an Apostle in my name;

2 For thou art an emissary, a teacher, a messenger and a special witness of me; and I called thee in thy youth, and thou hast been a witness in my name for many years, and thou hast faithfully served.

3 And now I have called thee out of the many apostles in these, the last days, for the benefit of my Churches, to help build up and unite my people, to help build my Fellowship and the daughters of Zion.

4 And I say unto thee: Many trials hast thou faced, and in these thou were not alone, for I was with thee in the fire, and I walked with thee, and I surrounded thee with mine angels, yea and these did and do watch over thee.

5 And why shouldest thou be placed in the fire? Was it for the sins of thy youth or to test thy worth? I say unto thee nay, these were not to prove thee nor to reprove thee,

6 For I knewest thou before thou wast born, and there I called thee and there did I set thee apart, and I know thee better than thou could ever understand by the understanding of this world.

7 But all these things were done that the world may know what I know of thee, that thou art a diamond in my crown, and thou hast shined forth in all thou hast been through, and for this thou art blessed.

8 And now it is given thee to help prepare this generation for as long as thou art able, and to prophesy unto this generation of the goodness of God.

9 And behold, there are many youth born in this day and even unto this very hour, that await thy words, to hear thy story, for it is sacred; for thy story is my story, and in it shall these gain strength.

10 And thou art a daughter of Zion, and thou art called to help gather my daughters unto me, to cry teshuvah to my people that they might cry no more in the wilderness, but to see that their salvation is come,

11 Therefore, tell thy sacred story, even the story of thy faith, that through thee others may be empowered and illuminated by my Spirit.

12 And now I say unto thee: My work has been placed before thy feet, and thou hast been given thy mitzvah, therefore go forth unto thy duty; Even so, Amen.

Revelation 31

A Revelation to Allen

Revelation given to Allen J. Broadus February 2020 in Miamisburg Ohio. This revelation is Section 118f in Doctrines of the Saints.

1 Unto my servant Allen I say: Blessed are thee in this thy labor, and thou hast been called to lead my people and to build Churches in my name.

2 Yea, and I have called thee as a talmidim, a disciple, my shaliah; an apostle of the Seventy in my name, for thou art an emissary a teacher, a messenger and a special witness of me.

3 And know thou this: That if my works are to be done by this generation, then it must be done by they whom I have called, for thou has thy duties, and other duties have I given unto thy brothers and thy sisters;

4 And what are thy duties? To find others, my lost sheep and my shepherds, to set them apart as Pastors and Bishops, and Evangelists in my name, for it is these that shall labor in my vineyards.

5 Behold, not all fruits are fully ripe when they are plucked, therefore think not that thou must forgo and do all alone, yea some may fall but these must be free to do so.

6 Therefore, I say unto you: Seek out those that would do my work and advise them in their way, do not the labors for them.

7 Yea, and I have many awaiting thy call to help thee, even other Seventy, and the woman thou seeketh shall be thy helpmate in this thy calling, to preside as an equal over the Seventy, and she shall help build up the daughters of Zion.

8 But for now be patient and be ready, study the revelation on my priesthoods, be prayerful and ever watching for many are called and thou shall build up my kingdom throughout the earth.

9 Therefore, I say unto thee again: Go and do, be watchful, be ready, moving forward, ever forward with faith; Even so, Amen.

Revelation 32

A Revelation to Anni Rose

Revelation given to Anni Rose February 2020 in Miamisburg Ohio.
This revelation is Section 118g in Doctrines of the Saints.

1 Unto my servant Lorrian I say: I, HaShem, have called thee, and set thee apart, and all thy life have I been thy teacher, though I have come unto thee in many names and many guises,

2 And I have not always found thee well, and thou hast not always heard or heeded my voice; yet thou hast sought me diligently, and I have called thee and set thee apart, and thou art a Matriarch[a] in my name;

3 Yea, I have brought thee up and instructed thee that thou might help others find what they seek, even a balance between the earth and the heavens that are my creation,

4 And this that they might see my creation as I see my creation, to find the joy in my creation, even as I have created the heavens and the earth with such joy!

5 Behold, to those that seek me I say: Beware the double edged sword, for it is the sword of truth and the sword of truth sways neither to the right nor to the left, but is in perfect balance on the straight path;

6 Thus, thou too must find balance on my straight path; for narrow is the gate and one false step may cause such great pain unto many, even as if it were the shedding of blood.

7 Therefore, I say unto thee: It is better that thou never set foot upon my path than to fall to the right or to the left upon the sword, for the truth is a hard thing for mankind to bear;

8 Yet unto those that shall walk my path of truth and stay holy; unto these shall their joy be made full, and such joy it is!

9 Wherefore my daughter, find patience in thy heart; for all things shall be done in my way and in my time,

10 And those that shall not heed my word, to do my will to their blessing, shall do my will to their detriment, for my will shall be done in all things.

11 And thou hast walked my path, and carried my sword, and thou hast faltered; but I was there to pick thee up, yea, even now, and thy sins are forgiven thee:

12 And for this cause was Raphael, who is known unto thee as Melchizedek, sent unto you; that thou should be ordained as his hand,

13 For thou art Magdalene, and thou hast been called to carry the oil, and thou hast come prepared;

14 Therefore, I say unto thee: Share thy oil, even the knowledge that thou hast been given, with those that would be wise virgins,

15 Teach these that they are to keep oil to spare and be not like those foolish virgins that they should go out to buy oil when I, the Bridegroom, shall come at last unto my Shekinah.

16 And who are these virgins? I say unto thee that all those that come unto me with a pure heart and a contrite spirit are virgins, for these are made whole in me, and these are pure of heart.

17 Yea, and thou need not do this work alone, for I shall send others unto thee, and thou shalt work together with these to teach them; yea serve with they that I shall send unto thee, and together teach teshuvah in my name.

18 And for this cause have I called thee and others: to help raise up these, my people, in this wicked generation; to bring my Israel[b] to teshuvah, and to teach in my name:

19 For I have given thee to eat of the fruit of the tree of the knowledge of good and evil, that thou mayest eat freely and without consequence, for thou hast waited to partake with my blessing and my permission, for thou art mine;

20 And thou hast eaten too of the tree of life with my blessing, and unto thee there shall be no curse, except thou should forget me, thy first love, and in so doing should shed the blood of the innocent.

21 And if ye abide in my Law, which is the Law of Love (to love the Lord thy God and likewise love thy neighbors as thy self),

22 And if ye shall keep my Covenants, all those that I have made between me and thee,

23 And if thou shall shed not innocent blood, to lead others away from their first love[c],

24 Then ye shall come forth in the first resurrection, to inherit thrones, kingdoms, principalities, and powers, dominions all heights and depths, and thy glory shall be a fullness and a continuation of thy seed forever and ever.

25 Therefore, I have called thee to teach my people, even my Israel[b], my Law, and to teach of the balance between the heavens and the earth that my people might gain their inheritance;

26 For thou are a prophetess and a judge in my name, yea even a Matriarch[a], like unto my servants Sarah, and Thecla, and Eliza Snow, to teach, and to preach teshuvah in my name;

27 Yea, thou art my Church; therefore, seek thee my kingdom, and all good things shall be added unto thee.

28 And now I say unto thee: Go fourth, O my Daughter of Zion; for thou hast been given thy mitzvah and it is thy duty; Even so, Amen.

Notes:

a   See DoS 114.

b   See 2c.

c   See Alma 19:1-18 RAV, 39:1-12a OPV.

Revelation 33

A Revelation to Johnathan

Revelation given to David Ferriman February 2020 in Miamisburg Ohio. This revelation is Section 118h in Doctrines of the Saints.

1 Unto my servant Johnathan I say: I have called thee and set thee apart in these, the last days, to organize the Low Priesthood, or the

Levites[a], yea and this because of thy lineage, for thou art of Levi and of Ephraim,

2 And so, I have set thee apart to be mine right hand, to gather those of the lineage of Levi and of Aaron, and those called to the Low Priesthood[b], both the male and the female;

3 And thou shall be even as Aaron, to watch over my peoples, to help gather Israel[c] for this the last time, and to help unite my Churches.

4 And this thou shalt not do alone, for thou shall call councilors to aid and guide thee, and I have set apart a woman to help thee in gathering the daughters of Miriam, be they the literal descendants of Levi, the sons and daughters of Aaron and of Miriam[d], or be they called to the Low Priesthood.

5 And none shall call these but me, and I shall call them through thee, my chosen servant, and thou shalt anoint the men, and the daughter of Levi that thou shalt call shalt thou anoint, and she shall then anoint the daughters of Miriam.

6 And thou shall call two brothers to counsel with thee in me, for when two or three gather in my name, there am I; and the Daughter of Miriam that thou shall call, she shall call two daughters as councilors to counsel with her in me;

7 And together these five shall lead the Levites as the High Priests and High Priestesses with thee, even the Archbishopric[e] of my Churches.

8 And ye shall call upon others of the house of Ephraim to sit with thee and advise thy council, but all decisions are thine, yea thou art the one I have called and set apart,

9 And when thou art great of age, or no longer fit to bear the burden of thy calling, thou shalt call another in thy stead.

10 And ye, my council of Levites, shall send out emissaries unto the Churches of Christ, to represent my Levites, and these shall report back to thee,

11 And if a Levite feels called to one church over another, unto that church shall thou send them,

12 And if a church should reject my Levites, thou shall send unto them an emissary in peace and in righteousness, that my will be done in all things.

13 And when thou shall gather the Levites, thou shall call upon wise men and women rich in the knowledge and wisdom of God,

14 And these shall teach the Levites of their duties as they have been instructed in the Torah and in the Doctrine and Covenants, and in other revelations of this day that ye shall find pleasing unto me;

15 But condemn not any of the writings nor any of the Churches, for should these repent and come to me in teshuvah then shall all rejoice, therefore speak not ill of any of the Churches that no ill will should be born.

16 And thy people shall be my judges, and keep the peace; wherefore prepare thee my Levies to be my peace keepers and the mediators of my Word.

17 And I say unto thee, my servant Johnathan, thou are to join none of my Churches that thou should be an impartial judge.

18 Yea, but all they of my Churches that accept thee and my Levites may anoint thy head with oil as a sign that they shall heed thy word and the word of thy counsel.

19 And there have and there will be those that try to persuade thee to follow them, and to be the head of the Levites in their churches, and to forsake mine Churches, unto these shalt thou say: Nay, but I am for the Lord.

20 And thou shall not sit in the councils of any Churches, but shall appoint others to represent thee in such works, even as called by the Holy Spirit through prophecy and revelation.

21 Therefore I say unto thee now: Go and seek and thou shall find, for thou has been called to raise up this generation in righteousness,

22 Yea, thou are a High Priest in my name, and a Bishop of Bishops, even an archbishop[e], and I shall not call another should thou reject thy call until thy passing, for thou shall do my work or I shall work through thee in manners of which thou shall not be aware,

23 For I am God, and all things are done, even as I will, yet so much the better it is for those I have chosen if they should follow me.

24 And now I say unto thee: My work has been placed before thy feet, and thou hast been given thy mitzvah; therefore, go forth unto thy duty; Even so, Amen.

Notes:

a   See DoS 112.
b   The Priesthood of the Earth or given to prepare the Earth.
c   See DoS 2c.
d   See Exodus 15:20, Megillah 14a.
e   Archbishop is a Greek term for High Priest or High Priestess, a simpler way of saying "High Priest in my name, and a Bishop of Bishops.

Revelation 34

A Revelation to Doug

Revelation given to Doug Hatten February 2020 in Miamisburg Ohio. This revelation is Section 118i in Doctrines of the Saints.

1 Unto my servant Doug I say: Thou hast been a traveler in my name, and a teacher, and a healer; for thou art a choice disciple;

2 And I have called thee and set thee apart to do a work in my name, and behold this is not a work of the world, to judge the actions of men, but to unite my people, that they may be one as my Israel.

3 And to this end hast thou been born, to unite my peoples; and to this end has thou been called to the Levitical Priesthood[a] as a traveling Bishop and a High Priest in Zion, and this because of thy lineage, for thou art of Levi and of Ephraim.

4 And by thy blood[b], thou art born into the Levitical Priesthood, as a son of Aaron, and not by the laying on of the hands of men;

5 And by thy covenant that thou didst make with me as a son of Ephraim I have called thee to the High Priesthood[a]; not of men but thou hast been ordained by the angel to hold the High Priesthood.

6 And all these things that I have set thee to hath been for thy good, and for thy experience,

7 That thou may know of a surety, both in the spirit and of the flesh, that no man may lead my Churches, except that man be the very Son of Man, yea the Great I AM, and I am He.

8 And I have called thee to work with Johnathan^c the Levite, my High Priest, to seek the unity of my Saints; to call men and women to teshuvah, and to teach them of me that they might accept the gifts that the Spirit has bestowed upon them.

9 Behold, thou hast seen the trappings of men: Ego, pride, greed, and sin pitting brother against brother, and sister against sister, and Saint against Saint;

10 But the time for such trivial matters has passed, for the Hour of the Gentiles has come and gone^d and the earth has been found wanting,

11 Wherefore, I have called thee, and I have set thee apart that no man may lay claim upon thee, and I ask thee to unite my Saints in teshuvah;

12 Yea, I ask thee to be a bridge as a Bishop and talmidim, as one of my shaliaḥ; for thou art an emissary, a teacher, a messenger, and a special witness of HaShem.

13 And two tasks shall I give thee to help thee fulfill my call: and the first is that thou shall remind my Saints of mine Holy Days, yea even the days of remembrance of the Everlasting Covenant that I have made between me and my Israel;

14 For behold, the days of the sacrifice of animals are past, and all that is required of thee in sacrifice is a broken heart and a contrite spirit, and this sacrifice shall be given again on my Holy Days.

15 And the second is that thou should be a bridge between the Saints of the Restoration between the Levites and Churches that thou would be sent to.

16 And I have spoken unto my servant David, and he has known that thou art a Bishop; but if thou art to fulfill his desire that thou should sit upon the Council of Fifty in the Fellowship, understand that this is

something between me, and thee, and my servant Johnathan, if thou shall accept this call,

17 But know that it is my will that thou should be a bridge between my Levites and my Churches, and I have called both the Levites and the Church of Jesus Christ in Christian Fellowship to be parts of this bridge;

18 Therefore, I would ask thee to be a leader of men in helping my people on their journey in teshuvah, expanding the scriptures for the benefit of my Saints,

19 Watching over the storehouses, and preparing my people for trials of famine, both of the spirit and of the flesh.

20 And this is the work that I have called thee to do, and I see that thou hast been about my business, but think not that thou hast been sent alone, for there is much work to be done in gathering mine elect and the building of my temple.

21 Wherefore, go thee now and the Levites have been given their charge[a], and thus to hast thou too been charged with thy mitzvah; therefore, go forth unto thy duty; Even so, Amen.

Notes:

a   See DoS 112.
b   The Priesthood of the Heavens. See Revelation 114:4-5.
c   See Revelation 113f.
d   See Revelation 2c.
e   Archbishop is a Greek term for High Priest or High Priestess, a simpler way of saying "High Priest in my name, and a Bishop of Bishops."

Revelation 35

Of the Priesthoods

Revelation given to David Ferriman February 28, 2020, in Miamisburg Ohio. Words in italics were changed by Matriarch Anni Rose by inspiration from the Holy Spirit to give a clearer understanding of the intent of the revelation. This revelation is Section 119 in Doctrines of the Saints.

1 Thus saith the Lord unto my people of the Church of Jesus Christ in Christian Fellowship: Hearken, O ye people of my Church!

2 I see that ye have questions on those things which are written, and that ye wish to know of things not written, in regards to my Priesthood; therefore, I shall give unto thee this day these things for thy profit and learning.

3 Behold, come and see, and I shall show thee things that are of me, that are a mystery unto the world, but not a mystery unto me, and after this day no longer a mystery unto thee.

4 It has been said that there are, in my Churches, two priesthoods[a], namely: The High Priesthood, called the Melchizedek and Magdalene, and the Low or Levitical Priesthoods of Aaron and Miriam,

5 And the High Priesthood is of the Heavens, and the Low Priesthood is of the Earth, but all priesthood is of me;

6 For behold, in the beginning was the Word, and the Word was with the gods or the elohim[b], and the Word was YHVH, I AM, and in the beginning was created the elohim, and the heavens, and the earth;

7 But my *power and my* Priesthood is eternal; without father, without mother, without descent; having neither beginning of days nor end of life;

8 Therefore, all priesthood is given by God unto mankind from the eternal Elohim[c], and not by descent from father nor mother:

9 Know ye this: That all priesthood is as eternal as the Elohim, and that thou too are eternal, having neither beginning of days nor end of life, and ye are elohim[b], and ye are given of that which ye are called from before the foundation of this world.

10 What then is the High and the Low Priesthoods? The Low is of the Earth, and the High is of the Heavens, which is to say that the Low priesthood is to prepare the Earth for the things of Heaven, and the High is to bring the Heavens to the Earth; this that all may be one, for all is one in me.

11 Yet these are one priesthood, how then can this be if all are one in me? I say unto thee that thou, O man, thinkest plainly and understand not the things that are of me.

12 In aforetime[d] here upon this earth all these were one priesthood in my name, and the Low Priesthood was given to men and women and pasted[e] down father to son, mother to daughter, unto those that were worthy and called by the Holy Ghost in the Patriarchal and Matriarchal order,

13 And many grew, Grace by Grace, in their ministry from the Low to the High and used the gifts of the Spirit as moved by the Holy Ghost, for the Holy Ghost is my messenger to administer in all priesthood, or all they to whom these gifts have been given.

14 But after the Flood my people were scattered and divided, and to keep out priestcraft and that mankind might have my power and priesthood, these things were hidden from the world and became lost and deluded.

15 And when I came in the flesh, I came to restore order to my people, and thus it is that there are three orders of priesthood:

16 One is the High Priesthood of Melchizedek, the King of Salem, and of Magdalene, the Apostle and fisher of men, given by an oath and covenant, having power and authority over all given from the Heavens to the Earth, holding the keys and the power of endless life, and the Keys to seal on Earth unto Heaven.

17 One is of the Patriarchy and Matriarchy, of the marriage of Abraham and Sarah, passed down in the blood from father to son, mother to daughter; and it is by this priesthood that the true Levites are called and anointed unto me.

18 One is the Low Priesthood, or the Levitcal as it is now called, to administer in outward ordinances, preparing mankind to receive their King.

19 And I am Yeshua HaMashiach, Jesus who is the very Christ; the heir of the Kingdom, the only begotten of the Father according to the flesh, and I hold the keys over all this world, giving all glory to the Father.

20 Of the Low and High Priesthoods ye are aware, and these have been made known, what then of the Patriarchy and Matriarchy? I say unto thee that thou dost not know, nor dost thou comprehend these things!

21 For behold, thou seest through the eyes of the churches of men, and not of me, and so I say unto thee that men give keys to the workings of their flesh, but I give keys to those that are prepared to receive them.

22 And so it is that the Patriarchal and Matriarchal Priesthood gives men and women the power to pass down both the Low and the High Priesthoods by the laying on of hands,

23 Were it not so then only those who were born from the loins of Aaron and Miriam should hold these keys to prepare the Earth, and only those ordained by an angel should hold the High Priesthood.

24 For as it says in the Book of Melchizedek^e: And thus, having been approved of YHVH, Melchizedek was ordained a High Priest after the order of the covenant which God made with Enoch, this being after the order of the Son of God, which order came not by man, nor the will of man, neither by father nor mother, neither by beginning of days nor end of years, but of Elohim; and it was delivered unto men by the calling of the voice of Ruach Elohim, according to His own will, unto as many as believed on Hashem.

25 Yet men are called in the Churches of Christ to be ordained to this High Priesthood, and they are called of men and women, and ordained of men and women,

26 And by the power of the Patriarchal and Matriarchal Priesthoods these things are of me, so long as they are done in my name and in righteousness.

27 And behold, the keys to the Patriarchal and Matriarchal Priesthood are that of prophet, seer, and revelator; were it not so men and women would know not who to call and who to ordain,

28 And this is why I say unto thee that ye shall call a Patriarch and Matriarch to be in thy council, even the Council of Elders, and to lead the High Councils over the other Evangelists, or the traveling Bishops

and Pastors; to be a bridge between the things of the Heavens and the things of the Earth;

29 For these are offices of the High Priesthood doing the works of the Low priesthood, for first shall be last; and the last shall be first, and the Heavens are all around thee, yet the Earth is yet unaware,

30 For all things are a straight line unto me, beginning with the outward ordinances and the offering of sacrifices, growing in my Grace unto the works of power and blessings, and know ye that all these things are of me.

31 Therefore, now I say unto thee again: Build my temple up that I may send Elijah the prophet unto thee, and there ye shall learn more of the Patriarchal and Matriarchal Priesthood,

32 That thy covenants may be made to seal the hearts of the fathers to the children, and the children to the fathers,

33 That thy anointings and sealings given unto all those that have been called and elected in my name are made sure, or in other words, that thou might see me face to face, that ye may know that I AM from everlasting to everlasting;

34 Yea, I invite thee to come unto me, that ye may know me, and that, being doubtless, thou might feel of my hands and touch thee my wounds.

35 These words are given unto thee to be received by they that are pure before me; therefore keep these things in thy hearts, that the wisdom of the eternities may rest upon thy minds. Even so, Amen.

Notes:

a   See Doctrines of the Saints 5a:1.
b   Elohim (lowercase "e"): "gods," here denoting the Children of Elohim (the children of Yah, God the Father & Mother, or the Masculine and Feminine aspects or God.), or the Children of God.
c   Elohim (capital "E"): "Gods." Can denote the Godhead or Trinity as a whole, God the Father & Mother, or the Masculine and Feminine aspects or God.
d   DoS 5b:1-4
e   See Appendix 1.
f   See Melchizedek 1:3-5 in the plates of brass.

Revelation 36

Together in Sisterhood

The following revelation was given to Kristine, the Elect Lady and co-president of the Church of Jesus Christ in Christian Fellowship in Ohio as early as November of 2019. She did not, however feel the time was right to write this revelation down. On May 19, 2020, being in the Spirit of the Lord in Miamisburg, Ohio, she felt the time had come and recorded the following revelation, recorded as Section 10g in Doctrines of the Saints.

1 Listen Israel to the voice of the Lord: I, the Lord your God, am displeased with the patriarchal hierarchy that has been besieged upon My daughters for generations upon generations.

2 My daughters have too long been pushed down, their voices silenced, and their priesthood power and authority ignored.

3 In these, the latter days, I have set into motion the circumstances and have provided the tools needed for My daughters in Zion to reclaim their spiritual power and their birthright.

4 I command My daughters to amplify their voices, together in Sisterhood, and uplift and enrich one another so that balance between My sons and daughters can be found on the earth once again.

5 My daughters; do not seek to be more powerful or mightier than your brothers, yet you should stand with strength and steadfastness next to them, as equals, and join together as one to do My work.

6 My sons; open thy spirits and thy minds to My daughters, hearken ye unto their voices, seek ye to uplift and work one with another, and seek ye not to dominate over them.

7 This assembly of spirits and minds is fundamental in order for My plans to be fulfilled.

8 I have more to say to My daughters, but for now this is enough; organize yourselves, together as a Sisterhood, and I will further make My will known as it befits My work. Amen.

Revelation 37

The Council of Fifty

Declaration of the purpose and function of the Council of Fifty of the Church of Jesus Christ in Christian Fellowship, given by inspiration through David and Kristine Ferriman June 3, 2020. This revelation is Section 50a in Doctrines of the Saints.

1 In the Church of Jesus Christ in Christian Fellowship, the First Presidency over the Church may call men and women of all walks of life, from any of the Churches of Christ upon the earth, or any of those sympathetic to the Christian teachings and way of life;

2 And these shall be called to unite the Saints, to unite God's creation in all that has been revealed and all that will be revealed, from the creation of the earth to the return of Christ our King:

3 And this Council shall exist as a part of the Order of the Ministry, consisting of twenty-five brothers and twenty-five sisters; and the First Presidency shall be their presidency.

4 And these shall be brothers and sisters, one to another and to the World, working in the Order of the Ministry under the direction of the First Presidency, being sent forth to represent them and the God that has called them unto all the world.

5 And these shall endeavor to proclaim peace and unity in the face of adversity, to act as representatives of the Living Constitution of the Kingdom of God, to be a force of peace and order in the midst of chaos;

6 To assist in the Works of the Lord as the Saints and those that would call themselves Saints, move from the creed of the Church to the Kingdom of God, where all that desire shall find a home and a place to dwell to find rest for their souls.

7 And this Council of Fifty shall be organized to run and to teach in the School of the Prophets, as organized by the First Presidency of the Church of Jesus Christ in Christian Fellowship;

8 And to assist the Presidency in all things they stand in need, to help them fulfill their duties and callings;

9 And, when necessary, to represent them in the judgment seat, by letter of appointment, which letter may only be used of the case to which it shall be assigned, and any judgment rendered may be taken to the First Presidency for approval or acquittal.

Revelation 38

The Seventies

A revelation given to David on June 3, 2020, with further revelation given through Kristine and David, as moved by the Holy Spirit. This revelation is Section 70a in Doctrines of the Saints.

1 Thus sayeth the Lord unto His servants: Behold my son and my daughter regarding the Councils of Seventy, ponder these things upon thy hearts and thy minds and I shall guide thee and show thee and inspire thee on how these things should be done in my Kingdom;

2 And thou shall take these to thy councils and together ye shall perfect them, and this shall be that my will shall be known unto my people by the voices of my servants: Even so, Amen.

3 ¶ There shall be appointed in the Brotherhood of Christ Seven Presidents of the Assembly of Seventy called the Assembly of Seven, and these shall be special witnesses, High Priests to the Most High God.

4 And in the Sisterhood of Christ, there shall be appointed Seven Presidents of the Council of Seventy called the Council of Seven, and these shall be special witnesses, High Priestesses of the Most High God.

5 And of these, one shall be named President of the Seven Presidents in both the Assembly in the Brotherhood, and of the Council in the Sisterhood, respectively;

6 And these two presidents shall be the co-presidents of the Seven Presidents of Order of the Ministry; also known as the Quorum of Seven, and these shall five others from the Council of Seven and the

Assembly of Seven, and the Spirit shall move them, as councilors over all of the Seventy in the Fellowship.

7 And these five, with the first two shall be the Seven Presidents of the Council of Seventy, and these shall call from their ranks thirty-five High Priests and thirty five High Priestesses each to join the Order of the Ministry; to preach the Gospel to the whole earth as special witnesses of the Resurrected Jesus, and to the Church upon the Earth.

8 And the Seven Presidents, as a quorum, are equal in authority to the quorum of Apostles, who are equal in authority to the three Presidents, who are the First Presidency; and their duties are spoken of in these Doctrines of the Saints.

9 And the Seven Presidents shall be given their jurisdiction from the co-presidents of the Quorum of Seven.

10 And the Seven Presidents are to be called by the First Presidency and the Council of Elders, and these shall assist the Seven Presidents in calling the other Seventy.

11 ⸿ And, as it is stated in the Book of the Law of the Lord: The twelve Apostles shall select seventy Elders.

12 And these shall be the Seventy Elders, thirty-five from the Brotherhood and thirty five from the Sisterhood;

13 And they will hold the office of Elder, even if these have been ordained a High Priest or a High Priestess.

14 And these chosen men and women will work in the Order of the Ministry, teaching the Word of God, and preach the Gospel of Jesus Christ to all peoples; working to unite the Saints, under the direction of the Apostles.

15 And the Apostles will call one from the Brotherhood of Christ and one from the Sisterhood of Christ to sit in council with the Apostles, but not to vote with them;

16 But they will provide council and will lead the Seventy Elders, as the Law of the Lord states: shall set them in order.

17 And these Seventy Elders are not required to travel but should remain where they are and seek to serve their families and are called to represent the Apostles as they travel throughout the world.

Revelation 39

New Year of the Trees

Revelation given to Ruth Mauldin of the First Presidency of the Church of Jesus Christ in Christian Fellowship, by divine decree, to reinstate the Full Moon services. This revelation is Section 123 in Doctrines of the Saints.

1 In December of 2020, The Sisterhood of Christ was working on their Tu BiShvat service.

2 Tu BiShvat is the holy day originally celebrating the Divine Feminine, our Heavenly Mother; her symbol is the tree and the full moon, and thus this holy day is known as Rosh HaShanah La'Ilanot literally New Year of the Trees.

3 As Ruth Mauldin was working on the program, and feeling overwhelmed, Heavenly Mother came unto her, saying: If you do this, I will take care of the rest.

4 On January 27, 2021 the Sisterhood of Christ held the first known modern Full Moon service, restoring this holy day to Israel and allowing Saints everywhere to properly worship the Lord in celebration of the Divine Feminine.

5 In doing this the Sisterhood of Christ fulfilled the words of King David: Blow the shofar at the time of the New Moon, at the Full Moon, on our solemn feast day; for this is a statute for Israel, a Law of the God of Jacob.

Revelation 40

Apostles in Fellowship

The following revelation was given to David January 22, 2021, on the will of the Lord for the Apostles of the Church of Jesus Christ in Christian Fellowship. This revelation is Section 12g in Doctrines of the Saints.

1 Thus sayeth the Lord unto his servants, the Apostles of the Fellowship of Christ, and His friends: Be ye one, even as I and the Father are one, that ye may glorify my name.

2 Behold, I say unto thee at this time, four of ye have been called and one has been taken, and another too shall be soon taken if they do not repent of their transgressions.

3 And I say unto mine apostles: I have called thee to be fishers of men, to call men and women of all walks of life in my name; therefore, seek out my sheep and find them that they know that I love them even as I love each of thee.

4 It is the duty of mine Apostles to seek out other Apostles that shall hear and heed my call; twelve men and twelve women to represent me, as special witnesses of the Lord Jesus Christ in my Fellowship:

5 And until six men and six women are found, all of my Apostles shall remain as a part of the Council of Fifty to support the First Presidency.

6 And once these twelve are found, the six brothers shall council together, as the Apostles for the Brotherhood of Christ; and the six sisters shall council together, as the Apostles for the Sisterhood of Christ; and by the unanimous voice of these shall their presidency be chosen.

7 And they shall meet once a year to choose by the voice of my Spirit and by prophecy and revelations their respective presidents.

8 And these presidents shall be the co-presidents of the Quorum of Apostles in the Fellowship of Christ, in the Order of the Ministry;

9 And these shall bring with them five brethren and five sistren, selected by them and unanimously sustained by their fellows, and these shall form the Quorum of Apostles of the Church of Jesus Christ in Christian Fellowship.

10 And the duties of the Apostles in the Order of the Ministry are to unite[a] my Saints in Fellowship and to call, and teach, and train, and lead the Council of Seventy Elders that shall assist in my works.

11 Behold, each of thee are my Light in the world, ye are not the Light, but ye have been sent forth as fishers of men, sent forth to bear witness of that Light; and I AM the light and life of mankind, and ye are mine;

12 Therefore, go forth and do my work, seek out those called to serve in my name, be they of the Seventy Elders or fellow Apostles, and seek ye my face that where thou be, there am I also; even so, Amen.

Notes:

a   See Appendix 6

Revelation 41

The Lord's Supper

Revelation given to David Ferriman January 24, 2021, on the Sacrament of Communion. A question was asked about incorporating the Divine Feminine into the Communion prayer. David has asked the Lord about this before with no clear answer. Because of this, he advised that the service stick to the prayer in the Book of Mormon given by Moroni, in the Book of Avahr has reviled by God to Oliver Cowdery, and in the Doctrines of the Saints as reveled to Joseph Smith Jr. After partaking of the Sacrament of Communion, David received the following revelation, recorded as Section 15f in Doctrines of the Saints.

1 Thus saith the Lord: Behold, the Sacrament of Communion represents the marriage supper between the Shekinah and the Father, between the bride and the bridegroom, between the Saints of Zion and their Christ;

2 Therefore, these, the words[a] of the Eucharist, shall not be altered, nor shall they be changed; for they represent ordnance of the marriage covenants between the Creator and His Creation, between the Church and myself, even I, Jesus Christ;

3 For this ye do as a Sacrament, in remembrance of me; and I Am the Lamb that was sacrificed.

4 Yea behold, both masculine and feminine elements are presented in the Supper of Communion: the plate representing the Earth, my creation, and the cup representing my mercy;

5 So too doth the bread represent my body, which was broken for ye, from the things that had been planted and grown from the Earth; and the wine, the New Covenant made in my blood, which was shed that all might live again with our Elohim;

6 Therefore, this ye shall do in remembrance of my life, my death, and my resurrection; to renew the New and Everlasting Covenant, in fellowship with the Saints of Zion gathered at my table; and this too, in memory of the supper yet to come:

7 Do this and the gifts of the Spirit shall be made manifest in the presence of thy faith in the hearts of the daughters of Zion, for those that do so faithfully and in obedience.

8 Behold, it is not good to overstep beyond the mark that has been set, but see that ye do all things in both knowledge and wisdom, finding balance in all things;

9 Do this in reverence and rejoicing, and ye shall see that the heavens and the earth are one, and God in the creation; Even so, Amen.

Note:

    a.   See Moroni 4-5, Avahr 34:21, 23, and Doctrines of the Saints 2a:68, 70.

Revelation 42

Of Tabernacles and Temples

The following revelation was received by David on the morning of January 30, 2021. This revelation is Section 124 in Doctrines of the Saints.

1 Verily, verily I say unto you, my friends of the Fellowship of Christ: Your prayers have been heard of the Lord of the Sabaoth; therefore, fear not my children of the everlasting covenant;

2 Let your hearts be comforted and rejoice evermore; for ye have been sealed in the renewed testament; give thanks therefore, and all things shall work together for your good and to my name's glory, saith the Lord of Hosts.

3 I have said unto thee: Build mine house, and you have come before me asking for instructions on building the Tent of the Congregation, even a tabernacle to take from place to place that I may have a house therein to dwell;

4 And even though this was not as I asked, it is for a wise purpose in me that ye shall do this thing; therefore, I shall guide thee even as I guided mine ancient Israel, with a cloud of smoke by the day and a fire at the night, for I AM the light and the life of the world.

5 ¶ Behold: the inner court of my temples, or the Holy of Holies, shall be set to the westernmost end, and it shall be 20 cubits, by 20 cubits, by 20 cubits, which is to say 30 feet, by 30 feet, by 30 feet;

6 But for thy purposes at the present, it shall be 15 feet, by 15 feet, by 15 feet; and this too ye shall do for my synagogues, but my temples shall be 30 feet, by 30 feet, by 30 feet in my Holy of Holies.

7 And the Holy of Holies shall no more be kept hidden, but shall be used to house my bride, my Shekinah, even the congregation of my Church;

8 For ye are my body, wherefore ye are worthy to enter and partake of the supper of the covenant of our marriage, yea even the Sacrament of Communion:

9 Have I not asked thee to wear the tzitzits? And are these not a sign that ye are a royal generation, even a royal priesthood in my name?

10 And ye are the kings and queens, even the Priests and Priestesses of the Most High God, and therefore ye are worthy.

11 ¶ Set ye four poles to hang the four sheets, with an opening to the east that all might enter, and an opening to the west; and this shall be thy Eden as thou returneth unto me in teshuvah.

12 And in it ye shall place an altar, the ark of my covenant with thee, to be used to store the tools of thy ministry; and upon it ye shall bless all things that ye should bless unto me, and ye shall use it for the Sacrament of the Endowments, as ye have been instructed in the Book of Remembrance; and there ye shall read the words of my prophets.

13 And when it is not in use, ye shall keep the Book of the Law of the Lord open to my commandments there upon the altar, beginning even with this: I, YHVH thy Elohim, which brought thee out of the

land of Egypt, from the house of bondage; thou shalt have none other gods before me.

14 And this ye shall do, for this is mine house and my tabernacle; therefore, ye shall do this that all shall be reminded of my Law, my Torah.

15 ¶ And to the East of my Sanctuary shall be unto me an outer sanctuary, the outer court; yea, even the Holy Place, for giving instruction, and for times when there are people so numerous that they flow out from the Holy of Holies;

16 ʼ (Yod) And at the West part of this room, upon the sheet that shall divide the Holy of Holies to the west, and the Holy Place to the East, thou shall place upon the curtain the emblems of the Ministry:

17 The square for the justice of Elohim, and the compass for my mercy, and the symbol of my Holy Spirit and also a sign unto them and to all generations that every knee shall bow and every tongue confess that I, even Jesus, am the Christ: Son of the Living God.

18 ה (Hei) And at the north part of this room, ye shall place a table that shall house my shewbread, in remembrance of my Shekinah; and it shall be kept fresh at all times that my congregation shall be nourished;

19 And behold, if any shall come in, in want of bread, this thou shall give unto them to eat; therefor thou shall keep food aplenty that all may be edified in my name.

20 ו (Vav) And at the East part of this room, ye shall place an altar of incense at the entrance, in remembrance of the Father (and I am the Father, and the Father is in me);

21 And the altar shall be one cubit wide, and one cubit deep, and two cubits high; which is to say, one and a half feet wide, and one and a half feet deep, and three feet high;

22 And it shall bear rings upon the opposite sides, through which my priests and priestesses shall use poles to carry it;

23 And it shall be hollow, with a grate upon the top to collect the ashes; and it shall be cleaned upon the first day of every week.

24 And upon the altar ye shall pour oil for a dedication; but after this, it is pure, and no more oil shall be poured; but it shall be used to burn incense that a sweet savor shall be in mine house.

25 ה (Hei) And to the south ye shall place a table that shall house my menorah which shall hold seven lights which shall burn brightly to be as a light unto my people, in remembrance of my Spirit, that it may be with all they that shall enter;

26 And the menorah shall house seven lights for the seven days of my creation, and the seven archangels over the seven dispensations, for this is the time of the restoration of all things; and it shall be in the shape of a tree in remembrance of Eve, the mother of all living.

27 ¶ And behold: this outer court in my temple shall be 20 cubits, by 40 cubits, by 20 cubits, which is to say 30 feet, by 60 feet, by 30 feet;

28 But for thy purposes at the present, it shall be 15 feet, by 30 feet, by 15 feet; and this too ye shall do for my synagogues, but my temples shall be 30 feet, by 60 feet, by 30 feet in my Holy Place.

29 ¶ And to the North there shall be a Court of the Sisterhood, and it shall be for instructing the women and those that identify as women; and it shall open to the South into the Holy Place.

30 And this court shall be 20 cubits, by 40 cubits, by 20 cubits, which is to say 30 feet, by 60 feet, by 30 feet;

31 But for thy purposes at the present, it shall be 15 feet, by 30 feet, by 15 feet; and this too ye shall do for my synagogues, but my temples shall be 30 feet, by 60 feet, by 30 feet in this, the Court of Women.

32 And this Court shall have a curtain in the middle—two curtains that may be drawn apart for the whole of the Sisterhood, or closed that the Sisters of the Low Priesthood may meet to the East, and the Sisters of the High Priesthood may meet to the West;

33 And there shall be two openings to the South, that my Sisters might travel to and fro the outer court;

34 And there shall be an opening to the East and the West of this court, that my Daughters might enter as they please from the east and depart as they will from the West.

35 ❡ And to the South there shall be a Court of the Brotherhood, and it shall be for instructing the men and those that identify as men; and it shall open to the North into the Holy Place;

36 And this court shall be 20 cubits, by 40 cubits, by 20 cubits, which is to say 30 feet, by 60 feet, by 30 feet;

37 But for thy purposes at the present, it shall be 15 feet, by 30 feet, by 15 feet; and this too ye shall do for my synagogues, but my temples shall be 30 feet, by 60 feet, by 30 feet in this, the Court of Men.

38 And this Court shall have a curtain in the middle—two curtains that may be drawn apart for the whole of the Brotherhood, or closed that the Brothers of the Low Priesthood may meet to the East, and the Brothers of the High Priesthood may meet to the West;

39 And there shall be two openings to the North, that my Brothers might travel to and fro the outer court;

40 And there shall be an opening to the east and the west of this court, that my Sons might enter as they please from the east and depart as they will from the West.

41 ❡ And beyond the walls of my temples ye shall grow unto me sacred groves of oak trees, and of nut trees, and of trees bearing all manner of fruits;

42 And this ye shall do that my people and all of my creation may find nourishment and be filled of the good things of my creation.

43 And in these groves ye shall plant an altar, even as did my servant Jacob, that ye shall have a place to offer thy libations[a], and that my daughters shall once again have a place to sing and dance and have joy in their creation, as they did in the days of Miriam.

44 And it is my will that my daughters shall listen to my voice to know mine ordinances, and that they might restore the daughters of Israel to my ways;

45 Therefore, listen ye to my voice as spoken to my Elect Lady, and my Daughter of Zion, and my Dove bearing the olive branch; for these are the Miriam of thy days: the judge, and the restorer, and the bringer of peace.

46 ¶ And Behold, ye shall build also a place to baptize and wash clean those that would come unto me; and this ye shall do with wisdom, and as suited to the lands wherein ye shall dwell;

47 And if it shall be that thy mikveh[b] shall be built under the inner court, to the West, before the curtain of the Holy of Holies in my temples,

48 Or if ye desire to house thy mikveh in a room to the East of the outer court, in a court of the Gentiles, this too ye may do;

49 Therefore, do so as ye see fit as to thy mikveh for thy washings and thy Sacrament of Baptism in my synagogues and in my temples.

50 ¶ And this too shall ye build unto me, saith the Lord thy God: The Tent of the Presence; and this shall be as a meeting place for the Council of Elders and to know my will.

51 And at the first, this may be a small tabernacle unto me, even as a Holy of Holies being 15 feet, by 15 feet, by 15 feet;

52 But I would command ye to build me a house in the Center Place, even in Zion—that is Missouri—that ye may meet together once a year, that my will be known;

53 And this too shall be used by they that seek my face, and desire to dwell in my presence;

54 But behold, it is my will that all shall have a temple in their homes, that these might too be my synagogues and ye may seek my face wherever ye may be each day.

55 And when ye shall build the School of the Prophets in Zion, there shall thou build the Tent of the Presence, and then it shall be 30 feet, by 30 feet, by 30 feet.

56 And there too, at the School of the Prophets, ye shall build a mikveh for mine washings and anointings;

57 And there the tabernacle shall stand when it is not in use, that it may be used by the School as they see fit.

58 ¶ Behold, I say unto thee, David, and what I say to thee I say unto all the Saints of the Fellowship of Christ; and what I say unto the Fellowship I say unto all those that would be Saints, or that would call themselves mine:

59 Do not think that I ask this of thee that I might have a place to dwell, for all the earth is the footstool of my creation;

60 And think thee not that thou must enter mine house to know me or to dwell in my presence; for behold, I say unto thee: Where thou art, there am I also;

61 Thou doeth not come into my temples to be in my presence, but thou and thy fellow Saints bring my presence into mine house.

62 Yea, and why then do I ask thee: Build me a house that I may rest? This I do for thy sake, that my people may together find rest in fellowship in my presence;

63 Therefore, go ye and build a house in my name, that ye shall have a place to worship in my name, and to celebrate with thy fellow Saints the new moons, the full moons, the Sabbaths, and all other Holy Days that I, the Lord, have given thee.

64 And now I say unto thee: Go now, and build me a tabernacle, and build my temple, and unite my Saints in my name; even Jesus Christ, the Great I AM; Even so, Amen and Amen.

Notes:

a.   Libations: the pouring of liquids in ritual worship; libations were part of ancient Judaism, as mentioned in the Bible: "And Jacob set up a pillar in the place where he talked with him, even a pillar of stone: and he poured a drink offering thereon, and he poured oil thereon" (Genesis 35:14). When receiving this part of the revelation, David was given a vision of the door or curtains of the Holy of Holies being opened and a Priest declaring the new moon and pouring oil on a altar in a small grove outside the temple, after declaring the new month. And he saw a Priestess during a full moon as the altar, pouring water to nourish the grove after declaring the full moon.

b.   Mikveh or mikvah (Hebrew: מקווה /מִקְוֶה): a bath used for the purpose of ritual immersion (baptism) to achieve ritual purity.

Revelation 43

The Church of Jesus Christ in Christian Fellowship

On April 13, 2021, three members of the Council of Elders sent a list of nine items concerning the direction of the Church of Jesus Christ in Christian Fellowship. David took these questions and concerns to the Lord. In response, the Lord gave him the following revelation, which was first sustained by the First Presidency and then sent to the Council of Elders. This revelation is Section 125 in Doctrines of the Saints.

1 My son, David; thou hast come to me asking to know my will regarding the Church of Jesus Christ in Christian Fellowship:

2 Is the Fellowship of Christ a church? a religious movement? an idea? or is it something else altogether?

3 ¶ Behold, O man, the will of your God: The Church of Jesus Christ in Christian Fellowship is all these and more, for it is the very Kingdom of God.

4 ¶ Did I not tell thee: Unite my people in Kabbalah[a]? And thou didst seek to know the meaning of this.

5 And at the first thou thought Kabbalah meant the power of God, then thou thought Kabbalah was a way to help mankind understand my Word,

6 And then understood Kabbalah to be the holy traditions given to mankind of me through my servant Moses, and still thou thought Kabbalah to be something more.

7 And I say unto thee: it is all these and more: Yea, Kabbalah is a mysticism[b], a theology[c], and a thaumaturgy[d];

8 Kabbalah is the tradition of Israel, it is my doctrine, and thus it is a mysterious art, for my doctrine is too simple for mankind to comprehend.

9 ¶ And behold, therefore, I shall ask thee: What is the Church of Jesus Christ in Christian Fellowship? Did I not tell my servant Joseph Smith Jr. the meaning[e] of my Church?

10 My Church are all they that repenteth and cometh unto me; and this is my doctrine, for the spirit of contention is not of me, but is of the devil:

11 And they that cometh unto me shall humble themselves before me and be baptized in my name and shall be saved, for so is the Kingdom of God;

12 And the Church is my body, and the priesthood, or the power given me of the Father, is my blood; therefore, the Kingdom is the Church, and there in ye shall find many mansions.

13 ¶ How then shall ye of my Fellowship unite my people, my Israel, in Kabbalah? Doth not thy own laws[f] that ye wrote out and agreed upon say that the very purpose of the Fellowship of Christ is to establish a Christian Church with a School of the Prophets?

14 And how can ye be a Church and build up my Kingdom if ye do not teach they whom I shall send unto my Church?

15 And I did say[g] unto the First Presidency, through the mouth of my servant Joseph: Through you shall the oracles be given unto another; yea even unto the Church.

16 And how were these oracles to be given? Again, said[h] I through my servant Joseph: Through your administration the keys of the School of the Prophets, which I have commanded to be organized, that thereby they may be perfected in their ministry for the salvation of Zion, and the nations of Israel, and of the Gentiles, as many as will believe.

17 ¶ And this is thy ministry, and the ministry of all that are called of me unto all the Churches: Feed my sheep, seek out the lost and the lonely;

18 Therefore, find they that thou callest the spiritually homeless and shelter them in the bonds of my love, for this is my Law.

19 And I have one Law[i]: thou shalt love the Lord thy God with all thine heart, and with all thy soul, and with all thy might; and thou shalt love thy neighbor as thyself.

20 All they that add to the Law and to my Doctrine do so to their own peril, for I am a God of order and not or contention; therefore, fight not over theologies of man, but love one another in me.

21 ¶ As to those called to serve me in my Fellowship, I say: Thou, David, hath trodden too quickly, thou hast tried to walk further than thou art able, as I have warned[j] thee against.

22 Behold, how can my Fellowship have a quorum of Apostles with but so few acting apostles? But as I have told[k] thee, all are called to the Council of Fifty at the first;

23 Therefore, worry not about the Council of Elders, but the First Presidency shall oversee and care for my Fellowship, until such time as twelve are called and these chose[l] for themselves two to represent them in the Council of Elders.

24 Behold, I have given these, my commands; and until these are met there can be no quorum of Apostles, but Apostles within the Council of Fifty.

25 ¶ And thou and my servant Victoria did right to dissolve the Seventy, for they were too few in number;

26 Therefore, even as I have said[m], find and call seven brothers and seven sisters to be Seventy within the Council of Fifty;

27 And these shall be righteous, and as the Apostles, trained up in me by the School of the Prophets;

28 And these shall choose from among themselves seven, be these four brothers and three sisters or four sisters and three brothers it mattereth not,

29 And these shall establish the Quorum of Seven of the Fellowship of Christ to be established within the Order of the Ministry,

30 And from among them, they may choose one brother and one sister to represent them on the council, being the co-presidents of the Seventy; and I shall advise thee more at that time.

31 ¶ And of those that were willing to heed the call, Allen, Matthew, and Christian; behold, I say unto these: If thou desireth to heed my call and be a part of this council of Seven, study my Words and my works in the School of the Prophets until thou art ready that ye should train up those that I will call.

32 ¶ And unto Christian I say: continue as thou are in thy call as the Priest of the Fellowship of Christ that my holy days may be observed, even until a Levite is found; and this shall train you up in preparation for your place in my Kingdom.

33 ¶ As to thy call, my Fellowship, to unite my people, I say: accept those that all others reject with hope, joy, and happiness.

34 Worry not that there are those that judge others by the color of their skin, or their gender or sexual orientation, or in any way, for those who

seek to hear my voice and heed my call must soften their hearts to these, my children.

35 Homosexuality is neither a sin, nor a confusion, it is an eternal principle, for thus did I create them; and so too are my transgender children;

36 Therefore, exclude them not, hide them not, and forgo them not; for these are my children, and I say unto thee: bring these children unto me.

37 Worry not what the world shall say unto thee for obeying my Law and my doctrine, but be thou obedient and thy tolerance shall be a light in the darkness;

38 But know that this is my light, the very light of Christ, and the darkness shall comprehend[n] it not;

39 Therefore, let my love and my light shine forth through the darkness that these, my children, shall no longer be lost, but be found in me and find a home in thee.

40 This is my commandment to my Church and my Kingdom, yea even all my Saints that wish to fellowship in my name; so mote it be, Amen.

Notes:

a. See 2 David 3:9.
b. Mysticism, as used here, refers to the Creation becoming one with the Creator through our growth in Grace allowing us access to the Gifts of the Spirit.
c. Theology is the study of the nature of God, applied to personal religious understanding as it evolves and continues to develop.
d. Thaumaturgy is the use of spiritual gifts, or "miracle working."
e. See Avahr 17:39 (DaC 3:16 CoC/10:67 CJCLdS).
f. See DoS 3c Article II 1.
g. See DoS 7b:4 (DaC 87:2a CoC/90:4 CJCLdS).
h. See DoS 7b:7 (DaC 87:3b CoC/90:7-8 CJCLdS).
i. See Leviticus 19:18, 33-34; Matthew 5:43-48, BoR 15:23-30.
j. See DoS 116:20-25.
k. See DoS 50e:22.
l. See DoS 12e:4-6.
m. See DoS 70:3-6.
n. See John 1:1-5.

Revelation 44

Revelation on the Plates of Brass

Revelation given to David Ferriman, June 21, 2021. David had prayed, asking for witnesses to the plates of brass he had been called to translate. The Lord responded with the following, recorded as Section 126 in Doctrines of the Saints.

1 My son, Thus saith the Lord unto His people, even Israel: When thou did covenant[a] to keep my Torah[b] and my mitzvah[c] thou did so as one, my child, and thou came to life, being filled with my Breath[d], yea, even the Holy Spirit;

2 And as thou moved forward ye did abandon my Torah and my mitzvah for the calf of gold that came from out of that fire:

3 And behold! Ye did repent, yet not out of faith but by fear; yea, I did give thee of that which is good, and ye did spit it out, and turned it away as ye thought it bitter and ye longed for the fine things of Egypt.

4 But not all, for I did send my prophets to teach thee, and to guide thee, and to save thee, O my rebellious child;

5 For the love of a parent is unconditional, and so it is that I will always make for thee a way back.

6 And now behold, here in the last days I have sent mine angel, Moroni[a], to sound the trump and to bring forth the everlasting gospel[b],

7 That it may be preached unto all that dwell upon the earth, and to every nation, and kindred, and tongue, and people: for the whole earth, she is mine.

8 And what is this good news[a]? Behold, it is the very same Gospel that thou, my Israel, did speak[b] and say, with one voice: All that YHVH hath spoken we will do.

9 And thus I did make thee a nation of kings and queens, and a nation of priests and priestesses; yea, even so did I make thee a holy nation,

10 And from thee I was born, even Jesus Christ: the King of kings, the Creator of the heavens and of the earth:

11 But ye did not keep my Torah, nor my mitzvah, for ye sought out the vain things of this world; and ye did seek for the treasures of this world, and the knowledge of this world, and the wisdom of this world:

12 Yea, ye did not leave Egypt behind.

13 Wherefore, I did create a way back[a] for thee, for I love Israel, my child; and so did I send ye out into that world that ye desired, yet I prepared a way back for thee that thou might come home;

14 And thus was the record of the Lehites kept, even the Book of Mormon, that my Gospel should be restored at the last days.

15 And some have asked: why then should they keep this record if my servant Joseph Smith Jr. should not read it, but keep it covered by his side and gather its words from visions I did give him by means of a stone that shone brightly in the darkness of his hat?

16 Yea, the record was kept as a testimony of that people, and that the gifts of my Spirit, that of prophecy and revelation, should be restored again upon the earth;

17 Yea, the plates of gold were given to those who were witnesses of the book, and others have seen it since, and others shall see it also, for there is more written upon it than my servant[a] was sent to give.

18 And now the Gospel hath been restored, and with it that spirit of prophecy and revelation, that all the gifts of the spirit might be enjoyed by my people, even Israel;

19 And there is more yet to come, but these could not come until my people were blessed with my Spirit, even the power of the Holy Ghost, and given that gift of prophecy and revelation; for my people must be a prophetic people.

20 And now, wherefore thou, David, have asked of me for witnesses of the plates of brass, that men and women should know and testify that thou art my servant, and of these records which I have given thee to translate by the gift and power of God, even as did my servant Joseph:

21 I say unto thee that I am thy witness, and that those that I have called, those that have read the Book of Mormon and know it to be true by the power of the Holy Ghost, and by the spirit of prophecy and revelation shall know, even as my Israel did know to answer together as one, saying: All that YHVH hath spoken we will do;

22 So too will these be thy witnesses, for they shall testify of me, and that the work that I have given thee is mine:

23 Yea, they shall read it and filled with my Spirit and rest in my Presence[a], they too shall say: All that YHVH hath spoken we will do.

24 And when they shall read it, I will fill them with my Spirit, even as I filled them with my Spirit when they did read and study the Book of Mormon, and they shall feel the burning[a] in their hearts.

25 And yet there will be those who shall deny my Spirit, and shall deny my testimony, using the things of this world to try to confound and confuse, for these are not yet out of Egypt:

26 But these shall know that they do kick against the pricks, for I shall build thee up, and make thee strong, for thou art my servant and I have called thee by my power to fulfill these things in righteousness;

27 Thou art a mighty nation, and those that read and study to understand that which is written on the plates of brass by the gift and power of the

28 Holy Spirit, these shall gain my wisdom, and my knowledge, and my understanding: That Zion might be built, and that I might return again to complete my creation, least I come again to destroy it.

29 And I gave these records, even the plates of brass, to the Lehites that they might build for themselves a nation like unto the city of Enoch;

30 Yet they did waste their probation building up gain unto themselves, warring over land and resources that I gave them to share in peace.

31 And now too, Satan has grabbed up Israel to pride and envy, and thus us the ground of my temple, the center place of Zion, is still empty.

32 When will my Israel heed my call? When will my Israel abandon the things of Egypt and receive that which I have given her?

33 When will she take up her role as kings and queens, as priests and priestesses to be the holy nation I called her to be?

34 Behold, I am God, and I know all things; thou art mankind and I say unto thee: Seek after Zion, that thou might know truth in all things;

35 Ye have suffered much in thy rebellion, O my Israel; and I say unto thee: Come home!

36 I have given thee both signs, and wonders, I have given thee the gifts of my Holy Spirit; now seek ye not to war one with another in thy pride, but be thou one in me, be ye Zion:

37 Read these plates of brass, learn from them that which ye should do; read them, study them out, for they are my works saved up and held back until now, in the fullness of times.

38 Behold, I am Jesus Christ; I am He who walked the earth, the Son of man, I am He who suffered that thou might live, I am He who gave up the ghost freely that Israel might not taste eternal death,

39 I am He who rose from the grave on the third day, that I might take thee from the darkness into the light of my resurrection, and that thou might stand at the right hand of the Father with me and inherit all things with me:

40 I am the Creator, and thou art my creation; and behold, I come unto thee quickly; make thee ready therefore, be ye Zion; even so, Amen.

Notes:

1a See 3 Moses 27:7, Exodus 19:8

b Hebrew, "Law," "Instructions," or "Teachings"

c Hebrew: "tradition," "commandment," or "obligation"

d See Ruach HaKodesh

6a Revelation 14:6-7

b The Book of Mormon

8a Gospel: Greek, "good news"

b See 3 Moses 27:7, Exodus 19:8

13a See Teshuvah

17a Joseph Smith Jr.

23a See Shekinah

24a Moroni 10:3-5 OPV; See Avahr 20:12, 35:53

Revelation 45

Divisions and Secret Combinations

Revelation given to David April 30, 2023. David had been praying on the Sealed Book of Mormon and the problem of causing a division by revealing the parts of the book hidden by its publishers. He had also been praying on the contradictions in scripture and how to deal with these differences. This revelation is Section 128 in Doctrines of the Saints.

1 My son, I say unto thee that thy questions are not unwarranted, you have been called to unite my Saints and at times the things I ask of thee may seem unto thee as divisive attacks upon thy fellow servants.

2 Worry not where the Sealed Book of Mormon brought into the world by my servant, Mauricio Berger, came from; as I told thee before, all things may be used for the good things of God, for my purposes shall prevail in all things.

3 Remember the vision I gave thee when thou didst pray upon the book: in vision I showed thee many Saints, and those that would call themselves Saints, studying as one in my name; and is that not the purpose to which thou wast called? therefore, know ye that any work that is used to unite my people in righteousness is of me.

4 Remember also the reminder of revelation I had given thee before: the Gold Plates shall not come forth by deception nor by force (*Doctrines of the Saints 113:8*); therefore it was good of thee to be weary of these things, for where deception lie so doth the adversary:

5 Yet this work is of me, as its purpose is to unite my Saints in me, as is the call I have given through Raphael to all they I have called to unite my people.

6 ¶ And be ye, all my Saints, warned and forewarned that there will be those that shall use that which I give unto the world to unite my Saints for secret combinations:

7 Look no further than my Church, even the Church of Jesus Christ of Latter-day Saints; did they not go forth into the deserts saying, Behold, he is in the desert! and, Behold, he is in the secret chambers! For these, my people, did gather in the deserts and did build up secret chambers as temples in my name.

8 Yet I had warned my servants of this when I said: If they shall say unto you: Behold, he is in the desert; go not forth: Behold, he is in the secret chambers; believe it not (*Matthew 24:26*).

9 For while I did gather a portion of my Saints in the West, I did first instruct all to gather in Voree where there was life and safety, but when the majority of my Saints rejected this (many because my truth was hidden from them) I did send them to the deserts to blossom like a rose:

10 And blossom they did; but not without thorns, for they did fear mankind and separate themselves from the rest of my people, bringing forth new doctrines—many of which were not pleasing unto me, as I have told thee before (*Doctrines of the Saints 13a:28-33, 49-59*).

11 And because of this, today I do declare unto thee and unto the world: There shall be no oaths of secrecy among my people—yea, and there shall be no secret teachings, rituals, revelations, scriptures, nor any of the like among my Israel.

12 Wherefore, to this end I shall reveal unto the world some of that which has been left aside by my servant Mauricio Berger, that he might know that in order to receive more light and knowledge he must share all the light and knowledge that he has been given.

13 ¶ Sealed Moses 4:63 talks of the idea of gilgul, which has been understood to be reincarnation or multiple mortal probations; I say unto thee: That thou shall worry not of these things, for this life is the time to know me, and I am Jesus Christ, thy advocate.

14 There have been many that come to believe that they are Joseph Smith Jr. or another prophet or apostle come again in the flesh, or even that they are Jesus Christ restored to the flesh:

15 Know that I have called these men and women to do even more, even greater things in death that they did in the flesh; and they, regardless of their guilt or innocence in this world, are saved by my Grace and have more to do in my name, and greater works are they able to do as they have moved beyond this mortal spear;

16 Therefore, those that have been called to move this work forward, they are not my servant Joseph Smith Jr., though they may be working in that same spirit of his calling, even the restoration of all things.

17 And know too that I did come but once in the flesh, and I did take up my body again, whole; for I AM God, even the Father and the Son; therefore, I shall not come again in the flesh, for I am eternally spirit and flesh—immortal and eternally I AM the Lord, your God.

18 ¶ Sealed Moses 13:1, 3: These missing parts were restored in 3 Moses from the plates of brass, and these were held back for my own purpose that when they should be known unto the world it will be

seen that these books share this same knowledge, and many other places that were excluded; therefore I say unto my servant Mauricio: Make all these things known unto the world.

19 ¶ Sealed Moses 14:3, 17:23 I have shared what is missing in these with my servant David, and I say unto my servant Mauricio: Do not hold this back any longer, that my servant David might testify that you have sent forth the true words that you have kept hidden; do this and my servant David shall be instructed to testify that you have brought forth that which thou hast kept back.

20 ¶ Acts of the Three Nephites 2:8 doth reveal the reality of the Divine Feminine of which the ancient world knew, but this portion of the vision was held back to be restored in this day, and this that all things may be restored in their proper order.

21 ¶ Acts of the Three Nephites 7:3 reveals many things, one of which is the restoration of the Priesthood to my daughters in the last days.

22 ¶ Acts of the Three Nephites 12:14 reveals why none, not even my servant Mauricio, were to remove these things, but that should he do so, they would be restored and he would be forgiven, for he did that which he thought to be faithful unto me.

23 ¶ And now I say unto my servant, Mauricio: Translate the Torah of Moses, as translated into English by my servant David, into thy native tongue, even Portuguese, that thou might learn from it more of thy mission, and understand that which thou hast been given.

24 Seek not to divide my people, but help to build Zion in the hearts of the Saints, that none shall rule over them but me, sayeth the Lord, that ye be of one heart and one mind, and truly my Church without walls or boarders.

25 ¶ And unto my servant, David, I say: Worry not that those I have called throughout time have not seen all things eye-to-eye, but know that human understanding is culminated through culture, experience, and Spirit; therefore, when things seem to conflict, it is a wise thing unto me, that all may be edified to their own cultures and understanding.

26 Yea, there is one truth, and I AM the Truth, the Way, and the Life, and all they that shall find rest in me shall do so by their own understanding; therefore, it is wisdom in me that my people should be a prophetic people that they might understand the things of God by the Spirit and not by the arm of the flesh.

27 ⁋ Worry not, fear not, seek truth, love one another; do this and the world shall know that ye are mine: So must it be; even so: Amen, and Amen.

Revelation 46

Revelation to the Churches of the Fellowship of Christ

Early in the morning of May 3, 2023, David was awoken by the Lord and conversed with Him regarding things that should come to pass. He was told to get up and write the following revelation to the future churches of the Fellowship of Christ. This revelation is Section 142a in Doctrines of the Saints.

1 In the Church of Jesus Christ in Christian Fellowship there shall come a time when the Saints shall gather in my name, and then shall people of all walks of life join together in churches, and synagogues, and congregations worshiping in the Kingdom as one in my name.

2 And in that day, many needs shall arise that shall be more than one church, or synagogue, or congregation can contain, and these will need to reach out to counsel and assistance;

3 There are many revelations given by my servant, Joseph Smith Jr. and others on these matters for those in their days, and I say that ye shall look to these, yet I wish to speak to you with more, my fellowship, for your days which are yet to come.

4 ⁋ And I say unto thee: That when this day shall come, a council shall be formed and it shall be called the Council of Churches, and any may join be they a part of the Church of Jesus Christ in Christian Fellowship, or any branch of the Churches of the Latter Day Saints, or any other part of the Church of Jesus Christ:

5 And these shall pay one tenth of their income as a tithe, and they that have more to give shall give more, even up to half of all that they have; and they that have less shall give less, and they that have nothing shall give nothing; and nothing shall be demanded of any, but all are to give as they are moved by the Spirit.

6 ¶ And the Council of Churches shall be established by election; yea, each body of Christ (every church, synagogue, and congregation) shall elect one to send as a representative of that body to sit on that Council, and it shall be organized based on the needs of the size and by revelation.

7 And this, the Council of Churches, shall be guided by the Holy Spirit and shall be the charitable arm of my Fellowship; to guide its way it shall be led by the Bishops Council, and this shall be the High Priest and High Priestess called as the Bishops and the heads of the Low or Levitical Priesthood of the Church of Jesus Christ in Christian Fellowship;

8 And these shall use all the funds at their disposal to feed the poor, house the homeless, to care for the widows, and the orphans, and any that are in need or cannot care for themselves.

9 ¶ And this council shall be as such: A High Priest and High Priestess as the Archbishops and Father and Mother of all the Levites of the Fellowship of Christ;

10 And these shall call a High Priest and a High Priestess as the First Deacon and First Rabbi (it matterth not which be the male or female or if they be nonbinary or unisex so long as they are called of me by the Holy Spirit).

11 And to sit on their council: the Patriarch and Matriarch of the Fellowship of Christ (even they that shall sit upon the Council of Elders), for these are the Father and Mother of the Church of Jesus Christ;

12 And the Quorum of Seven shall call two, be they any of the Brotherhood of Christ, of the Sisterhood or Christ, or of the Order of the Ministry (a nonbinary or unisex person), it mattereth not, so long as these two are called and sustained by the unanimous voice of that quorum;

13 And the Council of Churches shall elect from their membership a lay member as the ninth member of this Council.

14 And this Council shall work with the Council of Elders for the benefit of the Saints, and all they that call themselves Saints, or would be counted a Saints in my name.

15 ¶ And I say unto thee, my servant David, that thou shall set aside Sections 142 and 143 in the Book of the Doctrines of the Saints to house all revelations for this council, even as thou did set aside Section 12 for mine Apostles, and Section 50 for my Fifty, and Section 70 for my Seventy, and etc.

16 And thou shall set aside section 144 for those whom I has told thee, and it shall be revealed unto the world as these revelations are presented unto my Saints and the world.

17 ¶ And until the time shall come that the Council of Churches and the Bishops Council shall be formed, I say unto all my Saints: Be ye ready, for the need is great, even now; even so, Amen.

Revelation 47

Stirring the Water

After listing to an audiobook on the Gospel of John, August 13, 2023, David learn something about the place Jesus went to heal the sick and went to the Lord for further light and knowledge. The following is a portion of the revelation he was given that day. This revelation is Section 129 in Doctrines of the Saints.

1 **Question:** The Gospel of John, Chapter 5 verse four states that an angel went down pool and stirred the water, and that this water then healed the sick; was this angel Raphael?

2 ¶ **Answer:** Yes, it was Raphael that stirred the water, and as he did he blessed them to heal the sick.

3 ¶ **Question:** It has been said that this healing water was Asclepius, a Greek god of healing; why would Raphael bless the pool of a pagan god?

4 ¶ **Answer:** Why would I, the creator of all, not heal any that are in need and serve me people only?

5 And did I not, when in the flesh, heal my people without use of the waters?

6 Behold, I am a healer and I am not a respecter of persons; therefore, I will offer salvation unto any that ask.

7 And unto they know me not, I shall provide a way both tem-poral and spiritual,

8 For I am come to save this, my creation, first the Jew and then the Gentile;

9 Therefore, wonder not that I would send angels to those in need.

10 ¶ **Question:** What then of 1 Moses Chapter 15, verses fourteen through nineteen, Raphael was sent to heal, but when the people sinned Raphael left them; why then did Raphael help people at the water of Asclepius?

11 ¶ **Answer:** Those that sought help in banishing the sa'iyr and the shedd from out of their lands did know me,

12 And when they did reject me, my angel did leave their presence.

13 Yet he had taught they that did remain with me my word and how to heal, sharing with them some of the wood from the branches of the tree of life.

14 Those that were healed from the stirring of the waters when I was upon the earth in the flesh knew me not;

15 And unto they that did know of me, these did wait for me to come unto them to heal them myself, that they should be a witness of me.

16 Had the man not waited thirty-eight years? Behold, it is I, the Lord, that shall heal my people,

17 And they shall have faith in me, and my mighty hand shall heal them; and they will know that they have in truth been healed in my name.

Revelation 48

Revelation to Jason and His Wives

After speaking to Jason, David inquired of the Lord for a revelation as to Jason's role in the Last Days. As a prophet, Jason had received revelations and great strength from the Lord. Seeking guidance, on May 8, 2023, David received the following, recorded as Section 130 in Doctrines of the Saints.

18 My son, Jason: Thou hast sought guidance, and in this I am well pleased; for thou art strong, and one mighty among Israel, yet thou wast not called to do all things alone;

19 And for this cause have I, the Lord, sent others unto thee—some to help and others seeking thy care; yet not all those who I did send have helped, and not all those who have sought help have been given that which they did need.

20 I have many things to say unto thee this day, and I would that thou should harken unto my voice, even as I do speak unto thee through my servant, David, in who I am well pleased.

21 ¶ Behold, know that I have called thee, and I have set thee apart even as I did my servant, Abraham, and I have given thee land;

22 But know that no man can own any land, for all things do belong to me, the Lord thy God—

23 Yet I have made thee a steward in my name, even as I did unto Abraham, and my Israel, and Lehi and his children, to care for the land that thou hast been given dominion over, so long as thou art worthy of it, for there shall be no violence in the land.

24 And know that thou hast not been called to this task alone, for I have given unto thee wives and I have given you unto them, and of wives thou shalt have at least three, even as did my servant Enoch.

25 And I say unto all of you: Be ye one in my name.

26 Remember, O remember! the words^a which I did give unto my Israel: Hear and listen, O Israel: YHVH your Elohim is Unity; and thou shall love YHVH thy Elohim with all thine heart, and with all thy soul, and with all thy strength;

27 Therefore, I say unto you: Be ye one, even as I and the Father are one.

28 ¶ And now I say unto thee, Jason, my son: Thou art my Sharath[b] and my Ro'eh[c] a Sheliah[d], an Apostle;

29 For even as my servant Abraham, I did sent thee forth from thy home into my promised land, and thou art a shepherd in my vineyard and in my name, called to feed my sheep in these the last days—

30 Yet know that I did not call thee nor thy wives as Ambassadors[e] nor as Evangelists, for it is not your duty to travel but to prepare for that which is to come.

31 And I have given thee many gifts, even the gift of prophecy that thou should prepare and be ready; for the children of man do grow restless, and I am troubled of them, sayeth the Lord;

32 Therefore, I say unto thee: Build up my Zion, even a place of peace that my Saints shall find rest.

33 ¶ And thou and thy wives are called to be my Torah Chakhamimot[f], yea, each of you a Torah Chakham;

34 Therefore, study ye my Torah; yea, know[g] it that all may come to thee seeking knowledge, wisdom and to gain understanding in my name.

35 And it is by my Wisdom[h] that I have called you—yea, that I have called your family—into the order of plural marriage:

36 That in strength thou shall support one another, and that as one ye shall teach my Gospel to all they of every age who are ready to hear my Word, and to help prepare those to become ready to hear my Word that they might taste of the milk that they be ready for the meat when the time should come.

37 Line upon line, precept upon precept shall ye be given all things, be they lands, wives, children, knowledge, wisdom, understanding— even all things;

38 And behold, each of thee is a pillar to hold up a portion of the work that I have given unto you;

39 Therefore, that which I say unto one of thee, I say unto you all; for pillars that stand divided shall cause the house to come down in violence.

40 ¶ Wherefore, I say unto thy wives: Prepare thyselves to be anointed and ordained that ye should be given the keys to the Law of Sarah.

41 And the first wife shall be ordained first, and she in turn shall assist in ordaining the rest;

42 And in this ye shall be prepared to do all that which I have called thee to do, that everything be done by and in the proper order of all things.

43 And behold, my daughters of Zion: I have called thee to be teachers of men, and of women, and of children that my Gospel might be sent forth and preached unto the whole earth;

44 Yet I have not called thee to be sent out, but to bring others in and to make ready their endowments, that once prepared ye shall send them out in my name.

45 ¶ My son Jason, all Elders have been given the keys to seal on earth unto heaven, and to bind on Earth in my name and by my Word, saith the Lord, that these shall be eternally bound in the Heavens; to bless they who bless thee, and curse they who curse thee.

46 And I shall give unto thee more keys of sealing powers; know that thy calling and election have been made sure, for thou art of the church of the Firstborn:

47 But unto the Holy Spirit of Promise, yea, even the power to seal those of my people called up unto exaltation, this thou shall not be given; for only one[i] shall hold these keys upon the earth at any time.

48 And this, the Holy Spirit of Promise, can only be broken if innocent blood be shed by they who obtain it; therefore, woe be unto they who know me, and that are sealed by the Holy Spirit of Promise, and reject me for the covenant of Mahan[j]!

49 Wherefore, I say unto thee: Prepare thyselves and thy family for that which is to come, that lives may be saved, and that my Saints shall be protected from those that would make the oaths of the Mahan.

50 ¶ And now, I would speak unto thee of thy visions, for the gift of prophecy is one of thy gifts: Thou hast been warned, and thou hast been making ready thy preparation.

51 And I say unto thee: That thou should remember my servant, Jonah.

52 For after it was that the fish did vomit him out, he did heed my call and he did arise and go unto the city of Nineveh; and there he did cry out, saying that Nineveh shall be overthrown.

53 Yet the people did repent, and I did spare them; and in this was my servant displeased!

54 And I, the Lord, did prepare a gourd that I might teach him, and I did shew unto him to pity the people that I did send him to preach against,

55 That he would see that I, the Lord thy God, do shed mercy upon all they who repent, and to love those who I sent him to serve, for his work was not to destroy but to build.

56 And thou too wast not called to destroy, but to build; to preach teshuvah[k] that all might return unto me, and to love others without condition that ye might be an example of me and in my name.

57 ¶ Wherefore, I say unto thee: Thou hast taken my name upon thee, and thou hath not taken it in vain; be therefore wary of pride, in thyself and in those who would associate with thee and with thy family.

58 Call all mankind to repentance with love, not only by thy words but with thy deeds, that there be neither contentions nor disputations among my peoples, and see that everyone doth deal justly one with another in all things wherein I have given thee stewardship.

59 Lead my people, even my Israel, by thy words and by thy deeds; yea, show them the meaning of my words even by thy deeds that all might know me by knowing thee.

60 Seek to raise unto me a people who desire to have all things common among them, there being neither rich nor poor, neither bond nor free that all may be truly free and partakers of the heavenly gift.

61 Do this that the tribulations might be avoided, and if they should come that Zion shall be free; not by force, but by thy peace:

62 For the World shall fear my people not because of their weapons of war, but because of the love in their hearts; for the wicked cannot understand this thing and thus they reject me.

63 ¶ And it shall come to pass, sayeth the Lord, that all they who are Zion shall come to the New Jerusalem,

64 And all they who seek war shall flee from before Zion, and the desolation that the wicked shall bring shall cause all they who seek peace to flee from before the World unto Zion;

65 Therefore, be not like the men of Enmer Kar[j], nor as the judge[m] that did condemn the poor widow and her sons, nor as the chief judge, whose name was Laadan[n], but be wary of those that would act as such.

66 But be ye like the Twelve Righteous men, and teach unto my people the words of Tzophar, that the secrets[o] of my temple be made known unto the World.

67 And fear not what the World should do with my words, for those who are not my friends shall not understand my words,

68 And even as Laadan they shall be confounded by their power; for the more wicked the man, the more the words of Tzophar shall drive them to violence.

69 ¶ Use the gifts that I have given thee: the gift of prophecy to guide my people and in proclaiming my Word with boldness,

70 The gift of leadership to encourage and help others to build my kingdom and prepare the earth for my coming,

71 The gift of management to help in setting goals and staying on task.

72 The gift of teaching to instruct the people of my truths and my doctrines and my Word;

73 The gift of knowledge in teaching and in discipleship, the ability to learn, to know, and to explain my Word to the understanding of mankind;

74 The gift of wisdom to discern the works of the Holy Spirit, in both thy teaching and in thy actions, that men and women should learn from thee in all that thou doeth.

75 The gift of discernment that thou should recognize the truth in any situation, to see into the hearts of men and women, to see their souls, to assign them to their talents and to be weary of those sent to deceive.

76 The gift of shepherding that thou should strive for the spiritual welfare of others, and of service in helping those in need.

77 The gift of mercy that the World might see my compassion;

78 The gift of giving that others too should give freely and with joy to further my kingdom;

79 And the gift of hospitality that all shall feel welcome, appreciated, desired, and heard in my peaceful Kingdom.

80 ¶ Call upon my sealing power that the heavens shall be open to bless the lands that I have given thee, and I have given thee these lands that thy family and Zion shall be blessed.

81 Prepare those that should bear thy burdens that others shall be made ready to move the works that I have called thee forward as it expands, to seal them up unto thee and teach them to use these gifts that thou hast been blessed with.

82 ¶ Stand ready to serve thy wives and thy children, teaching them and encouraging them in my ways;

83 Strengthen them in their struggles, love them even as I love them and as I love thee, lend them thy support and thy strength that thy family should be the example of my ways.

84 ¶ Teach my Gospel, ye are called and have been sent to stand firm: for even as Abraham, I have taken thee out of Egypt and into my promised land;

85 Therefore, watch and be ready, even as I have told thee; even so, Amen.

Notes:

    a. See Deuteronomy 6:4-5

    b. Sharath: Hebrew: "servant" or "minister"

    c. Ro'eh: Hebrew: "shepherd"

    d. Shelah: Hebrew, "one sent out"

    e. See Book of the Law of the Lord 36:6-7

f. Torah Chakham (singular) Torah Chakhamimot (plural): Hebrew, liberally "expert of the Torah." A sage, one who is well versed in the Torah. Note: Chakhamim is the male plural while Chakhamot is the female plural, in this revelation the Lord combines these, which is not how Hebrew traditionally works.

g. Hebrew, "yada;" to know or understand deeply, enter into covenant together

h. A nod to the Divine Feminine, Heavenly Mother

i. See CJCLdS DaC 132:7b/Doctrines of the Saints 17a:15

j. See 1 Moses 7:31-32, 8:17

k. Teshuvah: Hebrew, "return;" often translated as repent.

l. 1 Moses 17-20

m. 1 Moses 18

n. 1 Moses 19

o. 1 Moses 19:41-45

Revelation 49

Revelation on the Urim and Thummim

On the morning of Saturday January 5, 2024, David was awoken around 4:30am and before falling back to sleep, he prayed, asking the Lord to teach him of His ways. He was then given a dream in which Raphael showed him an urim and thummim attached to a short wooden rod. In the dream, he was instructed on how to use the instrument. Upon awakening, he prayed to the Lord for understanding about the dream and was told to speak to Kristine, his wife. After doing so on the morning of January 6th, he prayed to the Lord for further light and knowledge about this tool. On January 8, 2024, he was given the following revelation, recorded as Section 131 in Doctrines of the Saints.

1 My **Question:** Is there only one or only one type of urim and thummim?

2 ¶ **Answer:** No, there have been many upon the earth: Adam and Eve were given an urim and thummim when they left the garden, and this was passed down to Enoch who took it with his city to the heavens when they were taken.

3 Noah and Na'amah were commanded to make an urim and thummim called the tzohar, and was passed down to Abraham; and I

did teach Abram how to use it, for his fathers had forgotten how to use it in their apostasy.

4 And Moses and Zipporah were given an urim and thummim, and they did teach my Israel to make the urim and thummim for themselves, and were instructed on its uses:

5 And Aaron the High Priest did place an urim and thummim in a pouch to be worn over the heart that it should sit between him and the breastplate;

6 And so too did they make an urim and thummim for Miriam, the High Priestess, and these did rest upon her shoulders; the urim upon the right shoulder and thummim upon the left.

7 ¶ And these are but a few of the urim and thummim given unto mankind, for I did give unto the brother of Jared also interpreters, being two stones; and these were a type of urim and thummim.

8 And these were given unto my servant, Mosiah, that he too did seek light and truth from them.

9 And these were connected to a chest plate that they should be near unto the heart of any I should give to wear them.

10 And behold, Moroni did give these unto my servant Joseph Smith Jr., and he did wear them at times to translate the portions of the plates he was given to translate, even that which contained the Book of Lehi, the very pages that were taken and kept hidden from him.

11 ¶ **Question:** What then of the brown seer stone, and seer stones in general, are these also a type of urim and thummim?

12 ¶ **Answer:** A seer stone is a stone used to help the seer, and an urim and thummim is given to any that desire to know.

13 I say unto thee: Any that are called to see may be given a seer stone, even as my servant Joseph was given stones to see and to interpret.

14 And this the Latter Day Saints did call an urim and thummim, but Joseph's brown stone was a seer stone and not an urim and thummim;

15 Yet his seer stones he did use, and I did grant him power from on high, and this power came from me and not from any earthly powers.

16 And the seer stones were as an urim, being gazelem, bringing light in the darkness, and as a thummim that they did give Joseph voice to speak my words unto the congregation;

17 But a true urim and thummim, these do represent the bond between the heavens and the earth, even the unity of that which is above and that which is below, for they do speak unto the earth the wisdom of the Heavens.

18 ¶ **Question:** Can anyone use a seer stone, how do they work?

19 ¶ **Answer:** Behold, I have said before: I will prepare unto my servant gazelem, a stone, which shall shine forth in darkness unto light, that I may discover unto my people who serve me, that I may discover unto them the works of their brethren; yea, their secret works, their works of darkness, and their wickedness and abominations.

20 And what then is this gazelem?

21 ¶ Behold, I shall tell thee: Gazelem is my servant and gazelem is the stone, for the stone can do nothing of itself, and my servants will only do my works through my power; therefore, gazelem is both the servant and the seer stone.

22 And even as I did say through my servant, Moses: And unto the seer shall be given the gazelem, which shall shine forth in darkness unto light; and any who are instructed to look into the stone, the same is a seer; for my gazelem is a bridge between the earth and the heavens.

23 ¶ And what can a rock do without the seer? and what can the seer see without the power of my Spirit?

24 Therefore, know this: The seer that uses the stone filled with my Spirit and my power is gazelem, and the stone too is gazelem, for there is life in all of my creation.

25 And the stone and the seer may only work through the gifts of my power, and these gifts are given of my Holy Spirit.

26 ¶ **Question:** Can anyone make a seer stone or an urim and thummim?

27 ¶ **Answer:** The seer stone cannot be made, but might be awakened by the seer; and this after the seer is called and awakened in me.

28 And I did teach the earth many of the secrets of her creation through my servants, Moses and Zipporah; therefore, study their words and ye shall learn of these, the seer stone and the gazelem.

29 The urim and thummim may only be made and used by those I call to do so; some are called to be seers, and some prophets, and some apostles in my name.

30 ¶ The urim is a stone of quartz, and the thummim of onyx.

31 The urim and thummim I gave unto the brother of Jarod was made of translucent quartz for the right eye, and translucent onyx for the left.

32 The urim and thummim made for the seed of Levi were of white quartz for the urim and black onyx for the thummim;

33 And these are but two types of urim and thummim.

34 ¶ And the urim and thummim are the manifestation and truth: urim is aleph or the alpha, thummim the tav or omega;

35 Yet these are not in opposition of one another, for they do show my oneness: Hear O Israel: YHVH is your Elohim, YHVH is One;

36 Therefore, the urim and thummim represent the oneness of the heavens and the earth, the Creator and His creation, the light penetrating the darkness, and the indivisible whole.

37 ¶ **Question:** What is the relationship between the urim and thummim and the breastplates of the High Priest and High Priestess?

38 ¶ **Answer:** These are given power by my hand through the urim and thummim.

39 Behold, the stones and their rods: behold a son, he has heard my suffering; he will unite Israel, and Israel will praise YHVH; YHVH shall bring justice for Israel through the struggle of Israel; the fortune of YHVH is the blessing of Israel, and the reward of Israel; the Honor of Israel shall be the indication of Israel, and YHVH shall add to Israel, even the right hand of Israel.

40 ¶ These stones, they do speak of me and of my love for my Israel; and in the hands of the High Priest, they do speak truth unto all my peoples by the power given of my Spirit.

41 These stones, they do represent the rods to be cast when they that wish to know should cast their lots; and in them shall my people know, and be warned, and be comforted, and be blessed.

42 And behold, it was by this casting of lots that mine apostle, Matthias was chosen, after Judas had left them.

43 ¶ And on the breastplates of the High Priestess sits carnelian and onyx with a pearl between them; carnelian for redemption, onyx for truth, and pearl for wisdom:

44 For behold, when the daughters of Israel were told of my salvation from the hands of Egypt, they did not seek a sign as did my sons, they heard my truth and in wisdom they did believe.

45 And therefore, carnelian is a help unto women, and onyx a shield, and the pearl wisdom granted by faith unto all they that do believe.

46 ¶ And this breastplate too is given power by my Spirit through that urim and thummim that does rest upon their shoulders.

47 And together, the breastplate of judgment and breastplate of mercy become the tablet of truth, or the tablet of goral:

48 For when the High Priest and the High Priestess do work as one in my name, to prepare the earth for the heavens and to bring the heavens to the earth, then they shall know by my Spirit what has been assigned, apported, and allotted unto my Israel.

49 When the High Priest wears the breastplate, the urim and thummim is worn over the heart, for it is by thy heart that I, the Lord, do judge mankind;

50 And when the High Priestess wears the breastplate, the urim and thummim is worn on the shoulders, for by your works shall the world know that you are mine.

51 ¶ **Question:** In my dream, I was given a rod with the urim at the head and the thummim at the tail of a rod, what does this mean? am I to make or use this tool in your name?

52 ¶ **Answer:** Should you make a rod with the urim and thummim or have such made for thee, even as in your dream, it shall only have power as all tools fashioned and used in my name, and that is power given unto the earth from upon high.

53 I do seek to teach the earth of my mysteries, for they are mine, and I do give them freely unto all they that would learn of them.

54 ¶ And behold, Satan doth teach the children of men of these things to corrupt them and to use them in pride, for their undoing.

55 And I say unto thee: All that is necessary between thee and me is our covenant, made by your broken heart and contrite spirit;

56 Yet in these last days, Satan shall and does move upon the whole face of the earth with his priestcraft to deceive even the very elect; and what does this mean?

57 It doth mean that Satan will give signs unto the children of men that shall please their egos yet shall wound their pride, teaching mankind that they should not seek my mercy nor my face.

58 ¶ What then of the urim and thummim and the seer stone, and the breastplates?

59 These are symbols of truth and the power of my priesthood, and these tools work only through my righteousness; therefore, all they that seek my face, and seek to call all mankind unto teshuvah, unto such do I give my priesthood.

60 And this that they might use these gifts to bring souls unto me, for the earth, she is mine, and all they that love me are given power to heal the earth.

61 ¶ And all these things are given as signs and as tokens unto they that do believe, and all they that will believe in my name; for I am the Lord, YHVH, your Elohim, and I do watch over Israel, even unto this day.

62 And I do give my outstretched hand unto all they that will take it, for salvation both spiritual and temporal; therefore, when you read these words, know that I do speak unto thee and unto all the world of things both spiritual and temporal.

63 ¶ And all my words shall be fulfilled, and all my truths shall be known, from the beginning of days even until the end of days, for I am Alpha and Omega, Aleph-Tav.

64 And you are mine, for I have called thy name, and you did hear me, and in this I am well pleased.

65 Now, go and do, even all the works that I have called thee to be engaged in; for your works are mine, for I did give them unto thee, my good and faithful servant; even so, amen.

Revelation 50

Revelation on the Miltabim

On Friday, January 12, 2024, David saw online a symbol that he had seen in the plates of brass, the seal to be engraved (cut, carved, or sewn) upon a holy coat: "...thou shalt engrave the seal upon the inside of it; and in the middle of the seal put the letters, and around the seal thou shall write: YHVH, may this chereb do Thy services, and may the Lord of it approach!" -4 Moses 32:42. This led David to learn more of Rabbi Moshe Cordovero and his ideas on the Sefirot, but in the short time he had to search all he found were commentaries. After praying and sleeping on what he had read and discussed with a friend on the topic, he retired to bed. In his evening and morning prayers, he asked the Lord to help him uncover more light and knowledge on this symbol. The following morning, David was praying and meditating on the topic when he received the following revelation. This revelation is Section 132 in Doctrines of the Saints.

The Sefirpot as drawn by
Rabbi Moshe Cordovero

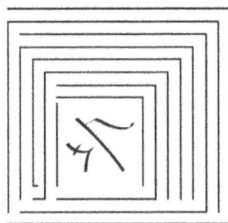

Recreation of the seal
on the plates of brass

1 My Thou has asked for more light and knowledge on the seal of coat of the chereb; yea, and for some time thou has studied and wondered on this chereb of Moses, and of this I shall tell thee this day.

2 When Moses and Zipporah were taken upon the mount, there I did give unto them crowns and I did teach them.

3 And what were these crowns? The crowns which I place upon the heads of my servants is that light and knowledge of things beyond the minds and comprehension of mankind.

4 This is why Keter is the crown on that tree of life, for it is all that is beyond comprehension.

5 And I have given thee to wear this crown at my pleasure, that thou should know and teach my people and all they that would be my Israel;

6 Therefore, I say unto thee now: All that was preserved in the chereb of Moses are that which Aaron and Miriam and others did preform in ritual that they should know me and see my face;

7 For behold, all that I desire of thee and of all mankind is a broken heart and a contrite spirit, and this shall set any on the path for in me they have found redemption.

8 Yet there are those that do seek this greater understanding, and did I not promise Israel that they should be a kingdom of kings and queens and priests and priestesses?

9 Wherefore, it was my desire from the beginning to give them to wear the crown.

10 Yet they desired not to step forth upon the mount when my servants, Moses and Zipporah did bring them unto me;

11 Yet there were those that did desire to know, therefore it was given unto Moses and Zipporah to teach them.

12 And any one, man or woman, may be taught to wear my crown and to see my face; therefore, this knowledge was saved upon the plates of brass.

13 ¶ And this was given unto the Lehites; and my servant Alma, son of Alma, did wear the crown and did see my face, as did Mormon, and his son, Moroni and others.

14 Wherefore, thou hast read and witnessed of the power of my Word in the record of the seed of Joseph that were led away into a new land, and in the record of the seed of Judah; therefore, thou might know my Word is true.

15 And as thou has read and seen, these things have been corrupted, and Satan has cast his illusions to deceive even the very elect, that as these gifts are restored unto my people, they shall be seen as not by some, and as priestcraft by others,

16 Yet those who shall partake of my Spirit and heed my Word shall know that it is of me.

17 ¶ Therefore, what then of these things? There will be those that ask: What have I to need of it? And should wonder if they are to partake of it, seeing that I have already given them salvation and exaltation.

18 Therefore, I say unto all ye this day: These things are of me, and they are not beyond the mark, nor do they that reject them miss the mark; for in me is Salvation found, and not in any works that mankind should do.

19 Those that do these things shall do them as they are moved by the Holy Spirit, and there is no salvation in them, but are given unto they who have already been saved and exalted in my name.

20 ¶ And all they that come unto me have already tasted of this chereb, for does not the scripture say:

21 Thou shalt be washed, fully immersed in living water, be it by a running stream or with the mikveh; and this thou shall do to fulfill all righteousness; for except that thou be born of the water, thou cannot enter into the Presence of Ha'Elohim; therefore ye shall wash with water that ye die not.

22 And when thou cometh up out of the water, thou shall be clean and the Breath a shall fall upon thee; and this thou shalt do that desire to be holy unto YHVH and walk in teshuvah before YHVH, thy Elohim, and to wear the mantel of righteousness.

23 ¶ And is this not what I did when I was upon the earth? For John did wash me in water, and my Father did say: This is my beloved Son, in whom I am well pleased; and the Spirit did descend upon me even as a dove.

24 Wherefore, if I should do this to fulfill all righteousness as is taught in the chereb, who art thou, O man, that this be beneath you?

25 ¶ Therefore, I say unto you: All they that come unto me and are baptized and that do receive the baptism of fire, all these are on this path to receive the chereb and to wear my crown.

26 What then of this path that hath been placed before you? Will those that read these, my words, walk this path and wear my crown?

27 I do welcome all they that would do so in my name, but remember my words: Greater love hath no man than this, that a man lay down his life for his friends;

28 Therefore, walk this path in love, for they that loveth their lives shall lose their lives, and they that will not run from death shall keep their lives into the eternities, for all they that will drinketh of the water that I shall give them shall never thirst.

29 And this water that I shall give shall be in them a well of water springing up into everlasting life.

30 And what is this water? It is the love of God that did pour out upon this creation from before the foundation of the world.

31 ¶ And now, I do say unto you: This chereb is a sign and a token, it is a physical witness of the spiritual reality that you are mine and of our oneness,

32 And the clothes do represent the priesthood, that you have been called and set apart to do works in my name.

33 Even as I told thee before: As a man putteth on one set of clothing to plow the fields and another to sleep, so too doth man put on another to do the work of the Lord.

34 And the garments that you are given, these do carry upon them the staff of Elohim, and you are as a staff in my hand; the motion upon that path to which I have called thee; the guidance of El Elyon, all those on my path do follow my words; and the house of the Holy Spirit, for thou art a holy temple unto me.

35 ¶ What then of the symbol of that coat, the Miktabim or in other words, the writings? Is it even as my servant, Rabbi Moshe Cordovero did teach?

36 Behold: I give my symbols unto all that are called to teach to use as they instruct all that would learn of me; therefore, it is even the tree of life,

37 And this it does represent the connection between thee and me, for you were created in my name and the tree of life is in you even as you are in me.

38 I am in all of the creation, and the creation in me, there is no part of this earth where I do not dwell;

39 Therefore, it is even as Rabbi Moshe Cordovero did say: The stone is a thing pervaded by divinity; and this I did show unto you when I did teach you of the urim and thummim.

40 That which is not of me is the darkness that lies in the heart of mankind; for these do reject my love and my grace and seek to hold to this life and seek immortality in their sins, even as Lilith did.

41 Yea, I am that light that penetrates the darkness, and they are the darkness that comprehendeth not my light nor my love; therefore, shed away thy pride and thy ego and be one in me and in my name.

42 ¶ And the letters, Tsadi and Mem; Tsadi does represent the righteous, and that veil that is penetrated by my light and that Holy Spirit that does guide all they that do follow me.

43 Mem does represent the living waters, the wisdom of my Word as given by the prophets and the prophetesses and my chosen seers.

44 These are together in the Miktabim that represents my pathways, and is this not the tree of life?

45 Have I not said that mankind should walk about the orchard and these pathways?

46 And thou knoweth that the orchard is my written Word, and and these pathways are the growth in my Grace.

47 And together, these become צם, or tsám: they who have fasted.

48 And what is to fast? It is to give up the things of this world, to give them to me as my servants have given themselves unto me; therefore it can be said: That thou hast given thy life for thy friends.

49 ¶ And now, I say unto you, and what I speak unto you I speak unto all those that should walk my paths, seek the chereb and the crown, and to see my face:

50 You do not walk this path alone, for I am with thee, and I do send my angels to comfort and watch over thee.

51 All those that come unto me have started upon this path; therefore, fear not: I shall give thee strength, and you shall not be weary.

52 Know that my Spirit is with thee and does rest upon thee, and this path is mine.

53 All those that have been called up to walk it shall not walk it alone, but I shall send others to help thee that thou should strengthen and watch over one another, even as I do watch over thee.

54 ¶ And now, I say unto all they that seek to see my face: Go and do; even so, amen and amen.

Revelation 51

Building Zion

Revelation given through David Ferriman February 18, 2024. This revelation is Section 133 in Doctrines of the Saints.

1 Over the past serval years, when pondering the idea of Zion as a city, I have been given visions of a city with lush vegetation, green technology, and a covenant of creation between the people, the Lord, and the earth and its creatures.

2 It is a utopia that when outsiders come to destroy it, they throw down their arms and beg to join its covenant peoples.

3 Whatever wars and strife, plagues and disasters that happen outside its walls, the people within are blessed by the Lord and one another not to be effected by them.

4 In prayer, I asked the Lord how or even if these things can or will come to pass; in response, I was given the following:

5 ¶ Behold, my son David; it is to this end that you are called, and that many others have been called also; yet the people have not harkened, for the fear of the adversary is great within them.

6 And I have spoken through my prophets and my prophetesses from the beginning of these things, and I shall speak of them again through you this day, for the time is ripe, and the sun is setting.

7 ¶ Behold, as I have said before, many are called and few are chosen, and I say unto you this day, that by this shall they who are chosen know of their call:

8 All they who shall read these words and feel of my Spirit that calling to which they have been called, gaining a sense of purpose, a yearning to unify in this, the restoration;

9 For behold, this is the time of the restoration, and it is a restoration of all things.

10 Yea, and some have thought this time of restoration was merely a return to the things of former days, yet were the former days better than these?

11 Many of every generation have waisted their probation away seeking for the days of their youth, or longing for a time that was before their time.

12 And these acquired not any wisdom in this; no, but they that learn from the past, and seek to build the present and a better future, these are they who I have called and have chosen.

13 ¶ Behold, all they that read these, my words, and do hear my voice, and that the Spirit giveth clarity to, that their understanding is opened up, these I have called.

14 Yea, and I am thy compass, that thou should be not afraid, nor pulled by the things of this world to the right, nor to the left; and I shall be as your liahona, giving you my wisdom that you shall know.

15 And if you should heed that call and reach out to build my kingdom, then you are chosen of me, for thou didst hear my voice and heed it also.

16 ¶ And to those who have been called to assist in these, my works, how shall ye know them?

17 My works are all that bring glory unto the Father, and to bring glory to the Father and the Mother;

18 Therefore, all they that seek to glorify me, and that seek to glorify the Father and the Mother, by this you shall know they have been called.

19 Look not to those that seek to glorify themselves, nor they who seek their own safety, for I am thy safety and I am thy peace.

20 ¶ Yea, and all they who have been called, you shall know them for they do my works; therefore, they who have been called but do not my works, they have not been chosen:

21 For I will lead they who will follow me, and I will lift them up and make their burdens light; therefore, they who do glorify my name, and the name of the Father and of the Mother, and do the works to which they have been called, these have been chosen unto me.

22 ¶ And what are my works? My works are that which restoreth all things, even from before the foundation of the world;

23 My works are to heal this, the creation, to seek out the lost and the broken and offer them healing, my works are even as I have asked all ye to do in my name: Feed my sheep.

24 For I am the good shepherd, I am the lord and the master of the vineyard, and all they that will work in my fields, tending to my sheep and healing my vineyard, these are my servants and my friends.

25 ¶ Yea, and in my vineyard and my pasture the plants nor the sheep are not alone, for there also is the soil, and the air, and the insects, and the beasts of the fields and the fruits of the garden, and the weeds;

26 And all of these have I put upon the earth for a purpose that is wisdom in me, for thou, O man, are not alone being in this world, nor are thou, mankind, alone in this creation.

27 Wherefore did I give Adam and Eve dominion to care for this, my creation; for ye are my creation, and when ye shall care for the earth and my creation, ye are in my service,

28 But when thou rejecteth my creation, and seek to force my creation into submission, thou doth reject me an my work, seeking not for my glory, nor for the glory of the Father or for the Mother.

29 And I say unto thee, O man: Forget not thy origins; for without me and without this earth, thou shall not survive;

30 Therefore, I say unto thee: Seek not to build up for thy own gain, for Zion shall not be there; but seek Zion in thy heart, and ye shall build Zion.

31 For Zion is a place of refuge, and thy body is a temple unto me, for there doth the Holy Spirit reside; and if my light, even the light of Christ, cannot pour out from the Mother, through the Son, into you, my creation, then it cannot flow from you to heal this, my creation.

32 But behold, if you, my people, will but open your hearts unto me, and let my light shine forth from within you, by your fruits shall I be known;

33 For your works will be my works, and my works your works, and we will be One, even as the Father and the Mother, and the Son are one in the Holy Spirit.

34 Wherefore, I say into you again, this last time: These are they who have been called and chosen unto me;

35 They who seek to glorify my name, and the name of the Father and the Mother, they who would do my works feeding my sheep and caring for my vineyard, and they who seek the unity of the Creator and the creation.

36 Seek ye out my people, even Israel, and be Zion, for if thou art a holy place, then the ground on which thou standeth will be holy; and if the ground be holy, then Zion shall dwell therein, and be lifted upon high; so mote it be, amen and amen.

37 ⁋ With the vision and revelation ending, I was left with one thought: Those that would be Zion will not live in fear, but seek to build others; this is Israel, and this is Zion;

38 We are one human race, one human family, and one with all of this creation, and to be Zion we must one with our Creator; amen and amen.

Revelation 52

The Symbolism in the Temple and Ritual Clothing

Revelation given through David Ferriman February 26, 2024. This revelation is Section 134 in Doctrines of the Saints.

1 In discussing the revelations I was given when I first received my call to the Fellowship of Christ, I commented that I believed the reason for the white garments in Doctrines of the Saints 106:50 was because up to and even after this point, this was a part of the tradition I was raised in.

2 Seeing that the Church of Jesus Christ of Latter-day Saints also sold garments of different colors for military use, it just made sense to me that this was not a requirement but preference.

3 White was my preference at that time, and so I continued with that, and this was likely the reason for the revelation stating I should take a while cloth to make my new garments.

4 Shortly after this, a friend requested I take this matter to the Lord so verify this idea, I agreed and began to pray to the Lord for further instructions.

5 In taking this to the Lord, I was given the following revelation:

6 ¶ David, my son, I shall answer this thing unto thee this day and I shall tell you even more.

7 Behold, white is to symbolize purity; therefore, I say unto thee: Make thy garments white, and place the holy symbols upon them;

8 And these may be even as the symbols of the Masons used by so many of my Latter Day Saints in these, the last days, or they may be the symbols as thou hast found them inscribed upon the plate of brass, for both share the same meanings;

9 Yea, and this is what giveth the symbols their power: the heart of they that do wear them.

10 ¶ Behold, if thy garments, that is to say the state of thy soul, be white, being made clean by the blood of my sacrifice, then ye be clean also;

11 But if thou doeth not come unto me even as a child, with a broken heart and a contrite spirit, then the color of thy garments mattereth not.

12 And if my people do desire to wear colors that are not white, I say unto my people: Come unto me, and ask me for to know of thy own garments.

13 And I say unto all of you this day: That it is the soul that mattereth to me, saith the Lord; therefore, be thou clean, O man, washed in my mercy and my grace, and this shall be sufficient unto me.

14 ¶ And now, I would speak unto thee of the the tabernacle and the temple: Behold, in the times of Moses and Zipporah, and Aaron and Miriam I did command my people in all things;

15 Wherefore, I did command them to build my tabernacle down to the very buckles that did latch shut the curtains.

16 But in these, the last days, I would not command my people in all things, but would teach you, each of you, to seek me for yourselves.

17 Behold, each part of my tabernacle and my temples were given to represent the things of this earth and the bringing of the heavens to the earth.

18 Yea, the gold, and the silver, and the copper or brass; the gold to represent the transcendence of mankind, silver the flow of my light into this world uniting the heavens and the earth, and copper or brass my governance over this, my creation;

19 And the linen and the cedar wood to represent the plant life of this creation, and the wool and the skins the animals and the beasts of the earth;

20 Wherefore all of the creation is made into my house, and all that is seen therein are to represent the coming of the heavens to the earth.

21 ¶ And the colors: White for my purity; red the passion and the fire of the Holy Spirit; blue the eternal unity found in me, the Creator, and my creation; and purple, my compassion and kingship, for I am the king of kings; therefore, all of these to connect the heavens and the earth.

22 The Holy Spirit gives birth to the soul inside all that are born again, that soul shall live with me in my Father's kingdom for ever and ever,

23 And I am the bridge that does connect the heavens and the earth; therefore, I say unto thee: Wear what colors as thou wilt, but have meaning behind them and let them be a sign between me and thee;

24 And this I do say unto all they that seek the chereb or in other words, all they that I call to the ministry that are moved by my Spirit to partake in the rituals of my temples.

25 ¶ And that there be no confusion, I would say more unto thee: When I did say unto my people, even the Fellowship of Christ, how to build my tabernacles and my temples, I gave unto you the simpleness of the way.

26 And now, that there be no disputing among you, as shall say unto you a few things more:. There are some that shall ask about the four poles to hold the four sheets.

27 Wherefore I say unto you this day: That two sheets shall hang to the West and two sheets shall hang to the East, and this that they might be parted;

28 And the four poles are to bear them, two shall be to the East and two shall be to the West that the sheets be supported.

29 ¶ And there will be those that do ask: Are the sheets or veils to be even as Moses did teach unto Israel, or will they be as the veil used in the temples of my church, even the Church of Jesus Christ of Latter-day Saints, or should they be something different all together?

30 And behold, I do say unto you this day: That you shall make a veil like unto that of the Church of Jesus Christ of Latter-day Saints that these, my people, shall be welcome in my house and to use my temple even as they desire for their ordinances.

31 And ye shall make sheets even link unto that of the tabernacle of Moses and Zipporah, and Aaron and Miriam for the use of the Levites.

32 And should I require you to make other sheets, it shall be done even as I shall make known unto to, but for now, it is enough.

33 ¶ And when ye shall build unto me the tabernacles, the synagogues, and the temples, you shall do so prayerfully in my name, seeking the knowledge given by my servants Moses and David, and seeking further light and knowledge through prayer and deliberation.

34 But make not unto me vain and empty places, honoring the wealth of the things of this world, but see that my symbols are seen throughout in all parts of its creation,

35 For these shall be my house and a place for uniting me and my people, that my Presence shall be known;

36 Therefore, go and do; make a space for me amongst my people and teach my rituals unto all they that I have called to receive them. So mote it be, amen.

Revelation 53

A Revelation on the Tzitits

In asking the Lord about the tzitits, what are they, should he wear them, David received a revelation that he kept to himself as a personal revelation. A few years later, in March of 2024, in preparing the Doctrines of the Saints, he felt impressed by the Holy Spirit to revisit this revelation. Because he did not write his personal revelation down, he went back to the Lord to re-receive this revelation for the Saints of Zion. This revelation is Section 135 in Doctrines of the Saints.

1 **Question:** What are the tzitzits and are we to wear them?

2 **Answer:** In the repetition of the Law (*Deuteronomy 23:7-8*) my Servant, Moses, spoke unto my Israel, saying:

3 Thou shalt not abhor an Edomite, for he is thy brother; thou shalt not abhor an Egyptian because thou wast a stranger in his land; the children that are begotten of them shall enter into the congregation of the Lord in their third generation.

4 Now I shall say this unto you, that ye should understand it, the first generation of Israel is the dispensation of Moses, for in them did my people come up out of Egypt;

5 The second generation of Israel is the dispensation of John who is the Baptist, for at that time did the Gospel spread forth unto the Gentiles;

6 And the third generation of Israel is the dispensation of Joseph Smith Jr. now is the time of the restoration of all things; therefore my Saints in the Latter Days are the third generation.

7 And now, behold, I shall speak the repetition of the Law unto thy understanding:

8 Thou shall not abhor the world, because thou wast a stranger in their land; thou shall not abhor those of any of the seed of Abraham, for these are thy brothers and sisters; and now, in these the last days, Israel shall be gathered up in me, for this is the third generation.

9 And all they that do hear my voice, and that are moved by my Spirit to wear them shall put on the tzitits; and this is not to be seen but that my people shall see, and that those that wear them shall know their kin and where to find safety in my wings, for the tzitzits are my wings.

10 **Question:** Thank you Lord for your wisdom and guidance; what do you mean by stating the tzitzits are your wings and how are we to wear them?

11 **Answer:** In the Torah of Judah, In the Desert (*Numbers 15:38-40*), I spoke unto Moses, saying:

12 Speak unto the children of Israel and bid them that they make them wings in the borders of their garments throughout their generations, and that they put upon the wings of the borders a blue cord; and it shall be unto you for a tassel, that ye may look upon it, and remember all the mitzvoth of YHVH, and do them, and that ye seek not after your own heart and your own eyes, after which ye use to commit apostasy, that ye may remember the covenant, and do all my mitzvoth, and be holy unto your Elohim.

13 The wings are to be worn that thou should see them, and not for mankind; for behold, when I walked the earth, the Pharisees and the scribes did seek to sit in the seat of Moses, wearing long cords for their wings to be seen of men, and for the honor of man.

14 This ye shall not do, but when thou should wearest them, thou shalt put them on to be seen by thee and by me, and I shall reveal them unto any that I desire to seek them out;

15 Therefore, they should be visible as a sign, for the blue string doth represent the water of my mercy, and my Torah which is written on tablets of sapphire, and my sapphire throne;

16 And the wings of them do carry healing and protection in them, for they are of me, and the blue string is a reflection to remind thee.

17 Doth not the Torah of Joseph (*4 Moses 7:23-26*) say: Thou shalt make tzitzits in the four corners of thy garments throughout all your generations, and thou shalt put upon the tzitsit a blue thread; and it shall be unto thee for a protection, that thou shalt look upon it and remember all thy mitzvoth unto me and do them,

18 And thou shalt remember that Israel is a holy people, a nation of kings and queens, and of Priests and Priestesses; sanctify yourselves, therefore, and be thou holy; for I am YHVH, thy Elohim; and thou shall keep my statutes and do them; I am YHVH which sanctify thee.

19 And thou shalt wear them upon the for corners of thy garment for all of thy days, for am I not King of kings? and are you not my royal priesthood?

20 Therefore, wear them not to be seen of mankind, nor out of fear of me, but thou shall wear them as a sign of the covenant, and that thou shall remember that I am the Lord, your God, and you are mine.

21 **Question:** Is everyone required to wear the tzitzits?

22 **Answer:** Behold, thy mitzvoth is written in my Torah, and I did shew unto thee the Torah lived in me, as I walked the earth and taught my people, and did keep all the Torah;

23 Therefore, I say unto thee that all that read this should come unto me with a broken heart and contrite spirit, and ask the Father in my name, even as thou did, David, to know my will for themselves.

24 For behold, look ye at the churches of man, do they not quote my words, even the scriptures? And do these obey every commandment? I say unto thee: Nay.

25 Yet my Grace doth cover them, for the wings of my atonement are wide, and I shall bring thee in, even as a mother hen doth gather her chicks;

26 Worry not, therefore, what others do, and seek not to rule over my people with the burdens of the flesh, but teach them to come unto me and to pray to the Father in spirit, that my people should be a prophetic people.

27 And behold, this mitzvah was not given as a burden unto my people, but in celebration, and as a reminder not to place one person above another in wealth nor station, but to have all things common;

28 For in me, as in Zion, are all things as one, and my people are to have all things in common, even as the Lehites did after I did visit them in the days after my resurrection.

29 Wherefore, do this thing in joy and jubilee, and in patience, and in peace; place the blue thread upon thy garments in a way that is pleasing unto thee, and let it blossom, that thou shall remember the covenant between thee and me: Amen.

Revelation 54

The Tent of the Presence

David was asked to pray on building a Tent of the Presence before building a temple or a tabernacle. After much prayer and meditation, the following was received on July 8, 2024, in New York state. This revelation is Section 136 in Doctrines of the Saints.

1 Unto my servant David, and unto all they that do desire to worship in my name; behold, I did say unto my people: Build a temple unto me that I may come into my house, and that my people shall have a place to worship[a].

2 And when thou didst come to me asking of the tabernacle, I did say that this would do until a temple could be built, and I did give unto you instruction, though not as great as the instructions I did give unto my servant, Moses[b].

3 And now thou doth come before me to ask of the Tent of the Presence, for if my people cannot build a temple, nor a tabernacle, what should ye do?

4 Behold, I say unto you this day: The Tent of the Presence is also the Tent of the Meeting, and if thou should build this and meet in my name, then I shall fill it with my Presence;

5 However, this is not a temple, but a house of meditation; therefore, though you may perform your ordinances and your rituals there in my name, I shall not send my servant, Elijah, there, and it is but a place of worship until the temple shall be built in my name.

6 ¶ And I say unto thee and to my Fellowship: There needs be a temple built in Missouri, and there ye shall meet once a year in my name^c.

7 And another shall be built in the Great Lakes region in North America, be it in the United States, in Illinois, Indiana, Michigan, Minnesota, New York, Ohio, Pennsylvania, or Wisconsin, or if it be in the Canadian province of Ontario or Quebec mattereth not to me, saith the Lord;

8 But know that this will be the very edge of Zion on the North American continent from which the Third Degree Apostles shall teach their Seventy Elders under the direction of the School of the Prophets or the School of Elders, and where the Fourth Degree Apostles shall teach the Seventy High Priest and High Priestesses,

9 And from there shall these evangelists and missionaries be sent forth unto all the world; to gather Israel, and to preach my gospel, and bring hope into this world.

10 Whether my apostles teach them, or if they shall work with the School of the Prophets to find teachers to teach them mattereth not to me, so long as they are taught in my ways and prepared that they not be sent forth in ignorance.

11 ¶ And from there, there shall be temples build upon every continent whereupon my people do dwell and these shall be houses of bread that will feed all they that do hunger and thirst after righteousness,

12 And you shall feed the poor among you that the wickedness of the Sodomites shall not be found within the gates of my house.

13 For even as I have said before, the wickedness of the Sodomites was even that of her pride, and her fullness of bread, yet she was idol in that her hand did not reach out to feed or help the poor or the needy[d].

14 And by this shall the stakes of Zion be stretched forth to heal this creation.

15 But behold, I say unto you: That this cannot be done in the Tent of Meeting, for it is a house of meditation and a house of prayer.

16 ⁋ And now I say unto you: There are five temples built up into me, the Lord your God, and these are the temple body, the temple of your abode, the synagogue or the temple of the congregation, the temple of Zion, and the temple of my house, or the temple of heaven.

17 And the temple of the body is the house of the Holy Spirit, for it is where my spirit doth dwell that mankind might be one with their God.

18 And the temple of your abode is the home temple, for it is where the family may gather in my name, even with all they that you should desire to invite to worship in your homes they you may be one in my name.

19 And the synagogues or the temples of the congregation are to be local temples where many might gather in my name, and break bread together, and tend to my gardens, and care for the poor and needy.

20 And the temples of Zion are where my people shall meet three times a year, that ye might all be one in my name, and honor the Holy Days of the covenant, and remember to love one another and be my Zion.

21 And the temple of heaven is even my house, where my Father and my Mother doth dwell, and there do I, even now, prepare a house for you, my good and faithful servant.

22 And the temple of the body is even the temple of heaven, for it is first build in thy heart, for there is my kingdom found.

23 And the Temple of your abode is even the first temple of the congregation, for the family is the community of Christ.

24 ⸿ And now do I say unto my Fellowship: The Tent of the Presence should be constructed near all of the temples of Zion that my people shall have a place to go and speak to me, and hear my Voice and know me by my name; for my people are a prophetic people and upon this rock shall Zion be built.

25 For all of my temples have the steps that are the straight line into my Presence, for first are the waters of life, then the Holy Place, and then the Holy of Holies.

26 And in the Holy Place, when all they that enter in do enter, they first pass the Altar of Incense for by the very Breath of YHVH is mankind awakened.

27 And to the right or the North is the shewbread, which is the bread of life and all ye would do well to remember that is it not by bread alone that mankind shall live, but by the very word of God;

28 Therefore, it is placed to the side, and you shall depart to the right or to the left only upon my instruction, for is this not the covenant: **All that YHVH hath spoken we will do.**

29 And to the left or the South is the Menorah which is to represent the tree of life and that fire of the fruits of the Spirit that doth light your way;

30 Therefore, it is placed to that side that you shall not come upon it in your distress and be burnt, yet it should light your way, and be a flame of purification from which you shall eat of the fruit of it when I shall teach you.

31 And the veil that stands between the Holy Place and the Holy of Holies is even the veil between mankind and the Lord, your God; therefore behind it lay the truth of all things, and all that read this shall gain access to me through the veil, should they seek it, for my people are a prophetic people.

32 ⸿ And in this, you do see that the temple is but a symbol of your body, which is your mind, your heart, and your spirit; wherefore I did say: Thou shalt love YHVH thy Elohim with all thy heart, and with all thy might, and with all thy strength[e].

33 And all the rituals that I do move you to perform are but a symbol of your growth as you return back into my Presence;

34 Therefore, when you should meet to stand before me, be it to hear my voice or to seek my Face, this tent shall be the Tent of the Presence, but when you should use this place to meet one with another it shall be known as the Tent of Meeting, but this shall not be known as a temple nor as a synagogue .

35 ⁋ And should then the temples of the synagogue and of the congregation have too the Tent of the Presence? Behold, this shall be based upon the needs of my people.

36 And I say unto you: That if the people are too small and there is not a house to meet in my name, but you can procure land enough for which to build a building there upon, then build a place for your dwelling that you might worship and feed those in need.

37 And if you cannot yet build the tabernacle; behold, I have given you the dimensions; therefore, if you have gold and silver enough to buy tents that you should dedicate them unto me as a tabernacle, this is enough.

38 Was not the temple of Nephi built like unto that temple of Solomon in Jerusalem save it be without all the riches? And what need have I for gold and riches? for all of the creation, she is mine.

39 But if you desire to use these tents as tabernacles unto me, then you shall see to it that they are set up properly as you have been instructed, and that they be set apart for my use.

40 And this thing must be done that your needs be met, even as I have instructed you, until such a time that my house may be built, and I say unto you that this must be done that I shall send my angels unto you, and that you should speak unto me again face to face.

41 For now I say: Go and do, for behold, I come quickly; even so: Amen and amen.

Notes:

    a. See Doctrines of the Saints 107:3

    b. See Doctrines of the Saints 124

    c. See Doctrines of the Saints 124:52

    d. See Ezekiel 16:49

    e. See 4 Moses 3:2

Revelation 55

The Court of the Brotherhood and the Court of the Sisterhood

David and Kristine were discussing the temple when returning from Missouri, October 20, 2024. While still in Missouri, Kristine asked what the purpose of the court of the Sisterhood and the Court of the Brotherhood. Taking this question to the Lord, David was given the following revelation. This revelation is Section 138 in Doctrines of the Saints.

1 Behold my sons and daughters: As I have told you before, the Court of the Brotherhood or the Court of Men shall be for instructing the men and those that identify as men,

2 And the Court of the Sisterhood or the Court of Women shall be for instructing the women and those that identify as women.

3 Yet be it known unto my people that even as I have said unto you, my temple is built for thy sake,

4 That my people may together find rest and fellowship in my presence; therefore, know that the temple is build for mankind, not mankind for my temples.

5 ¶ And it is because the Shekinah is represented by the North and the Holy Ghost by the South that these Courts of Instruction are made,

6 For my house is a map of the world and of the human body, for both are my creation.

7 And when my people do stand as one in my Presence, all are one in the holy place which is the center of my house,

8 For the mikveh, or place of baptismal washings, is to the East and the Holy of Holies to the West representing the Father and the Son.

9 And as you do walk my path from baptism to the Holy of Holies know that your Mother is with you to the North and the Holy Ghost to the South, that you not be alone but that I am with you on all sides.

10 ¶ And know too that my house is even as the tree of life, with Keter in the Orchard, and Da'at outside the door of the Court of the Brotherhood, and Chokhmah outside the door of the Court of the Sisterhood, for these are from before the creation.

---

11 And the Holy of Holies, this is Binah, for there do my people become one in my name.

12 And in the Court of the Sisterhood, Chesed is in the house of Magdalene, and Netzach in the house of Miriam, for these are upon the feminine pillar of that tree.

13 And in the Court of the Brotherhood, Givurah is in the house of Melchizedek, and Hod in the house of Aaron, four these are upon the masculine pillar of that tree.

14 And the High Priesthood are my hands, and the Low Priesthood are my feet, and in these are all my works completed.

15 And Tif'eret is found in the Holy Place, in there is found my compassion, and there shall you feel all they that come seeking substance.

16 And Yesod is found in the waters of baptism, therefore this is represented by the mikveh.

17 And all do enter my house at the gates of Malchut, for at these doors do you enter my house, and my kingdom, and into exaltation, which is to say, my rest.

18 ❡ And ye did ask if men should be permitted into the Court of the Sisterhood or Women into the Court of Brotherhood, and behold, I say into you:

19 These rooms are for your good and for your instruction, therefore these rooms are to be used for your needs;

20 But know ye that when the sisters do need to meet without the brethren, or the brothers to meet without the sistren, these shall be a place for your meetings, and let not any in uninvited.

21 ❡ It is not pleasing unto me that you should be commanded in all things, nor is it pleasing unto me for my sons to watch over my daughters, to rule over them or to command them unrighteously;

22 I have already told you of my displeasure of the patriarchy that has oppressed my daughters, I have warned you and forewarned you that Zion shall not be found in such unrighteous dominion.

23 Yet these courts are to be used for your good and to teach my people in my ways, and not for secret plots or secret combinations;

24 Therefore, use these Courts as you see fit and as doth meet your needs, and this is the purpose of all my temples.

25 Secret combinations are not of me, and exclusion is not of me, yet I, the Lord thy God, do understand the need for safety and peace in my name.

26 ¶ And behold, all do have both the masculine and the feminine pillars within, as all do desire to both give and to receive;

27 Therefore, do not separate yourselves by gender that you are not one in me, but create a safe place in my name that my will be done in all things: Even so, Amen.

www.ingramcontent.com/pod-product-compliance
Lightning Source LLC
Chambersburg PA
CBHW031234090426
42742CB00007B/201